KENNETH CLARKE

KENNETH CLARKE

Malcolm Balen

FOURTH ESTATE • London

First published in Great Britain in 1994 by
Fourth Estate Limited
289 Westbourne Grove
London W11 2QA

A catalogue record for this book is available from the British Library.

ISBN 1–85702–206–8

Typeset by York House Typographic Ltd
Printed in Great Britain by The Bath Press, Avon

Contents

Acknowledgements

This book has taken me on a journey from the Nottinghamshire border to 10 Downing Street, and I have incurred many debts along the way. Despite the demands on his time, Kenneth Clarke has granted my repeated interview requests and replied to further queries by letter. He has also allowed me to speak to his personal and political friends, and has provided many of the photographs in the book. At no stage has he discussed its contents, which is to his credit. He has broad shoulders.

My erstwhile employers, Independent Television News, were good enough to grant me a five-week sabbatical to begin my research, for which I thank them. I owe much to my Editor at Channel 4 News, Richard Tait, for his civilised intellectual leadership; to the programme's political editor, Elinor Goodman, for her sage counsel; to Sue Tinson for her support and advice; and also to Sue Brooks. I owe a longer-term debt to Derek Dowsett. Most of all, I am indebted to Jon Snow for his sheer journalistic enthusiasm; without him, I would not have started this project.

Thanks, too, to my literary agent, Anne McDermid, at Curtis Brown; to Miles Litvinoff; to John Barnes of the London School of Economics for his astute comments; and to Clive Priddle, at Fourth Estate, who has offered a constant stream of acute observations. I have relied greatly on his sharpness, percipience and good humour.

Finally, I have many family debts to repay: to my parents Bobbie and Henry Balen; to the indefatigable Deborah Meager; and, most of all, to Karen Meager and our two children for their love and support.

In August 1993, after Kenneth Clarke had become Chancellor of the Exchequer, I saw the following exchange on Channel 4's teletext service:

'It's the story of a fat dinosaur who ravages a country, destroying homes and factories as he pleases.'

'Are you reading Jurassic Park*?'*
'No – Kenneth Clarke's biography!'

I hope the real biography includes some of the humour of the imaginary, with perhaps a touch more political analysis.

Malcolm Balen
London, 1994

Illustrations

Note: No photograph may be reproduced without the written permission of the copyright holder. Where no credit is given in the full caption, the copyright is the author's.

CHAPTER 1

The Journey

A vast substratum of colliers; a thick sprinkling of tradespeople
intermingled with small employers of labour . . . then the rich and sticky
cherry of the local coal owner glistening over all. Such is the complicated
social system of a small industrial town in the Midlands of England.
                    D. H. Lawrence, *The Lost Girl*

Great political journeys must start from humble origins. Otherwise the
distance between birth and political glory is foreshortened, the road to
high office runs too smooth and the achievement appears diminished.
Perhaps for this reason any self-respecting politician feels happier if he
or she can claim a smattering of ancestral poverty.

That this applies to the Conservative Party as much as it does to its
opponents is reflected in its choice of leaders. Its MPs have turned to
leaders of humble stock ever since Lord Home descended from on
high to claim the keys to 10 Downing Street, only for Harold Wilson to
pick them up at the next general election. As in a game of political
happy families, the Conservatives have chosen Ted Heath, the
carpenter's son; Margaret Thatcher, the grocer's daughter; and,
somewhat more exotically, John Major, son of a circus artist and
gnome-maker.

Kenneth Clarke too can claim a modest upbringing – and his
political journey is more remarkable than most. He was born in 1940 –
on 2 July, the same day as Lord Home. But his family circumstances
could not have been more dissimilar from those of the one-time Earl.
Indeed, so varied was his father's career that in the game of political
happy families Kenneth Clarke can play three cards: the watchmaker's son, the miner's son and even the piano-player's son. By the
end of his life, Clarke's father had established himself as a small
shopkeeper; but the family, if not poor, was never rich. They
belonged to the backbone of England, the lower middle class, and so

1

Clarke's political journey started in circumstances as modest as any of the recent party leaders.

It is a background which will appeal to Tory image-makers. In his curious 1992 election broadcast, 'The Journey', John Major toured the streets of Brixton to retrace his youth from the back seat of his prime ministerial limousine. It was an exercise in image-making to show that the journey to No. 10 had not changed the essence of the man, that he still shared and understood the problems of the little people. When Major passed his old house he exclaimed with unconvincing surprise: 'Is it still there? It is, it is!' and then stopped to buy a pound of tomatoes and some kippers in the market.

To film the Clarke version of 'The Journey' the image-makers would have to travel to a world far removed from cosmopolitan inner-city life, to the small pit village of Aldercar, some half a dozen miles north-west of Nottingham, where a small stream, the Erewash, marks the county's border with Derbyshire. The broadcast would start with Clarke firmly ensconced in the front seat of his car, where he always sits, as it sweeps along the Kimberley bypass out of Nottingham, past the modern industrial estates which have sprung up to replace the mines of his youth.

As the car turns off the main road to begin the climb to Clarke's first home, the papered-over window of a long-since-gone upholstery shop would pass by in the background. The camera would dwell on the damp, faintly decaying landscape of post-industrial blight. It would then pan along the rows of red-brick Victorian terraced houses which mark the way as the road from the old pit village of Langley Mill winds uphill across a railway line. And then, where pub faces church halfway up the climb, the car would take a sharp left-hand turn into the wide expanse which is Upper Dunstead Road. Here Clarke, dressed in the least crumpled suit his media advisers could muster, would step out of his car and knock on the panelled door of No. 73, the modest home of his earliest years.

As Clarke stares at his old family home, relatively unscathed amid the Georgian wired windows and stone cladding of the neighbours' houses, he would express amazement at how small it is. He might even cast a wistful glance at the Horse and Jockey pub, a plastic creation which has sprung up in his absence, though his media advisers would not let him be pictured anywhere near a pint, much as he might feel like sampling one. The pictures would say, without the need for any words, that this is the man-next-door, a man of the people, a classless man, a man you can trust, a man who has travelled far but who has sprung from humble roots.

Unlike during John Major's journey, however, there are no markets here to visit, only a distant car-spares shop. The image-makers would doubtless decide that asking for a spark plug is an even less believable activity for a politician than asking for kippers. So they might instead decree a walk for Clarke through the fields to the little village of Stoneyford – along the path he took in his youth to visit friends – to muse upon his homecoming, with the countryside at his back.

At the end of the walk, it would be time to pay homage to his father. Eastwood is but a couple of miles' drive away, a small mining town perched in the midst of the countryside, where D. H. Lawrence was born. Lawrence could never escape the hold Eastwood had over him, nor the town him; Clarke's car would pass the tributes to its famous son, the Lawrence tea-room and the Lawrence veterinary centre. Then, as the setting for a few words of filial piety, Clarke would arrive at the site where his father once ran the town cinema, next to an imposing hotel which advertises proudly in large letters 'All Rooms with Colour TV, Satellite and Trouser Press'.

Clarke would then be driven through the town to Engine Lane, the scene of his father's wartime employ. The producers would have to take care here. The scene is one of blight. The pit where his father was an electrician has long since been erased from the landscape, the only indication of its past life a set of rusty rail-tracks curving into the thistles, and a broken National Coal Board sign which swings in the wind, struggling to escape the hawthorn bush which is trying to choke it.

But a touch of voice-over from Clarke about industrial renewal should do the trick: the old jobs have gone, but new jobs, genuine jobs, jobs in fridge-freezer warehouses and industrial cleaners, are being created in their stead. For where the Coal Board sign points to the pit's stores, a small industrial park has risen. The old colliery winding wheel, cut in half and painted an incongruous green, juts out from a coachwork factory which boasts 'Bodyworkers & Repairers, Signwriting & Vinyl Letters'.

3

Here the camera can see for itself the 'green shoots of recovery', depicted on the park's logo as if they spring from the pit-head itself, complete with a trumpeter heralding revival. Clarke would note with evident satisfaction the names of the factory units – Oak, Ash, Maple and Willow, planted for strength and growth, and Apple, for its promised yield. Times, he might reflect, have changed for the better since his father's day and his own impoverished youth.

And then Kenneth Clarke would retreat into his limousine, away from Engine Lane where the miners' terraces straggle down the hill, away from Upper Dunstead Road and its youthful memories, away from the concerns of middle England, doubtless expounding a line or two of cheerful philosophy for the benefit of the camera as he leaves the scene of his childhood behind.

There are only two problems with this journey for the film-makers. First, the immortal line 'Is it still there? It is, it is!' would sound even more hollow coming from Clarke. He knows full well what Upper Dunstead Road is like, because he still drives down it and, whatever else he has done in his political career, he has held to his Midlands roots. Second, it's not altogether clear that he would make the film. 'Were times tough? No. I've never gone in for this barefoot stuff,' he says.

The answer is typical of Clarke, who has made a career out of debunking theories and conventions, both political and personal. A gregarious man who is intensely private, he is an uncomplicated enigma – 'more self-contained than anyone I've ever met', according to one of his former political advisers.

To some, Clarke has about him the air of the market-stall grocer whose cheeriness lifts the spirits of his customers as they part with their money. But they will nevertheless wonder whether he is as affable as he seems or whether his *bonhomie* is a calculated act which is good for business. As Lord Parkinson puts it: 'Just listen to that laugh. It's not at all genial. There's not a lot of humour and jollity in it.' Would John Major have counted his change if he had purchased his tomatoes from Clarke's of Brixton?

Where charm ends and calculation begins is central to Clarke's character. Despite his many accomplishments he presents the image of an ordinary bloke, with a liking for jazz and beer. His suede shoes are the greatest political gimmick since Harold Wilson's pipe. Pure happenstance? Or a calculated act of image-making, a kind of *anti-image*, which has given him more publicity than any blow-waved minister who has been through the hands of the advertising men?

The answer, indeed the constant refrain, from Clarke's friends is, 'what you see is what you get'. Straight. Honest. Ambitious, yes, but not a plotter. A man who is true to himself with all the contradictions that may imply; but, for all his approachability, a self-contained man, confident in himself. One former minister compares Clarke to an egg: 'There are no gaps or seams. You can't figure out where he hurts.'

A strong man, it seems, for difficult times. A man who just happens to wear appalling shoes. And a political survivor who, for all his protestations, came up the hard way, but who also found a gilded path.

Kenneth Clarke was not born to be a politician, but he was brought up to succeed. His father, who had few ambitions for himself, had high hopes for the son who shared his name. Where Kenneth senior had been deprived of a decent education, Kenneth junior's path was mapped out, ordained, by his intelligence and schooling, which fused with his father's support for his brightest child to make his future clear. Clarke's perception of his father is of 'a talented man who'd obviously never been educated to do better; he was ambitious for me'.

The family came from humble stock, and lived in the unchanging world of middle England, the essential tap-root of any Tory politician. Indeed, Aldercar has changed little in the forty years since Clarke left. It is border country, unsure whether it is Nottinghamshire or Derbyshire, industrial or agricultural, a mixture of mining villages and countryside whose clash caused D. H. Lawrence to embrace 'the countryside of my heart' while fulminating against its 'ugliness, ugliness, ugliness'. But the young Clarke remembers fondly the wide expanses of countryside, with 'great fields all around', and as a little boy he would walk down an unmade track to visit his friends a mile or so away in the little village of Stoneyford, a road now scarred by open-cast mining.

Today, as it heads towards a modern housing estate, Upper Dunstead Road itself yields some clues as to what life was like for the young Clarke half a century ago. Its concerns are the small, unchanging ones of a Midlands village. A notice for the Aldercar and Langley Mill Horticultural Society advertises an all-embracing fruit, flower, vegetable, home produce and arts & crafts show, as well as a car treasure-hunt. 'Clare lvs Sean' and 'Helen lvs Matt' adorn the walls which line the road, faded white but engrained beyond the power of any graffiti-remover.

It is a small community. The corner of Upper Dunstead Road is marked by St John's Church where a cross commemorates the men of Aldercar who fell in the two world wars; two families lost two men each, and one family lost three. The inscription reads, 'May they rest in peace', but the traffic affords them little chance. The road is a long, wide, busy one and the buses which wind their way between the surrounding communities of Alfreton, Heanor, Eastwood and Hucknall pass just a few yards away from the little cross standing proudly at the graveyard's edge.

Upper Dunstead Road has a smart side and a poor side. Its better-heeled residents live in a line of 1930s semi-detached houses, with peaked roofs, mock-Tudor wooden beams and a view of the rolling hills of Nottinghamshire beyond. The Clarke family lived on the poorer side, in a small semi-detached house, planted where a line of flat-fronted terraced houses comes to a halt. It was here that Kenneth Clarke senior and his wife Doris brought their young son, Kenneth Harry, soon after his birth at Peel Street Women's Hospital in Nottingham.

Clarke and his mother were never close. But he would inherit much from his father: not just his name, but much of his character – his easygoing, rarely punctured affability, and his independence of spirit. And from his humble background, which would become wrapped in a privileged education, he took an ability to get on with a range of people whatever their status in life.

Although the ambitions Kenneth Clarke senior had for himself were strictly limited, he led an independent life, in keeping with his middle name, Horatio. He was a small, rotund man, five foot four at most, one of seven brothers from his father's two marriages. He was both genial and determined, learning to look after himself from an early age. At fourteen, he left school to join the watch-repairing firm of Gibbs in Nottingham's Goosegate as an apprentice, picking up the trade so quickly that he was soon training newcomers himself. He could look after himself and knew his own worth, or so he thought;

when he threatened to leave if he wasn't paid more, he was sacked instead.

Kenneth Clarke senior was determined to stand on his own two feet. He left home after a row with his stepmother when he was sick in his bedroom after a night's drinking, and found his own lodgings. His one great ambition, instilled perhaps by the peremptory treatment he received at the hands of his first employers, was to work for himself. The Depression years of the 1930s were not a time to be looking for employment of any sort. But he would not rely on the charity of others. 'I'd sweep the streets rather than be unemployed,' he recalled in later years. He found a job to match the exotic part of his name – in the cinema trade.

The growth of the leisure industry between the wars was rapid, and Nottingham was no exception. By the 1930s there were forty cinemas near the city centre alone. The scale of their popularity can be judged by the size of the Ritz, which opened on Angel Row in 1933. It had 2,500 seats, and the audiences poured in to watch Charles Laughton in *The Private Life of Henry VIII*. Fortunately for Clarke senior he had a talent he could offer this burgeoning industry. He was able to play the piano and organ by ear, although he lacked any formal musical training, and he started work in the pits of the Elite cinema, accompanying the silent movies until the first talkies were shown. From here he moved on to a second cinema on Trent Bridge, progressing to be a projectionist and picking up a knowledge of electrical maintenance as he went. He could turn his hand, it seemed, to almost anything.

On St George's Day 1939 Kenneth married Doris Smith, a secretary from the Lenton area of Nottingham, the eldest child of a toolmaker from the Raleigh bicycle works, who called himself a communist. Doris was pretty and blonde, and her parents thought she was marrying beneath her. It was certainly a marriage of opposites. Clarke remembers his mother as being far less outgoing than his father: 'She was a little bit quick-tempered, more emotional and less at ease with the world. It was a rumbustious relationship, but it was perfectly happy.' Mrs Clarke's life, however, was to end unhappily.

Kenneth senior was by this time firmly established in the cinema business, and Eastwood's plush new cinema offered to make him its manager. So he moved his wife and new-born son out to the Derbyshire border, to take up his new job.

The Rex was Eastwood's best. It was opened in November 1938 by a clutch of local dignitaries, with a free show for all the pensioners and disabled ex-servicemen who lived within a four-mile radius.[1] For this was very much Eastwood's own cinema, financed, built and designed by local people. It was seen as a matter of congratulation that almost everyone connected with the cinema lived within a mile of the place; the architects came from Eastwood, the builders, Langley Mill. It was a large, modern rival for the Eastwood Empire down the Nottingham Road – plusher by far than the Ritz in Langley Mill or the Cosy in Heanor.

The concerns of the wider world were now crowding in on this little community and an air-raid siren was fixed to the cinema's highest parapet. But even when the war began, the local newspaper, the *Eastwood & Kimberley Advertiser*, continued to reflect the unchanging life of its readers, with only a passing reference to the conflict itself. Its front page determinedly stuck to the editorial policy of advertisements only; its inside pages were devoted to the stuff of local life: to golden weddings and centenarians, whist drives and drama festivals, the Saturday-night dance at the Miners' Welfare, and the vegetable show by the Eastwood and District Garden and Allotment Association.

By the standards of the time, it was a stable, unexciting period for the family. Clarke senior stayed at home for the duration of the war, and there was nothing to disrupt his son's secure upbringing. Indeed, the politician remembers that the only dramatic event of his youth was that a bomb landed on a cow shed, killing its bovine occupant, a few hundred yards from where the family lived. There was little to trouble the readers of the *Eastwood & Kimberley Advertiser* unless members of their families were serving in the forces.

Kenneth senior did not serve. To be near his wife and young son, he took up a job at the local Moorgreen colliery as a miner, and as this was a reserved occupation, the family stayed together. Moorgreen colliery lay a mile out of Eastwood, past the miners' cottages of Engine Lane, and it was then owned by Barber, Walker & Company – a family firm which, before nationalisation, ran several pits across the country. Today the colliery has been turned into an industrial park, and few traces remain of the pit, except for a huge pile of bricks stamped 'NCB

Watnall', a tribute to the time when Britain could support not only a coal industry but one which personalised its bricks. The pit closed in 1985, but in the war years it was well established.

Shortly after starting his new job, Clarke senior broke his arm in a cave-in underground. When he recovered he was allowed to become a surface electrician, using the electrical knowledge he had built up through the cinema trade. Technically he can be called a miner and he would have had to join the union. But colliery electricians are a breed apart from the miners who hew the coal, and the men at Greasley Miners' Welfare, a mile from Moorgreen, recall Clarke as 'a gaffer's nark'. They claim they played a spiteful practical joke on him, not out of dislike, but because of his exalted status. One day he fell asleep on a wooden gantry, according to one ex-miner, wearing his raincoat; the miners nailed it to the wood, so that when he awoke he could not get up.

Most of his contemporaries, however, recall Clarke with respect as the man who escaped the pit, setting up a jeweller's shop in the village, a man from whom they bought their engagement rings. For during the war years, Clarke senior repaired watches in his spare time, and with the money he saved from this double income he was able to return to the trade for which he was trained. When the war ended he started a small shop in the centre of Eastwood. He had realised his ambition to work for himself.

Eastwood has grown up where three roads, from Mansfield, Nottingham and Derby, meet on the brow of the hill. On a large island, surrounded by a sea of traffic, stood the Rex cinema and also the Sun Inn, where in 1832 local businessmen met to found the Midland Railway. The main shopping area is further into Eastwood, where the Nottingham Road flattens out and straightens. But this was too expensive a location for Clarke's shop – so he took a less favoured location, down the hill from the Sun Inn, on the Mansfield Road.

It was a tiny shop, one room at the front and one at the back, with a large plate-glass window divided into three sections. Yet despite its small size and unfavourable location, business was good. By December 1949, 7 Mansfield Road was calling itself Clarke's *the* Jewellers. 'You could pretty well sell anything you could get hold of in those days,' comments Clarke's former assistant, Andrew McCulloch.

'The miners had money, and anything Kenneth could buy on a Friday he'd sell on a Saturday morning.'

By this time, the family was expanding. Kenneth's sister Pat, who is married to a Sussex farmer, was born in 1945. His brother Michael, a car salesman in Lincolnshire, was born two years later. Kenneth junior himself was growing up; at war's end, he was five and had started going to the local school. Two things were already clear about him; he was bright, learning to read before he started school, and he was extremely self-confident. For five years he had been the only child of an assertive mother and a gregarious father, and the combination made him self-possessed. On his first day at school, his mother started out to walk him the few hundred yards from Upper Dunstead Road to Aldercar Infants' School, and he simply left her behind. The next day she didn't bother to take him – he just set out on his own.

Two years later, Clarke junior moved up to Langley Mill Boys' School, housed in an imposing, old-fashioned building, long since closed, where the large rooms were divided into smaller classes by black curtains. Here he took his first steps on the educational path which, through academic achievement, would lead him far from Aldercar. Three teachers over the next decade would harness his intellect, turning a bright, if occasionally inconsistent, pupil into one who would win a Cambridge award. Clarke was quick to recognise that education was the key to his future: 'I was born to the purple of the working class. Education was my escape route.'[2] But it also showed him the rougher side of life.

Langley Mill Boys' School, which was established by the Church of England in the nineteenth century, had Victorian standards of discipline to match. If a boy was late more than twice he was beaten three times on each hand in front of the whole school. 'There was no messing about,' according to Bryan Eley, a former radio and television sales manager, who was one of Clarke's classmates. 'If you stepped out of line you got the stick. It was that sort of school.' It needed to be. Several pupils who were arrested for house-breaking were sent to Borstal and they were regarded as heroes by many at the school. Clarke himself remembers it as 'a rough old school'. Many of the games played by the boys 'seemed to involve running around socking each other in the playground'.

The school had seven classes of more than forty pupils who were taught in a rigorous, traditional way. Clarke was put under the wing of Geoffrey Burnett, whose enthusiasm made a big impression on the young schoolboy. Burnett ran an old-fashioned classroom with the desks in rows; the pupils were seated according to their form position, the brightest at the back and the weakest at the front. Clarke, who was always either first or second, would sit at the back with his closest rival, who is now a farmer in nearby Stoneyford. Clarke's fellow pupils remember him as the boy who was top, and who had a special talent for maths and English. 'He was more serious than the rest of us. He seemed to have a mental age that was older than us. He just got on with his work,' says Bryan Eley. But although Clarke was brighter than the other pupils, he mixed freely with them after lessons, jumping over the little stream at the back of the school to indulge his passion for football in the big fields beyond.

The young Clarke was also in the grip of another ruling passion – politics. From where this passion grew he is not sure, and he chooses not to analyse it. His father, like many a small businessman, voted Conservative, but his mother voted Labour: 'She probably thought people like us didn't vote Conservative.' Even so, there was little political talk in the family. Instead, the young Kenneth occasionally discussed politics with his grandfather, Harry Ernest Smith, who claimed he'd sold the *Daily Herald* for George Lansbury. When the Labour Party rejected Lansbury as leader in 1935, Harry Smith broke with the party. Thereafter, he always called himself a communist and the only newspaper he allowed into his house was the *Daily Worker*.

Harry Ernest Smith was a quiet, cultivated man, an accomplished artist who read widely and collected books on any and every subject. He also had a talent for making money in national competitions, winning an immense sum, £2,000, in 1925. When the Depression cut a swath through local businesses, he saved a garage, a fishmonger's and the rose grower Harry Wheatcroft with interest-free loans. Frequently he would reply to begging letters by sending off a £5 note.[3]

If asked, but only if asked, Harry Smith would argue quietly and logically that communism was an ideal form of government, although he recognised too that it was a Utopia which could not come to pass because of the flaws in human nature. He carried with him the strength of his inner convictions. Most weekends, when mushrooms were in season, he would walk the fields with another grandson,

Robert Smith, who is now a Nottinghamshire businessman: 'If he said a mushroom was edible, it was edible. You wouldn't question it – he knew so much about everything. But he wasn't a ranting type of communist, and he'd never drum his politics or his beliefs into anybody.'

Grandfather and grandson met mainly to go to football, Nottingham Forest one week and Notts County the next, and sometimes Clarke's great-grandfather would go too, meeting the young Kenneth off the trolley bus from Langley Mill. Sometimes the little group talked politics, but not often; Harry Smith, despite stories to the contrary, had little impact on his grandson's political development. Clarke's brother, Michael, remembers few political discussions in the living-room between Ken and his grandfather: 'Ken just seemed to have a natural interest in politics. When he was fifteen or sixteen, I remember him talking to me about pensions policy!'

Clarke's early interest in politics and his ability at school were, in time, to coalesce with the ambitions his father had for him. He recollects that by the time he was six or seven he had already decided to be a politician and he followed parliamentary reports, as well as football, every day in his parents' newspaper, the *Daily Mail*. In one lesson at Langley Mill Boys' School, some of the pupils were asked to stand up and say what they wanted to do when they left school, and Clarke replied that he wanted to be a Member of Parliament. He kept a scrapbook on the 1950 general election, and he can remember listening to the radio as the results of the 1951 election came through; every declaration seemed to be followed by the words, 'the Liberal candidate lost his deposit'. One of his half-uncles, Norman Clarke, now a pensioner in Nottingham, remembers that when Clarke junior was seven 'he'd already set himself up as a future Prime Minister – or at least a member of the Cabinet'.

Many theories are advanced to suggest how political leaders are formed. Lucille Iremonger, the wife of a former MP, made a study of British Prime Ministers and 'the search for love'. She found that a large number of British Prime Ministers had lost a parent in childhood, and many had been deprived of love in their early years. They accordingly demonstrated the most powerful drives for attention and affection, and were 'abnormally sensitive, reserved and isolated'.[4] None of those epithets appears to apply to Clarke; he is his father's son by name and nature, although he has added to that the steel of ambition.

Clarke mentions his mother rarely, however. She was, he says, just a normal Nottingham housewife, and he regrets that they were not closer: 'My mother was less of an influence on me. She might have settled for me being a bit more ordinary. She had a slight feeling about people being stuck up and snobbish.' By the time Clarke reached his teens, his mother had developed a drink problem; in the words of his younger brother, Michael:

> In my formative years my mother was always someone who would go off into irrational temper tantrums – which were due to alcohol. She'd just keep on going up and down to the bedroom to drink bottles of whisky or gin – anything, basically. It was what kept her going. But I don't think that was apparent in Ken's early years at all.

As for Clarke's father, he saw that his elder son could gain the educational opportunities he himself had been denied. This was the spur for the young Kenneth Clarke: 'Why was I ambitious? It was just the whole process of going to school. It sounds terribly arrogant, but I just found I was brighter than most people at school, and I found this interest in politics, and I read like crazy. I just got the bit between my teeth.' He set the pattern himself, but his father had given him the wish to succeed. Five years older than his nearest sibling, the young Kenneth struck out on his own within the family. His brother and sister remember that 'Ken was very much a loner when he was young. There was no brotherly love. Ken is normally very detached, emotionally and everything else; he's normally very much apart.' Clarke never lost his self-containment as he progressed in politics.

The schoolboy's educational horizons did not stretch much further than the local Heanor Grammar School, where the brighter of his contemporaries could expect to head. But his father's shop was faring well, and Clarke senior decided to move his family to Nottingham. This had the twin advantages that he would be nearer to his roots, and he would be buying a shop in a better position, one they could live above. So just before Clarke's tenth birthday, the family moved from Aldercar to Bulwell, on the northern outskirts of Nottingham.

The shop they moved to at 25 Highbury Road still bears the legend 'K. H. Clarke, Watchmaker & Jeweller' on a white sign, half painted out, beneath the black clock which protrudes from the shop front. It was one of half a dozen shops lining the side of a busy main road, and at the end of the garden lay a railway line, which was to provide a happy hunting ground for another of Kenneth junior's enthusiasms. His sister, Pat Chalmers, remembers him as having 'obsessive interests': 'He'd go train-spotting, or make model trains, or invent his own games for hours and hours. He lived in a world of his own.'

Highbury Road was home for the rest of Kenneth's schooldays, and beyond that in his holidays from university. The shop, which was not large, was the front room of a 1930s semi, so the family effectively lived behind and above the small area where watches were sold or repaired. The home was still modest, with three bedrooms for the five of them. Kenneth junior had to share a room with his brother all the way through school and university.

It was a time of rapid expansion for Clarke the businessman. A year later, in March 1951, he moved the Eastwood shop to the better end of town. There was a third shop, too: initially in Chilwell, south-west of the city centre, and then, when that proved to be a poor site, in Beeston, where Mr Clarke rented an old sewing-machine shop on the High Road, next to a greengrocer's. Yet, despite the expansion of his business horizons, Clarke senior had no grand plans. He never seemed much of a go-ahead businessman to Ron Robinson, who worked in the next-door shop in Beeston: 'He was quite happy to live and make a bob or two.' Indeed, his character was almost incompatible with his job; he was generous and soft-hearted, and by the time he had established himself as a modestly successful shopkeeper his assistants were being driven to despair at his lack of financial drive. Andrew McCulloch, who worked for him for half a dozen years, remembers him as 'a very kind man, very helpful to anyone and too easygoing to be in business, because people would often take him for a ride. They'd say they couldn't pay for it today and Kenneth would say forget it – so he was always struggling for money.'

Like his father, Kenneth junior would never be obsessed by making money, content to achieve academically and politically, not financially, to make the most of his educational opportunities. His brother Michael Clarke, who had a less distinguished academic record, felt the need to compete in a different way: 'I was materialistic. I realised I couldn't achieve scholastically what Ken could do, so I went into advertising. I had a Rolls by the time I was twenty-three, and then a Jensen Interceptor. Ken couldn't understand why anyone would *want* anything like that.'

It has stayed that way. The backbench MP Nicholas Budgen, who has known Clarke the politician for more than thirty years, observes: 'He's not at all avaricious. He's never lived in smart houses, and his idea of entertainment is to have a couple of pints in the bar.'

By now Clarke senior needed help in his Bulwell shop so that he could keep an eye on his other outlets. For the next eighteen years he worked with Ivan Deacon, who still runs the shop. Deacon found his new boss to be a chain-smoker, likeable and generous, unconcerned with politics, but with firm views none the less. The small shopkeeper had a strong distaste for the Labour leader Harold Wilson, the power of organised labour and the might of the trade union movement. Ivan Deacon remembers him as being strongly anti-union: 'He was against the closed shop and he didn't like having to join the mineworkers' union during the war.' Clarke's son also developed a sceptical view of the way unions exercise their power.

Kenneth senior eventually made enough money for the family to live comfortably, and when he died of throat cancer in 1974 he left a little under £21,000. Running three shops also meant that he had to work long and hard to make ends meet; Ivan Deacon would frequently walk past the shop window late at night, to see Mr Clarke hunched over his work, the little light in the repair room playing on to the pavement outside.

There was a price to pay. 'My mother died an alcoholic,' says Michael Clarke. 'Piecing it together now, I must have first realised something was wrong when I was about eight, and Ken was fifteen or sixteen. My father was a workaholic, and my mother would want attention, and so she had to resort to the bottle.' Michael Clarke's view of the family is very different from his brother's:

Her drinking was less apparent when Ken was young, so it was almost like two families. When Ken was in his formative years, I imagine there was a more stable family background. For me, it was normal to realise that my mother would go into enormous highs or lows. My sister and I can remember the occasions when my mother would spend two days drinking on her own in the bedroom. If you suggest that to my brother, he won't accept it.

Michael Clarke says that, although his mother's drinking started while Kenneth was still at secondary school, his brother seemed to shut himself off from the problem: 'He wasn't approachable about it, Ken is like an iceberg. Seventy-five per cent of him is underwater. To get where he's got he must be like that. I'm not saying his personality is a façade – it isn't – but there's a very large inner person. He can be very emotional, but he tends to detach himself.'

Mrs Clarke's drinking became worse after Kenneth senior died. Four years after her husband's death, on 15 October 1978, she died from cirrhosis of the liver and kidney failure. Michael Clarke says that even then his brother refused to accept that their mother had been an alcoholic:

I remember my sister and I having an argument with him on the day of the funeral. Ken got very upset and angry when we said it was bound to happen because she was drinking so much after my father died. We always say that Ken was detached from the reality of it. He never, ever, accepted that she was an alcoholic, because when she was really suffering, he'd left home.

The move to Bulwell was the single most important event in Kenneth Clarke's early life. He can still remember the exact date the family moved, 1 June 1950. It was important not just because it disrupted the family's quiet Aldercar world, but because it changed the young boy's educational horizons and forced him to adapt to a new and different environment. He was able to succeed at the highest scholastic level, and yet survive at the lowest, roughest, level in his new school playground.

At first, Clarke junior went to Highbury Junior School, which lay between an old tannery and a working men's club, just down the main road from the Bulwell shop. He had to adapt to survive, having acquired a strong accent from his time in Aldercar that, to his new classmates, was hard on the ear. Clarke would use 'thee' and 'thou' instead of 'you', and phrases like 'tha' wouldna'', which perplexed his fellow pupils. Within a day of arriving he was the target for the playground bully. But as he was able to defend himself with a degree of success, a truce was declared and Clarke was admitted into the fold – 'I was never very sporty, but I was always perfectly robust,' he recalls.

It was also clear, even to the boy himself, that he had a mental ability which surpassed the rest of his class. One day the headmistress summoned his parents to the school and they feared that their son had been in trouble. But she told them that she had never had such a bright boy in her school and that she almost needed a class for him on his own. From then on, Clarke was taken under the wing of his form teacher, who was determined that his young charge should win a scholarship to the top independent school in the city, Nottingham High School. No one from Highbury Junior School had done it before. Two pupils sat the exam – Clarke and the head boy – and only one of them won the scholarship. Clarke's fellow pupil, Andrew Macklam, remembers the morning the results were announced: 'The headmaster, Sam Spencer, said: "We have one pupil who we are very proud of. Can you come up on stage Kenneth Clarke." That's my outstanding memory of him.'[5]

Clarke had won one of only twelve Nottingham city scholarships, beating several hundred other applicants. While his contemporaries moved on to the local grammar schools, the new scholarship boy would spend the next seven years being educated in the independent sector, with all fees paid. His new school would be the passport to his future, and for Clarke the process was almost automatic: 'You expected to do well at school, and if you could, you carried on doing well. When your schoolteacher told you the next thing was the eleven-plus, you tried to pass it. If the next thing was O-levels and A-levels, you did that. If the next thing was Cambridge entrance, you did that.'

Nottingham High School is a vast castellated pile set in its own grounds some two miles from the city centre. More than twenty wide steps wind their way from ground level to the main entrance on the first floor, and to the young Kenneth Clarke the building must have seemed like some vast stately home. When he put on his regulation black blazer and grey trousers for the first time in September 1951, he was under no illusions that he was on a privileged path.

There were two types of boy at Nottingham High School: those who had come up through the preparatory school, and whose parents paid fees, and another fifty or sixty who had, like Clarke, won places in the main school at the age of eleven. In the first year, the boys were still divided according to whether they had come along the corridor from the 'prep' or won a place from outside. By winning a scholarship, Kenneth Clarke went straight into a form consisting entirely of scholarship boys from the city, like him, or from the county. For a young lad with a strong Derbyshire accent, he was in an even stranger environment than at Highbury Junior School. For the first time, he was mixing with boys from widely differing backgrounds. In Clarke's class of scholarship boys, the difference may not have been marked. There was a clerk's son, a window cleaner's son, an engineer's son, a farmer's son, a building surveyor's son and a french polisher's son. The prep school boys had richer parents, and overall the four forms of Clarke's year had a relatively classless mix, but a more refined one than he had left behind.

Among so many scholarship boys, the academic competition was intense. Clarke, for the first time at school, was by no means the brightest in the class. It was, in fact, the start of an inconsistent academic career. In his first term he was twentieth out of twenty-eight pupils in the form, bottom in religious education and French. But within a year he came top in the RE exam and was fifth in French. One year he was third from bottom in physics; the next year he was top. He seemed to work when he was interested, and showed an early tendency to prefer concentrated periods of pressure to more humdrum, everyday study. One master wrote on his report that he 'needs the stimulus of exams to bring out his best'. Clarke himself says that he wasn't a star pupil and that he never had to work hard, and the two doubtless went together: 'I think perhaps I could have done better if I'd acquired the habit of working harder – all the way through, and at university, I did the work that was necessary and relied on being a professional examinee really.' By and large, his approach worked. Only the occasional report is critical; in his second year, when he came twenty-sixth in maths, his performance was termed 'disappointing' and later he was accused of being 'rather easygoing' in the subject.

Nottingham High School set itself high standards and it didn't like to see its brightest pupils falling below their best. The school motto, inscribed on blazer pockets below the school badge, is 'Lauda Finem', which translates (somewhat ambiguously as far as the pupils are concerned) as 'Praise for the End'. But the school had no doubts as to its meaning. It prided itself, and still does, on the number of pupils who win awards at Oxford or Cambridge university each year. Eight in Clarke's year would eventually win Oxbridge awards. So through his very presence in the top form, Kenneth Clarke was effectively being told from an early age that such prizes were within his reach.

The subject which captured Clarke's imagination was history, and when he reached the third year he was taught the subject, along with religious education and English, by his form master, David Peters, who was new to the school. Clarke made a big impression on the schoolteacher for a quality he still possesses. Peters, who took Clarke for a total of ten periods a week, remembers there being 'other people in the form who were as bright as Ken, but he had something about him which most of the others perhaps didn't have . . . I think that he was unflappable.'[6]

Within a year, Clarke had begun to record a string of first places for history and English, including six consecutive first places for history in term work and exams, starting in the fourth year and taking him all the way through O-levels. So by this time, the shape of Clarke's future education was clear. The school's notes record: 'To History 6th? Top in English and History.' In 1956 he won a school prize for a topic on the history of the British Empire and he took his first General Certificate of Education exams, passing in eight O-level subjects: English language and English literature, maths and advanced maths, French, Latin, art and history. Physics and chemistry he gave up after the fourth year – an early sign of his lack of interest in science. He was knuckling down academically at the school, but only in his own individual way.

All schools like to bask in the reflected glory of the deeds of their famous sons or daughters, and the High School is no exception. Clarke returns the compliment to a limited extent. For he was already showing signs, which he would demonstrate in his political career, of his taste for debunking the system, playing the outsider on the inside. He feels he was 'never a great one for the school spirit', never wholly conformist or a model pupil: 'They wouldn't have dreamed of making me a prefect.' There were several reasons why he didn't win

19

preferment: he was never very keen on duties; he was frequently told off for not wearing a cap, which was then compulsory for all except sixth formers; it was clear from the nicotine stains on his fingers that he was smoking by the time he was in the sixth form; and he had started going to pubs 'as soon as I was old enough to pass for eighteen'. The sixth formers organised their own snooker league at the Mechanics' Institute, and Clarke and his friends would sneak off down the hill into the city centre during their free periods to play.

Clarke had three great passions at the High School: politics, a passion exhibited at the school debating society; train-spotting, a love fulfilled by running the school locomotive society; and football, which he couldn't play anywhere except in the playground, because the school played rugby union. The most vivid memory his High School contemporaries have of him is as a football player in the school yard, sweaty and dishevelled, chasing a tennis ball which was being used as a football, and kicking it between the blazers which were used as goalposts. At weekends, he played a more organised game, turning out for Sherwood Amateurs in the Midland Alliance League, usually at left-half in the second team, unless someone was injured in the first team.

The passion for steam was regarded more benevolently by the school. Clarke put all his considerable energy into running the locomotive society. Steam engines became an obsession for him and he travelled round the country train-spotting with other pupils. But this interest in locomotion revealed, too, his desire to be an organiser-in-chief. In 1956 he reported in the school magazine, *The Notting-hamian*, that he had run a trip to the Derby locomotive depot and repair shops: the day 'went without any outstanding occurrence until the Society took control of the historic locomotives preserved there, closely scrutinising all working parts of these two veterans which fortunately survived our invasion, none the worse for wear'. Three years later, at the end of his stay at the school, Clarke was still running the society, proudly recounting the boom in membership and still organising coach trips – to the Welsh borders in the summer and after Christmas to Sheffield, Doncaster, Scunthorpe and Immingham.

Yet this was no quiet, retiring boy huddling into a train-spotter's anorak, interested only in the obscure details of a locomotive's workings as he munched his sandwiches. His enthusiasm for trains was part of a wider enthusiasm for life, and the desire to know the precise but dry details of a train's component parts did not isolate him from the less easily defined wider world. He was at heart a participant, not a mere watcher; it was not enough just to be train-spotter, he had to run the club. 'He invented a game which, I think, sums him up,' says his brother Michael. 'He used to make up his own football league, and hold cup finals based on the roll of the dice. He'd work out averages and percentages. We would play, the three of us, but he'd make no allowances for age. He'd have to organise it – and win.'

Clarke's main passion was still politics, and it was at school that he made his first visit to the House of Commons. David Peters took a party from the school history society to Westminster in March 1956, when Clarke was nearly sixteen. The boys were taken round the House by James Johnson, then the Labour MP for Rugby. It made an impression on Clarke, the more so because Johnson was still there when he himself was elected to Westminster in 1970. Clarke was struck by what he saw, even though he must have realised early on that the work of the Commons is not always at the cutting edge of politics. The business of the House, watched by the boys, was the Slum (Clearance) Compensation Bill.

With such a political interest, Clarke found a natural home in the school debating society, despite the mixed diet it offered. On one Friday the boys might be debating 'that this House would favour the unilateral banning by Britain of nuclear weapons'; on another they would discuss the motion 'that the secretary of this society be sent up in the first available Sputnik'. (The latter was carried overwhelmingly.) Despite the variety of subject-matter, and the variable quality of the speakers, Clarke was a keen participant.

It is unfair, perhaps, to make too much of a comparison between the utterances of a sixteen-year-old schoolboy and those of the adult politician, but there is an uncanny symmetry of view between the young debater and the politician who tackled the trade unions for Mrs Thatcher as Health Secretary and then Education Secretary. Not only that, but the actual style of the young schoolboy could be mistaken for that of his mature counterpart. On Friday 11 October 1957 the High School boys gathered in the hall to debate the motion 'that this House would abolish the Trade Unions'. The minutes of the debate record that 'Mr K. H. Clarke sweepingly declared all arguments against the motion were wrong.'

Similarly, on 5 December the boys debated the motion that 'this House does not believe that Trade Unions contribute to industrial efficiency'. The minutes show, with some amusement, that 'Mr Clarke objected to the motion as a truism and said the House was trying to condemn the unions for not doing what they have no intention of doing.' Like his father – the small shopkeeper who had stood on his own two feet and made his own way in the world – the son had no truck with organised labour.

Clarke's main speech of the autumn term of 1958 was when he proposed the motion 'that this House prefers despotism to democracy'. He began by quoting Shaw, declaring that democracy was a new craze which gripped the minds of many who didn't know what it entailed. The old phrase of 'government by the people', he asserted, was pure fantasy. For him democracy meant instability, vacillation and inefficiency, all of which could be resolved by despotism. Clarke's argument was larded with some of the ringing phrases which were never to desert him in his political career. Democracy was faulty, he roundly declared, because 'political parties were followed like Notts County' – by a handful of people and out of tribal instinct.

Indeed, Clarke's contemporaries remember that he was never lost for words. Bill Woodward, who is now a Nottingham Queen's Counsel, beat Clarke in the election to be the secretary of the debating society, although Clarke was chosen as one of six committee members. He remembers that Clarke 'spoke very quickly . . . even more quickly than he does now. He was able to pick up any subject and deliver a compelling speech. He was quick to master his brief and he had an independent mind. He wouldn't necessarily follow the line if he didn't like it or agree with it.' If that sounds similar to the Clarke of today, then the school debating records also record the Clarke's style has changed little. In one debate, a participant 'complained of Mr Clarke's rotary motion whilst speaking'.

Some of the debates tried to tackle issues which were far beyond the boys' comprehension or knowledge of the world. There was an inadequate discussion of immigration, in which one boy was moved to point out that he doubted whether the House had ever seen a black man. But Clarke's view of the world was not a narrow one. Living as he did over the little shop opposite the Bulwell council estate, he could hardly escape the realities of everyday life. 'He struck me that he was more political than the other boys,' remembers Norman Thomson, the teacher who chaired the debating society and taught Clarke economics and politics at A-level. 'He could hold his own in debates, although he wasn't to my mind outstanding, but I often had the feeling that he knew more about *real* politics than I did.'

Pubs and good music meant as much to Clarke at this time as the debating society did, and if any of his friends wanted to find him at weekends they knew they didn't have to look much further than the Mapperley Tea Gardens, the Trent Bridge Inn or, more likely, the Dancing Slipper in West Bridgford, where he would sit with a pint or two to listen to the visiting jazz bands. Every Saturday night he went there with the same group of friends to hear musicians like Chris Barber and Acker Bilk, before moving on to another pub or a party, sometimes in his father's car.

So yet another enthusiasm was growing, sharpened by a fellow pupil who introduced him to a Gerry Mulligan record, which the pair played over and over again in the school's sixth form centre: 'We all sat round and listened to "Walking Shoes", which was a long way removed from the trad jazz bands I'd been listening to.' Clarke started buying Charlie Parker records from a little shop in Arkwright Street, near Nottingham Station, and he steadily developed his knowledge of jazz.

That Clarke should turn to jazz was a reflection of his character, and it is an interest which he has never dropped – 'the only music than can ever arouse passions in me, that I get addicted to'. Jazz suited his natural instinct not to conform completely. He told a radio jazz programme: 'I am naturally rebellious. Jazz went with a slightly rebellious lifestyle . . . the kind of disorganised lifestyle of jazz people, the late nights, the strange venues, the approach to life, which is fairly laid back, of jazz people.'[7]

Clarke's fellow jazz fan, the Shadow Cabinet minister John Prescott, offers an acute analysis of the music they both love: 'It's about a kind of freedom. It's anti-establishment, it's free-ranging, free-thinking, not allowing anything to be of a convention. It's a disorder of things that has its own structures and conventions. It's a great leveller. You can be in all classes and enjoy jazz.' For a schoolboy

23

like Clarke who wanted to succeed within the system without becoming subsumed by the system itself, who was receiving a middle-class education in a working-class family, jazz was a perfect match. Like the music itself, he was becoming classless, succeeding in a class-ridden society, but kicking against the system, however mildly, from within.

That he wanted to succeed within the system there was no doubt. Clarke took his three A-levels, in History, English and Politics with Economics, in the summer of 1958; he gained an 'A' grade in each subject, and later that year he won an Exhibition in History to Gonville and Caius College, Cambridge. The first part of the educational journey, so clearly defined even at eleven, was now over.

There lay ahead of him the political ladder which Cambridge could provide. Clarke was already calculating the best way forward. There would be nothing accidental about his progress. During that summer, at the age of eighteen, he made three key calculations which would shape the whole of his adult life. First, he realised that Cambridge would be a good platform for his political career, a platform he would need because he had set himself a deadline of reaching Parliament by the time he was thirty. Second, he was going to change from reading History to reading Law, because he thought 'in a rather utilitarian way' that he could combine it successfully with politics.

Third, Clarke decided that he wanted a larger stage for his future legal career than Nottingham could provide. It was a calculation he made when he spent a few weeks that summer gaining legal experience at a solicitor's office in Nottingham's Park Row. The firm set Clarke to sit behind counsel at a couple of trials at the Nottingham quarter sessions. He so enjoyed the performance, the sheer theatre of it, that he quickly decided to become a barrister, not a solicitor. He also realised that the best cases seemed to go to barristers from Birmingham and made a mental note that Nottingham appeared to be only 'a branch line' of the bar. Birmingham it would be, when Cambridge life was over.

But if the road to the top was carefully mapped out, then like the jazz of which he is so fond Clarke would reject no source in the confusion of elements that formed his personality. There was high ambition but a down-to-earth relish for the beery side of life too. He worked not just in a solicitor's office but also for Home Breweries, as a

24

driver's mate. He still recounts, with evident pleasure, how the job suited his natural inclination but overwhelmed his constitution. Every time they stopped at a pub, the driver would go inside to start drinking with the landlord, leaving Clarke on his own to unload the barrels. He would then stagger into the pub, exhausted, and the driver would let him have a pint before they moved on: 'The driver could obviously take this on a grand scale, but I couldn't, and I used to get pretty smashed during the day.' He was never to abandon this engaging mixture of high politics and low life.

There remained, too, another constant in Clarke's life: the Midlands. Clarke was not to forget his roots, even as his political career unfolded. He neither discarded them nor dwelt on them. They were simply there, his political tap-root, the unchanging security of his days in Aldercar and Bulwell. His teacher David Peters pointed out that Clarke 'always kept in touch with his contemporaries at the High School . . . that's remarkable for someone who's gone so far up the political tree that he's out of sight'.

Indeed, although Clarke's later rise at Westminster would be launched by his debating abilities there, he would base himself firmly in the Midlands and he would not throw off his accent, unlike the future Prime Minister from Grantham. Many years later, as Chancellor of the Exchequer, he could tell the merchants and bankers of the City of London, with some justification, that his whole life had been spent in the industrial Midlands.

For the moment, however, poised between Nottingham and Cambridge, the first stage of the journey from the pit village of his youth was over. What happened next would pitch Kenneth Harry Clarke into a network of political friends who would move with him from university to the Cabinet table – even if the new undergraduate still wasn't quite sure where his political allegiances lay.

CHAPTER 2

The Right People

Cambridge: I had a mental picture of port wine, boating, leisurely discussions over long tables gleaming with silver and cut glass. And over it all the atmosphere of power, power speaking impeccable Standard English, power which was power because it was born of the right family, always knew the right people: if you were going to run the country you couldn't do without a University education.

John Braine, *Room at the Top*

Even as he stepped through the Gate of Humility which marks the entrance to Gonville and Caius College, Kenneth Clarke was calculating the best way forward, though unsure of his ultimate destination: 'I went there determined to take up politics. I realised Cambridge would be a politically active university, so politics was going to be my main activity. It was absolutely calculated.' He was ambitious, but for what? Cambridge would form his political mind; it would also provide him with the political cement of his career. There he would gain both an entry into a new world of Tory Party politics and a group of friends who for three decades and more have remained his closest political allies. So active was Clarke politically, in fact, that by the time he left he had run every university political club within the reach of his beliefs.

There were two main routes out of Cambridge for any aspiring politician. The first step was to join the student political clubs, Conservative, Labour or Liberal. The second was the debating society, the Cambridge Union. Kenneth Clarke joined everything, and for good measure he later added the Campaign for Democratic Socialism. It need not have been a sign of his political ecumenicalism – many students joined all the clubs to gain a full choice of visiting speakers – but it was; Clarke had no clear party affiliations. Determined as he was to make his political mark in the world, he was wrapped up in the style of politics and not its content. His beliefs were not fixed in the political firmament, but his character was. Even as an undergraduate, he was to court controversy, but he also showed himself capable of withstanding the trouble he provoked.

Clarke appears at first to have been discomfited by the academic atmosphere of Cambridge and by the university's all-encompassing embrace. For a watchmaker's son from the wrong end of Nottingham with a modest tendency to kick against the system, there was much to kick against: 'When I arrived in Cambridge, the first year I did find myself – not at ease. I think I arrived with what I'd describe as a slight chip on my shoulder – or at least I was slightly chippie myself, a bit difficult and I think, to be candid, daunted by the atmosphere.'[1]

It took a while to shrug off the need to chase mere educational success. Clarke was reading a subject which was totally new to him, under the tutelage of academics who expected much and who considered that undergraduate achievement should be measured by Tripos results. Initially, Clarke worked hard, as his director of studies, Michael Prichard, recalls: 'He was much quieter when he first came up. He took a little while to take his measure of the task. But it was very clear soon that he'd assessed it and realised he could do it.'

Clarke was not going to be lost in a grey academic crowd, however. If he was going to work, it had to be on his own terms. 'Some undergraduates want to be told exactly what they have to do for the next supervision,' according to Prichard. 'They have to have it spelled out and then they'll rush away and do it. Ken was never terribly worried about exactly what it was that I wanted him to do!'

Michael Prichard supervised Clarke and three or four other undergraduates around the large table in his room overlooking Caius Court. In the first year he taught Clarke Roman law, and in the second the intricacies of land law. There was usually a group discussion about the particular legal problem that had been set that week, and Clarke argued his corner with complete confidence and good humour, even if, in the opinion of his supervisor, he was 'a bit laid back' in the hour-long session, which some of the other students found irritating. But he also showed an ability to think on his feet, says Prichard:

With some students you can almost see their mind clicking into gear and thinking, now what is it I've been told to say on this? Ken might come well prepared with the facts and figures, but he would react to the argument put against him. You felt he was

28

taking up a point intellectually, not just 'what is it I've got to remember to say?'.

Clarke was seen as a bright student with an analytical mind; it was not an academic intelligence, but a sensible, down-to-earth, practical ability which would bear academic dividends if he got down to his studies. In his first year, he did. In his law qualifying exams he took a First and was awarded a scholarship. It was by no means a borderline decision – Clarke gained first-class marks on four of his five papers. But he seems to have taken it as a sign that he had proved himself academically, and that it was now time to concentrate on politics. Indeed, so busily did he pursue his political career that Michael Prichard was driven to some despair: 'I berated him from time to time. I'd sort of wag my finger at him. He didn't disagree about it. But having got one First, he set his mind to politics.'

By now Clarke was beginning to form the political alliances which have lasted him a lifetime and would help to shape his views. Each year the university's societies hold a fair where hesitant freshmen are persuaded to part with their hard-won grants by being asked to join everything from the Anglo-Irish Club to the Trinity Foot Beagles. The recruiting drive is stepped up at individual college 'squashes', where drink is frequently supplied to make the prospect of joining a more mellow decision. At one such occasion Clarke was recruited by an officer from the Cambridge University Conservative Association or CUCA. The officer was Norman Fowler.

Clarke started to go to CUCA meetings regularly. The first one he attended was held in the rooms of a Pembroke undergraduate, Peter Lloyd – MP for Fareham since 1979 and a Home Office minister, who worked under Kenneth Clarke when he was Home Secretary. It was here that he first met John Gummer. They struck up an instant friendship, as Gummer remembers:

He had this great quality of being an attractive companion to a range of different people. His trick is that he's perfectly able and happy to spend an evening doing jazz with people who want to do jazz, but if they're not interested in that, he can spend an evening with great pleasure talking about things they are interested in. So he's one of those people who doesn't impose his own agenda on a relationship.

Drawn into this circle in his first term, Clarke worked closely with Gummer, who was the CUCA registrar in charge of recruitment and the library, as his assistant. Between them the two undergraduates, both of them destined for high office, accomplished a feat which few, if any, librarians can claim to have equalled; they lost the library. When last seen by the pair, it was parcelled up in a suitcase and placed, or so they thought, on top of a wardrobe in the college room of Ben Patterson, a future Tory Member of the European Parliament. But when the time came to hand it on, it had disappeared. 'Not before time,' comments John Gummer, 'because it consisted mainly of out-of-date pamphlets which people had given to us because they didn't want them.'

Clarke's nascent political career survived this early setback, and he began to speak at the weekly CUCA gatherings, becoming, in his own view, 'fairly Conservative' as his first year wore on. He was beginning to make an impression. Leon Brittan, two years his senior, remembers 'two extremely bright freshmen who were making themselves heard at meetings' – Kenneth Clarke, and a Peterhouse lawyer called Michael Howard; their rivalry would form a centrepiece to Clarke's political career at Cambridge.

CUCA offered the chance for Clarke to meet the leading lights of the Tory Party, affording him the opportunity to talk face to face with government ministers of the day. No undergraduate with his heart set on a political career could fail to be impressed. Each Sunday, when national politicians would visit, the students gathered in the faded Edwardian splendour of the Red Lion Hotel, next to Heffer's bookshop, to hear the visitor speak. Then a more select group decamped for dinner at the Blue Boar with the guest. In this way Clarke met both Harold Macmillan when he was Prime Minister and the party chairman, Rab Butler.

The Conservative Party took its links with student politicians seriously. It saw them as its future and had made a policy decision to encourage them. Conservative Central Office even paid for speaking lessons for its new recruits, which it organised through CUCA. Each Wednesday afternoon in term time a formidable woman by the name of Mrs Howard Cusforth held court in a ground-floor room in Trinity College. A generation of future MPs were to pass through her hands at her weekly tutorial. In front of Mrs Cusforth, no speaker dared fail to make an impact through inaudibility or poor delivery; there was to be only clarity of expression. She expected and accepted only the highest standards. One very bright undergraduate, Tony Firth, who spoke confidently in Mrs Cusforth's end-of-term competition, expected to be told he had done well; but Mrs Cusforth was not impressed. 'If only Mr Firth had *stood up* to address the meeting,' she sighed. When the young tyros had been fully trained in the art of standing up and speaking at the same time, the deputy Conservative agent for the Eastern Area would bag a complement of them to speak in by-elections or in village halls as a warm-up to the main speaker.

It was clear to Clarke that, to pursue his ambition, he must commit himself to one party. He could not afford to diffuse his political effort. Clarke claims: 'I didn't actually know what my political opinions were for sure. At school I had gone through phases of veering around in my opinions almost from one extreme to the other. I arrived in politics a genuine agnostic.'[2] But while he was no Conservative ideologue, there was to be little inner anguish over which party to choose.

Several factors made the Conservative Party Clarke's natural home. His closest Cambridge friends were Conservative, and it was clear that the road to advancement lay with the Tory Party. As Macmillan's thirteen years of unbroken Tory rule wound on, one article in the *Political Quarterly* questioned whether Britain was on the road to one-party government; so, in the absence of any initial commitment except to political ambition, Clarke, in retrospect, seems to have been bound for the Tory Party as soon as he came up to Cambridge. Leon Brittan agrees: 'It was clear that he was then a left-of-centre Conservative.'

Clarke, perhaps reflecting his upbringing as the son of a small shopkeeper, says he was attracted by the individualistic free-market ideas of the Macmillan government, as well as by its readiness to contemplate joining the European Community. In contrast, he found Labour to be dominated by old-fashioned interests, in particular trade unions.[3] He certainly wasn't going to be a Liberal, as John Gummer explains: 'He hates Liberals. He feels strongly that they can't make up their minds about anything. He thinks they believe in every old bit of rubbish that comes. He thinks people of substance stand up for things. He's a very practical person is Ken. He's there to do something.'

Clarke now became a part of a Cambridge group which identified itself less with Macmillan, much as he was admired, and more with the younger generation of meritocrats in the Conservative Party – with Ted Heath, Reginald Maudling, and above all Iain Macleod. Macleod was an early hero for Clarke: an enlightened liberal, partisan, even aggressive, and on the Left of the party. These students believed in continuity but also in change, calling the magazine they produced the *New Radical*. They were broadly in favour of joining the European Community and supported 'the wind of change' view of Africa. Clarke, then as now, was to combine a belief in the free market with left-of-centre politics on social issues. But like his friends, he was driven less by ideological fervour than by middle-of-the-road managerial pragmatism: 'Iain Macleod used to talk about a just and efficient society, but he privately used to doubt whether it was actually practical to produce perfect efficiency with perfect justice. All politics is in the end a pragmatic means of getting as near to your desired objects as in the real world it is possible to do.'[4]

Several of Clarke's contemporaries, like him, were first-generation university students, and several were the product of grammar schools; Michael Howard went to Llanelli Grammar School, Norman Fowler to King Edward VI Grammar School in Chelmsford, Peter Viggers to Portsmouth Grammar School and Hugh Dykes to Weston-super-Mare Grammar School. 'University was such a liberation,' says John Gummer, 'because we all came from backgrounds which had been pretty restricted up till then. We came from small towns and grammar schools where the attitudes were very traditional.'

Cambridge itself, however, was dominated by conformist public-school conservatism,[5] a matter of great anguish to the student newspaper, *Varsity*, which questioned why it should be so: 'One would have thought that the combination of youth and intelligence would have resulted in a flood of young radicals, anxious to change the world for the good of mankind.'[6] Clarke and his friends, despite the name of their magazine, and their background, were no such radicals, except in the vehemence of their pro-Europeanism. They wanted to succeed within the established order. They were, none the less, liberal Conservatives; after the Sharpeville massacre, none of his group would drink South African sherry, even though it was cheap and had been, until then, the staple drink to be kept in any self-respecting undergraduate's college room and offered to visiting friends.

With academic success under his belt, Clarke committed himself to CUCA at the end of his first year and was determined to be elected its chairman. As Peter Lloyd says: 'If you had an interest you joined a political society, and if you had an ambition you sought office.' This was important because it gave a shine to the dullest curriculum vitae, brought you into contact with the brightest of the Conservative Party's luminaries and could lead to even greater things – such as the presidency of the Cambridge Union itself. It was also very time-consuming.

Varsity warned would-be politicians that they would get nowhere 'unless you are willing to live Cambridge politics up to the hilt and to act and be judged according to twisted standards of behaviour, and endure the trivial self-importance and small-mindedness these engender'.[7] By going to Caius, however, even though he didn't realise it at first, Clarke had joined a college where a large group of activists did live politics to the hilt, and this helped him in his ambition to run CUCA. There were only two other big colleges where students were as politically active: St John's and Trinity. Colleges tended to operate a block vote in elections, although canvassing was officially forbidden. John Barnes, now an academic at the London School of Economics who was at Caius with Clarke, remarks that 'There were understandings between people as to who were on the same ticket, and the word spread that really this man was the right man for the post this year.' The Caius vote rolled for Clarke, and he was elected chairman. He had achieved his first ambition, but he stepped immediately into a controversy of his own making.

Clarke's invitation to Sir Oswald Mosley to speak to CUCA was the defining moment of his Cambridge political career. The fascist leader was seeking to regain respectability on the back of his support for Europe, and was then writing in a liberal magazine called *New Outlook*, causing some Liberals to declare his views on economics true. Yet to many members of CUCA the invitation was tantamout to countenancing racism. Clarke had no time for Mosley's views, which he denounced in trenchant language: 'They are so intrinsically ridiculous that no one will agree with him. There is not one fascist in

CUCA.' But he thought Mosley's visit would capture a big audience from the rival political clubs, even though Mosley had been in Cambridge only eighteen months before. 'He was a brilliant debater,' recalls Clarke. 'I'd seen him in Cambridge before, when someone threw a custard pie in his face, and he turned it completely to his advantage. So I did it partly because he would be a good draw, and partly I suppose because it wasn't a safe thing to do. I wished to have controversial speakers.' The ensuing row came to dominate the term.

The political fall-out from Clarke's invitation to Mosley was immense, and it did much damage to his incipient career in Cambridge politics. Condemnation spread across the university, with Clarke's supporters defending the right to free speech and his opponents denouncing Mosley's views. CUCA rebels tried to get forty signatories to call a special general meeting, and Michael Howard, who is Jewish, resigned from the association. He felt that it was impossible to remain on the CUCA committee, where he was an ex-officio member.

The chairman of JAGUAR, the university's Joint Action Group for Understanding among Races, also weighed in, writing to CUCA to demand that the invitation be withdrawn. A closed meeting of its affiliated societies was held to try to censure CUCA, and this voted to express JAGUAR's 'profound regret'. JAGUAR's secretary, Alan Watson, a Liberal from Jesus College, spoke of Mosley as the most dangerous racialist in the country, and condemned the visit as a propaganda stunt. But motions of profound regret affected Clarke then as little as they might today. He pointed out that only nine Cambridge societies were represented at the meeting, and only five had voted for the motion.

The main threat to Clarke's political prospects came from the Cambridge Union apparatchiks. Eight of the debating society's senior members, including its President, Peter Hancock, its vice-president, Brian Pollitt, and its secretary, Barry Augenbraun, wrote a letter of protest to the student newspaper: 'We are quite aware that the principle of free speech is involved here; but . . . while it is one thing to allow Mosley to speak from a British Union Movement platform in Cambridge, or anywhere else, it is quite another deliberately to afford him the respectability which is undoubtedly attached to any meeting organised by CUCA.' They decided to take their protest further, calling a special meeting of the Union.

There was no official connection between the Union and CUCA, although the former watched the conduct of all the political clubs with a keen eye. It was nevertheless extraordinary for it to debate the running of CUCA's affairs in this way. The result of this gathering, combined with Howard's resignation from CUCA, would sharpen the political rivalry between Clarke and Howard in their battle to become President of the Union.

The special Union meeting was chaired by the former Union President Colin Renfrew (now Lord Renfrew, the Master of Jesus College, and a friend of Clarke's). It had before it an unequivocal motion, calling on CUCA to withdraw the Mosley invitation. It was proposed by the Union vice-president, Brian Pollitt, and backed by Michael Howard, who was on the Union committee. Pollitt made the opening speech, accusing CUCA of exploiting racialism. He insisted it was not possible for CUCA 'to dissociate itself from Mosley . . . The motives for inviting him are dubious in the extreme.' The secretary, Barry Augenbraun, warned that Mosley was dangerous: 'He's one of the most brilliant men in British politics, not the ludicrous figure that the other side is trying to make out.' Michael Howard spoke out too, declaring that 'the only way in which CUCA's reputation can be enhanced is for it to withdraw the invitation'. Clarke defended himself vigorously: 'The fact that we invite Sir Oswald Mosley in no way means that we associate with him. We try to have as wide a range of guests as possible . . . Mosley is a serious political figure; racialism is rising – Mosley's candidate got 5 per cent of the votes at Moss Side; he's got to be faced.' Clarke was backed by Colin Renfrew and John Gummer. But despite his trenchant defence, he lost the vote by 49 to 36. It didn't seem to bother him. 'The only thing that will influence us is disagreement inside CUCA itself. The Union can't dictate to CUCA,' he declared.

CUCA and Clarke were now at the point of no return. For Clarke to back down would have been unthinkable, but equally his invitation was doing harm to CUCA's standing in the university, and more importantly to its officers' chances of Union success. So he struck a compromise, deciding that the invitation should stand, but that afterwards the former CUCA chairman John Gummer should propose, and he would second, the resolution that CUCA 'views with alarm the manifestation of racialism in this country and deplores any attempt to exploit this and affirms its belief in a non-racial society'. On these terms, Sir Oswald came.

Clarke was correct to think that the visit would pull a crowd; a thousand students gathered in the Examination Schools to hear Mosley speak, ten times the usual audience. The controversy generated by his invitation was made manifest by the degree of security which the university had to impose. Police patrolled the building outside; proctors lined the back of the hall; stewards staffed the entrance; and there were three separate security checkpoints.

Mosley spoke for about twenty minutes, arguing for a united Europe, to stand as an effective buffer between East and West. But he spoke too on Africa (one-third should be cordoned off immediately as 'white territory') and on race. He maintained that it was as natural to preserve the 'purity' of one's own race as it was to guard the purity and interests of one's own family. There was considerable applause when he sat down.

Clarke and Gummer then replied to Mosley's points before the audience's questions began. This last session was, however, divided into sections corresponding to the various subjects of Mosley's speech, and by spinning out the discussion on Europe he was able to avoid facing many questions about his racialist views. Some questions he evaded; others he answered with anecdotes; but only towards the end did Mosley lose his hold over the audience, with shouts of 'Irrelevant!' and 'Answer the question!' punctuating the last few minutes. At a quarter past ten the proctors stepped in to end the meeting at the prearranged time. Mosley said goodbye to Clarke, refused his invitation to come back to his rooms in Caius for coffee, was whisked through a side door which was shut as soon as he was gone and walked swiftly through the pouring rain to the waste ground two hundred yards away where his car was waiting to take him back to London.

Clarke had survived his first brush with controversy, much as he would survive controversy later in his career. But he seemed to have taken a risk. Ambitious though he was, he was no student politician climbing silently up the greasy pole. 'The experiment of giving Mosley a just and fair hearing was interesting but a second experiment along the same lines scarcely seems worth the trouble,' *Varsity* concluded. Clarke had cause to reflect upon the point. There would be a political price to pay as he pursued his next ambition, at the Cambridge Union.

If CUCA was the place to cut your political teeth, the Union was the place for serious ladder-climbing. A galaxy of serious young men, fresh-faced but preternaturally aged in their bow-ties and dinner jackets, saw the presidency of the Union as the key to their Westminster future. They were dedicated to the cause. To get on in political life, they realised, they had to devote themselves to their chosen career from an early age and they did so with an extraordinary degree of certainty. Of this generation, five Union Presidents would reach the Cabinet: Leon Brittan (President in 1960), Michael Howard (1962), John Gummer (1962), Clarke himself (1963) and Norman Lamont (1964). Norman Fowler also made it to the Cabinet, although he held office only in CUCA. This group of contemporaries would, in time, become known as the Cambridge mafia, friends but rivals over the next thirty years. Norman Lamont explains it thus: 'I think the emergence of several of us in the Cabinet at the same time reflects a change in the Conservative Party and a change in Britain becoming much more open and meritocratic.'[8]

Half the Cambridge undergraduates were still educated at public school, however, and only less than a third went to grammar school.[9] The 'mafia' were men from similar meritocratic backgrounds who advanced themselves not because the way to the top had changed but precisely because they explored and exploited the traditional gilded routes to power. 'Looking back, I did do the conventional things,' Clarke agrees. 'School, university, going to the Bar, and so on. I have to admit, I was very ambitious – it was quite obvious by my behaviour – but I suppose I was as nonconformist as was compatible with that. I don't see myself as the archetypal Conservative politician of every generation.'

The 'mafia' were right to choose the path they did, based on precedent. Senior membership of the Union was recognised by the Tory Party as a harbinger of Westminster prospects. From bow-tied pre-eminence in Cambridge could spring selection for a seat, albeit a difficult one initially, and contact with the great and the good who came to speak to the Union at Round Church Street.

It was hard work. Union politicians spent hours running the society, for it offered more than just debates to its student members; it provided luncheon, tea and dinner, a vast selection of periodicals ranging from railway timetables to the *Rhodesia and Nyasaland Newsletter*, and a lending library from which three to four thousand books were borrowed each term. It was, in short, the very model of what undergraduates thought a gentlemen's club should be, even if the undergraduates sometimes spoiled the effect. Among the most popular books borrowed in 1961 were *The Adventure of the Christmas Pudding* and *When the Kissing Had to Stop*, although some respectability was restored by the popularity, for whatever reason, of *Structural Inorganic Chemistry* (third edition).

All this took hours of organisation, and the political tyros threw themselves into running the place which might make their careers. There was a standing committee, a library committee, a kitchen committee, a newspaper and periodicals committee, a gramophone committee, a ball committee and a development subcommittee. It was not a place to be if you were seeking academic distinction. A politically ambitious student like Clarke made a simple choice. He was what the *Sunday Times* called a 'professional undergraduate', convinced that as an investment for success in post-varsity life an ounce of social, political, literary or theatrical distinction was worth a ton of academic honours. As the *Sunday Times* opined:

> The Professional Undergraduate has in mind that large white space – headed 'university social activities' – which decorates questionnaires distributed by impressionable future employers . . . Editorship of *Granta* or *Varsity*, Presidency of the Union or a nervously brilliant performance in *Footlights* – these are the things that count. First-class Honours come a pretty poor second.[10]

This was a view shared by the drily cynical 'Napoleon Boot' who wrote a weekly column of political analysis in *Varsity*, styling himself 'the cross-bencher of the Petite Bourgeoisie'. (It was analysis spiced with free-ranging comment; he memorably described Norman Lamont as 'a cherub expelled from the Vatican ceiling'.) What was it, he asked, that drew 'these lovable giants of the Cambridge scene' into the Union? 'Roll the word around your tongue. CON-STIT-U-EN-CIES.' But 'Napoleon Boot' himself was a reflection of the closed world of Cambridge politics; many of his columns were written by Clarke, Gummer and Renfrew themselves. Politics was a serious business, but it was also fun, and the student tyros were not averse to debunking themselves.

To get on in the Union, students had to impress with their debating skills. There were two kinds of speech they could deliver: either centre-stage, as the proposer or seconder of a motion, at the invitation of the hierarchy, or from the floor, the main business of the night done. Clarke needed to make three speeches from the floor before he could stand for election to the Union committee and he made his début halfway through his first year, in January 1960, speaking for just three minutes against the motion that 'The national press is not worthy of freedom.' The motion was opposed by Norman Fowler, who, perhaps with his eye on a future journalistic career, contended that newspapers were surprisingly good considering the limitations with which they had to work.

It is difficult in some of these debates to ascertain the real views of the student politicians who were speaking. If they were the main speakers, making paper speeches either for or against a motion, they might have been invited to do so by the President, and could thus have been arguing not from conviction but out of duty. However, students who spoke from the floor did so from the heart – Leon Brittan, for example, argued against the motion that chastity was outmoded, and John Gummer spoke against the legalisation of abortion, which Clarke supported. Clarke's views from the floor were certainly not main-stream, as John Gummer remembers: 'Even in those days he was a great debunker. He doesn't get taken in by things. If he's got a fault, it's that sometimes he overdoes the scepticism and doesn't accept things he ought to accept.'

As if to prove the point, in the fifth debate of the term, on 14 February 1961, Clarke spoke for nine minutes in favour of the motion that 'The Monarchy has outlived its usefulness.' His friends still consider that he is sceptical about the monarchy's value. Clarke denies it, but only to a degree:

I've never been an ardent monarchist. I'm not in the John Gummer camp. I'm not the sort of man who'd ever keep a scrapbook of royal pictures. The monarchy's been damaged by being turned into a soap opera. But if we had an elected President we'd probably end up with some rigidly boring member of the establishment, like a retired general.

Clarke spoke well at the Union but not memorably. His style was easy and conversational, reeking less of midnight-oil preparation than that of other speakers. Yet he had one priceless ability; he could think on his feet. 'He would never be thrown by interruptions,' says Colin Renfrew. 'He would relax into the debate.' Clarke also retained the manner of speaking which had irritated his Nottingham High School colleague; Renfrew mentions his 'very mobile style of addressing the audience in all directions'.

Clarke's first big speech came at the start of his second year, in October 1960, when he seconded the motion that 'The West is fighting a losing battle.' The following May he argued with Roy Jenkins MP that 'Censorship serves no good purpose', and in November at the start of his third year he was the main speaker against the proposal that 'This House would fight for West Berlin.' Not all his speeches were a success. This last motion was proposed by the Union secretary, Barry Augenbraun, in a speech which the Union's record of debates calls 'strikingly able'. Clarke's reply, it is noted, was 'somewhat unorthodox and the House feared an anti-climax was imminent'.[11] Nicholas Budgen MP, who was Clarke's contemporary at Cambridge, says that Clarke was not one of the best student speakers: 'You'd go to Ken for an intelligent, vigorous bar-room row in which a simple point of view would be put forcibly but without any malice and from time to time quite amusingly.' Clarke was not in the same league as Colin Renfrew or Leon Brittan, or even John Gummer, but was considered better than Norman Fowler.

Michael Howard, Clarke's rival, was also speechifying at the Union. He made his maiden speech some months after Clarke, in October 1960, and was one of the main speakers for the traditional motion of no confidence in the government at the start of the 1961 academic year. This speech was not one of his best – according to Varsity 'it betrayed signs of unpreparedness'.

Howard, unlike Clarke, came from an unfashionable college, Peterhouse, the smallest in the university, with only around thirty Union members. So in terms of standing for office, he was at a disadvantage. But the Mosley affair gave the battle to become secretary a keen edge. 'Napoleon Boot' reported that Clarke 'is powerfully placed, with the Conservative crocodile having received its instructions. Michael Howard, having thrown over CUCA, can expect CUCA to return the compliment. After all, did he really expect it to prefer Mike to Mosley?' The Union did. John Gummer became vice-president, and Howard beat Clarke in the key battle to become secretary. Clarke has no doubt that the Mosley affair was to blame: 'There were great ructions. I should have won it but the row over my inviting Sir Oswald Mosley was tremendous. It was a huge controversy. I fell out with everybody.' As 'Napoleon Boot', ever ironic, put it pithily: 'Strife's better with the Conservatives.'

This election spelled trouble for Clarke, pushing him off the Union ladder. New officers were elected each term, and with few exceptions each officer moved up to claim the post above every time. It required little foresight to see that Howard would be President in the summer term of 1962, the final term of Clarke's final year. He faced the prospect of going down from Cambridge without the golden title, President of the Union. It was a prospect with which 'Napoleon Boot' could sympathise, in his world-weary manner: 'Imagine susceptible old Tory ladies . . . falling back dazzled as the otherwise unremarkable young hopeful proclaims, "I wath on the Committee of the Cambwidge Union, actually, only the woters never gave me a thecond count for theckwetary."'

When the new term started, Clarke was given a second chance to win a Union post. The Union suspected that its new President, Augenbraun, had been canvassing illegally. A special committee of six, including Leon Brittan, was appointed to investigate the charges, and it found that cards bearing the words 'Union Elections, Wednesday' had been distributed in King's College before the close of poll, breaking the Union's rules. The election was declared void. John Gummer assumed the presidency without a contest, and a new election was held for vice-president. Clarke stood again, but was beaten by thirteen votes by John Dunn, a left-wing historian from King's. There seemed to be no way he could become President.

But Clarke had found a third route out of Cambridge and into the Tory Party nationally, and he pursued this, too. Not only did it give him a greater chance of political success when he left Cambridge, through the connections it would bring him in national politics; it also helped confirm the views he was developing on specific issues, especially on Europe.

The Federation of University Conservative and Unionist Associations was an organisation which brought together students from around the country, although its initials were the source of some embarrassment to its members. 'You can imagine what our opponents called it,' says Maureen Tomison, then an undergraduate at St Andrews University, who now runs an international London-based lobbying organisation:

> We always used to joke about it, but Ken was down to earth enough to see that we'd better try to change the name. So he sent me to see the two old biddies who ran the organisation, but they kept saying now what does this word stand for, my dear? I was so embarrassed I just went rushing back saying I can't do this, I'm not going to tell them, and Ken just hooted. Only then did I realise he'd set me up!

Although FUCUA was less of an Oxbridge preserve, the names which dominated Cambridge University politics also crop up. John Gummer was chairman, and so too in 1963 was Clarke. Leon Brittan, Norman Lamont, Michael Howard and Hugh Dykes – as well as David Hunt and Keith Hampson from Bristol University and John MacGregor from St Andrews – all passed through its doors.

As well as four regional conferences, FUCUA held two main conferences each year: a course for the committed each September at Swinton Conservative College and the annual conference each April at High Leigh, near Hoddesdon in Hertfordshire. Each affiliated university, from Aberdeen to Swansea, would send about half a dozen students. The meetings were highly structured, and as at CUCA or the Cambridge Union, the national Conservative Party sent high-ranking speakers to address the students.

The group shared a feeling that they wanted a federal Europe and a realistic peace to end the Cold War. According to John Barnes, who was a vice-chairman of FUCUA for two years, 'It was the mood of the time . . . you can almost precisely date it. There was this enormous Tory triumph in 1959 and the sense that we must now really get on with putting Britain back together, and you could only really do that in a much bigger context.' Clarke, like many students of the period, became a passionate European.

The political heroes of this coterie were men like Iain Macleod and Ted Heath, who as President of FUCUA came to speak to the students frequently. For all his diffidence as a speaker and his awkward personal manner, Heath was good with young people; he struck a chord with them, and they returned the compliment, backing by an overwhelming majority his controversial attempt to legislate against resale price maintenance. 'Ted was our hero,' Maureen Tomison recalls, 'because he stood for an awful lot of what was important to my generation. He stood for Europe, and he stood for what we called a sensible attitude, a centrist attitude, a non-ideological approach to every aspect of politics.' Clarke confirms this view: 'Heath impressed me. By the time he was turning up to FUCUA he was crusading for Europe, trying to negotiate our entry into the Common Market, and I was an early convert to my present European enthusiasms.' The Cuban missile crisis reinforced the students' view that only a united Europe could act as a buttress between East and West.

When de Gaulle refused Britain entry to the European Community, FUCUA voted by an overwhelming majority to urge the government to develop its political, economic and military links with every Western European country, to ensure a unified Western alliance. It was a theme Clarke took up when he spoke to the Conservative Party conference at Blackpool in 1963. The rejection of Britain's application to join the Common Market was not a disgrace, he contended:

In fact, thanks to the skill of Mr Heath and his team of negotiators we emerged with honour from that rebuff . . . I think people in Britain are extremely concerned at the role they want to play in the world and extremely concerned about the national sense of purpose this country is endeavouring to find, the national place we have to discover for ourselves in the world.

The Earl of Home, then Foreign Secretary and soon to be Prime Minister, responded that it was an 'excellent speech'.

The student group, if idealistic, was also pragmatic, defining the essence of Conservatism as never to carry anything to its logical conclusion. 'None of us were ideologues,' remembers Maureen Tomison. 'We were all very pragmatic, and Ken of all people is the essential pragmatist.'

While the student politicians took themselves seriously, the social side of politics appealed to Clarke, too. The conferences always ended with a cabaret, and one night the students decided to make fun of the British Council over its attempts to export culture to Africa. Future Cabinet ministers Kenneth Clarke and John Gummer pranced about on the High Leigh stage, performing a Morris dance to words sung by Miss Tomison – and also, unexpectedly, to words added by Michael Cook, who is now a diplomat in Istanbul. Maureen Tomison describes the scene:

> Michael had got this broomstick from somewhere and he was jumping up and down in the middle of this thing talking about spring fertility rites . . . and there's Ken Clarke and John Gummer doing what had suddenly become a deeply, deeply obscene dance in front of the assembled ministers. Ken was the first person to laugh – he ended up collapsing.

Despite his success in FUCUA, Clarke was still eager to land the one university prize which had eluded him. It was clear that, because of the impact of the Mosley affair, he would fail to become President of the Union as an undergraduate. But by asking to do a fourth year, to take a Bachelor of Laws degree, or LLB, he might achieve his aim. He says he stayed on partly because he wanted to get a First: 'I was annoyed with myself for not getting one, and I also decided I'd have another year enjoying Cambridge before going out and earning my living.' But his friends considered the decision had more to do with becoming President than with academic achievement. 'Napoleon Boot' had other concerns; 'Can Ken Clarke manage on a pension?' he asked.

At the third attempt, and in his fourth year, Clarke was finally elected to Union office, becoming vice-president in December 1962.

The presidency was now within his grasp and he seemed fearful lest he lose his chance. Clarke and his Union President, Ian Binnie, suspected that a canvassing campaign had been mounted to try to defeat his run for the presidency in his final term in favour of Alan Watson, the JAGUAR secretary who had crossed swords with Clarke over the Mosley visit. The student blamed for the canvassing was a freshman at Jesus called Martin Short, who would later make a name for himself writing books about closed brotherhoods like the Freemasons. Short recalls that he was asleep in his college room when he was woken up by Clarke and Binnie banging on his door: 'They proceeded to interrogate me about my role in the supposed affair. I couldn't believe that these grandees of the Union were coming into my room without any notice, as if I'd be overwhelmed by their presence and confess to these bullying police officers. Here was a man who would do anything to play the game of the institution he was in.' This time Clarke was not to be denied. In the final term of his extra year he beat Alan Watson by forty-two votes in a three-cornered fight in which only 385 of the Union's thousand-strong membership bothered to vote. The watchmaker's son from Nottingham had become President of the Union.

Clarke had risen to the top, but again he became embroiled in controversy, as he had at CUCA. *Varsity* reported that in his first utterance as President, Clarke had declared his opposition to the admission of female undergraduates to the Union. But he denied the remarks. The debates of the sixties were recorded by the Union and on a quarter-inch tape, more than three decades old, Clarke's voice is to be found – a little husky through laryngitis, but still recognisable for the trenchant manner with which he defended himself. He wanted, he croaked, to make a 'brief personal comment': the stories about him were 'extraordinary' and 'entirely mythical . . . the invention of a man in the *Cambridge Daily News* service'.

> Various people said they were rushing through urgent polls to get women in the chamber before I and the forces of darkness behind me are here . . . I hope that members will hurriedly assure their suffragette friends that all the assassination attempts, all the boycotts and all the sit-down strikes are quite unnecessary and will bear that in mind in future.[12]

It would not be the first time in a career founded on verbal talent but occasionally undermined by exuberance and misjudgement, that Clarke would claim he had been misinterpreted by journalists.

Clarke's personal life, however, was now fixed and secure. At a Poppy Day fund-raising barbecue, organised by Trinity College on Midsummer Common, he had met a young history undergraduate from Newnham called Gillian Edwards, the daughter of two Sidcup schoolteachers. Unlike Clarke, who was neglecting his studies for political activities, she was highly academic, later undertaking a postgraduate thesis on food supplies to Edward I's armies in Wales. They would marry young, soon after Clarke became a Tory candidate – a personal event which was wrapped into the Cambridge political scene; John Gummer was best man, and Brittan, Lamont and Howard were among those in attendance. The way ahead would be marked by the stability of family life and of a constant group of political friends.

This group of friends had forged firm ties at Cambridge: not just a political bond, but a personal bond, too. Their main topic of conversation may have been politics, but their shared college life was also important to them. For three years, conversation and coffee in a friend's room was never more than a cycle ride away. Clarke would play bridge until late at night, or bar billiards in the Rose, and would travel to London to visit Ronnie Scott's jazz club. There was a life to be had outside his choice of career but it was politics, and politics alone, that was vital to his future.

Four years at Cambridge had produced a student politician with a glittering curriculum vitae that contained, by Clarke's high standards, only one modest omission: he failed to get a First. Instead, he rounded off his presidential term with a third consecutive 2:1 and a debate which held that 'Conservatism is building a just and efficient society in Britain.' By tradition the vote was held by acclamation, and Clarke declared it a tie, casting his deciding vote in favour of the motion. As well he might: he would be welcomed on to the candidates' list of the Tory Party as the holder of two Cambridge degrees, the chairmanship of CUCA and FUCUA, and the presidency of the Union. To Lord Renfrew 'He always seemed a likely candidate as leader, just as Leon Brittan always seemed a future Lord Chancellor.' Within a year of leaving Cambridge, Clarke was standing as Tory candidate in Mansfield.

Appropriately, the most popular book borrowed from the Union library during Clarke's term as President was *Life at the Top*.

CHAPTER 3

This Little Socialist Outpost

In a sense, nothing in life is planned – or everything is – because in the dance every step is ultimately the corollary of the step before; the consequence of being the kind of person one chances to be.
Anthony Powell, *A Dance to the Music of Time*

On Whit Sunday 1964 the Mansfield miners, some 20,000-strong, marched along the Chesterfield Road out of the town as the warm sun streamed down on their faces. They were heading for Berry Hill Park, three miles beyond, and as they marched the music of thirteen different bands kept them company. Children lined the sides of Market Street as the rally passed by and yet more children sat on the crossbars of the union banners as the men, wearing their Sunday best, wheeled the vast frames uphill. At the head of the parade, on a mobile throne, sat the Nottinghamshire Coal Queen, flanked by her attendants.

At the park the festivities began with the judging of both human beings and animals. There was a dog show, with four separate classes for pedigree and non-pedigree animals; 730 rabbits assembled in the marquee to be inspected. The muscled miners of the Notts National Union of Mineworkers area and their sons showed off their bodies in the 'Mr Nottinghamshire of the Mining Industry' contest; and the women, with more modesty, did the same – the three finalists in the Miss Venus '64 competition paraded in their one-piece bathing suits and high heels. There was a Junior Miss contest, a Prettiest Grandmother competition and prizes for the Happiest Mother and Child.

As little boys sailed boats in the pond, and even smaller children poked their fingers through the wire of the rabbit cages, the miners' floats slowly gathered in the park. The floats reflected one general theme, that there should be better conditions for the mining community. Some of the 'demands' were pure fantasy; in a 'Miner's Delight' tableau a miner in full pit regalia was fanned and cosseted by flimsily dressed 'Turkish' maidens.

When a Hucknall housewife had been elected the new Notts Coal Queen, and the donkey rides had stopped, when the Bestwood Colliery Black Diamonds had been awarded the best band cup, and thirteen branch officials from the NUM had been given their certificates to mark ten years' service, the political speeches began. For despite the festive occasion, the miners of Mansfield were fearful of what progress might bring. They mined the richest coal seam in the country; the East Midlands division had produced a record 47 million tons that year. But thousands of mining jobs were disappearing, and the miners as they rallied in the park passed a resolution that 'under the Tory regime there is no wonder that intelligent men are asking if automation and mechanisation mean human bankruptcy'.

The Labour Party's chairman, Anthony Greenwood, accompanied by the four local Labour MPs, sought to reassure the vast crowd. After praising the party's long, historic links with the NUM and declaring that the iron and steel industries would be taken back into public ownership, he promised that Labour would on no account interfere with the union: 'It is not for politicians to advise trades unions on how they should conduct their affairs.[1] Greenwood's fraternal greetings were warmly received. The NUM's national President, Syd Ford, replied that there was no better example of consistent loyalty to the Labour Party than in the mining constituencies: 'Indeed, if party constituencies throughout the country had been as loyal to the Labour Party as the mining constituencies you'd have a Labour government today.' It was true. The Labour majority over the Conservatives in Mansfield was as solid as the mining industry itself, more than 16,000 in 1959, giving Labour two-thirds of the vote in a straight fight between the two parties. Since 1918, save for a dozen years, the MP had always been the miners' nominee.

It was for this hopeless seat, this Midlands constituency which lived and breathed the mining industry on which its prosperity depended, and whose miners could rally on such a grand scale, that Kenneth Clarke was selected only a few months out of Cambridge.

The Mansfield Conservative Club, accustomed to fighting losing battles, made not the slightest pretence to be the gentlemen's club that the Cambridge Union had striven to be. It was a working men's club, a distant outpost of the Tory Party, representing a seat in which Central Office had only a passing interest. But it was an opportunity for Kenneth Clarke to fight, to gain experience, to do battle in order to lose well, so that when a better seat came along he would be the experienced campaigner with an election track record, giving him a chance to beat his self-imposed deadline of getting to Westminster by the time he was thirty.

The young politician was neither overawed nor miserable at being thrust from his Cambridge clique into the coal-blackened camaraderie of Mansfield. He was a self-confident character able to get on with most people. 'There was a fairly wide gulf between a Highbury Road jeweller and this high-flying graduate,' comments his close friend Martin Suthers, a Nottingham solicitor, who met Clarke at Cambridge. 'But Ken was no different then from how he is now – he blends effortlessly into any background.' The candidate brought with him an energy and enthusiasm which revitalised the Mansfield Tory Party, declaring his intention to 'make a dent in this little socialist outpost'.

That Clarke was chosen at all was the first large slice of luck in a political career which has been marked by the kindness of fate at several key turning-points. Clarke was selected in March 1964, just six months before the general election, because the previous candidate, an old Etonian, fell ill and could not face the prospect of standing. So close to an election there was little time for the Mansfield Conservatives to choose a new runner. The field was accordingly smaller, and Clarke was handed a late opportunity to win selection. It was a chance he relished, for the rivalry among the Cambridge mafia was as keen as its friendship – Clarke remembers 'being very envious when John Gummer was adopted in Greenwich when I was still up at Cambridge'.

Traditionally, the Mansfield Tories had selected well-recommended candidates, with no local connections; they had fought the last general election with a man from Cornwall, Robert Elliot, who lost badly despite impressing the miners with his physical presence – six and a half feet tall – and his capacity for beer; he drank from his own two-pint mug. This time the association determined to pick a local candidate, but not one who was so local that the choice might cause rivalry and jealousy within the Mansfield party itself. It asked Central Office for a list of twenty approved candidates, and Clarke, from Nottingham, seemed to fit the bill. He was among the six hopefuls interviewed by the party executive in the town's Swan Hotel and he gave the panel what it afterwards deemed to be a 'marvellous' address. Clarke's wife, Gillian, who was not involved in the selection at Mansfield – the couple were then not even formally engaged – has heard since that the selection committee was 'impressed by his frankness and realism': 'He was asked why he wished to fight a "safe Labour seat", and he replied that, although he hoped to enter Parliament eventually, he did not think it wise at that stage in his career.'

There was another crucial factor in Clarke's selection; even in Mansfield, his Cambridge Union background counted. 'There was a debate about selecting somebody so young,' remembers Major Tim Martin, who was the local party chairman. 'But his credentials even then were so good – university and ex-President of the Union, which marks a man out usually. It impressed us. Presidents of university unions usually make their mark, don't they?'

The Mansfield Tories imposed a condition on the young Clarke, however. Traditionally, candidates had used Mansfield as a stepping-stone; none had fought the seat twice. The association wanted to discover what would happen if a candidate, after the ritual failure, stayed to fight again, and it told Clarke he would be adopted only if he accepted these terms. Clarke readily agreed; the chance of fighting a seat so young was too good to miss. While he was reluctant to tie himself to a hopeless cause, he must have calculated that the association could hardly stop him moving to richer pastures if his experience in Mansfield gave him the chance to be selected elsewhere – even if this meant breaking his word.

Clarke faced many disadvantages fighting in Mansfield, and he overcame these with the trenchant language which has never deserted him and with the personal affability which took the poison out of any fight. He himself admits: 'I did look terribly young. Not only was I only twenty-three, I don't think I looked any older than twenty-three. Some people thought I was canvassing for my father.' The next problem Clarke faced was the image created by the Prime Minister, Sir Alec Douglas-Home. If Mansfield was hardly a natural hunting-ground for Tory votes, then the miners could hardly be expected to identify themselves with the party's new leader, and they didn't. 'The trouble is', wrote the local newspaper's political correspondent, 'that the Premier is still very much the 14th Earl . . . when he "emerged" as Tory Commander-in-Chief we were assured that "everybody loves a lord". Well, that doesn't appear to be the case in Notts.'[2] But Clarke was a man's man, in a man's area. (The chairman of the Mansfield Woodhouse Labour Party, appealing for better support from women, said: 'We like women to be members of the party, because they do all the work.') And while recognising the hopelessness of his task, he went about it cheerfully: 'By the time I got to Mansfield, thanks to Cambridge and the Bar, I was quite gregarious, so I enjoyed pressing the flesh.'

The magnitude of Clarke's task was increased when the Liberals decided to put up a candidate for the first time since 1950, when they had lost their deposit. In standing, they could only damage the Tory vote. Yet it was a natural decision; for the first time in many years the Liberals had also chosen to contest the town's South ward in the local elections, which the Tories had managed to hold since 1947. To make his mark, the Liberals' new parliamentary candidate, Reg Strauther, a local men's outfitter and Methodist preacher, called on Clarke to stand down on the grounds that he had no chance of winning the seat and ran the risk of splitting the non-Labour vote. Clarke was up to the battle, replying in language which is now familiar; he was 'very amused' by the suggestion and condemned 'the irresponsible Liberal antics' in the South ward, where 'the silly Liberal intervention' was difficult to understand, 'unless they actually want to unseat the Conservative councillors and give Mansfield 100% to the Socialists for the first time'.[3] Clarke's forecast was correct; a local miner beat his party chairman, Tim Martin, by two votes for the council seat.

This was a reverse which hurt the local Tory Party, and Clarke gave them a pep talk at the Swan Hotel. The Conservative vote could still be increased in the forthcoming general election, he told them, giving the Socialists a slap in the eye for all the setbacks suffered in the municipal elections. If the Tories could win the election 'the Labour Party would be defeated for good. An attempt to impose a centralised Socialist state would be resisted by the people of this country. People remember the drabness of this state under Labour and don't want it repeated.'[4]

Clarke didn't have long to wait for his first election fight. In the autumn of 1964 Home went to the country.

On Friday 2 October Clarke handed in his nomination papers, along with the other Mansfield candidates, at Nottingham's Shire Hall. He threw himself into the fight, enthusiastically touring the constituency in a loud-speaker van – overenthusiastically, he would later conclude. He ate lunch in a different place each day, so that the diners would spot his rosette and come up to talk to him. Each evening the party held a rally in a different school hall, where Clarke would make a speech and deal with questions. It was a high-profile campaign, and as a Tory Daniel in a Socialist lions' den Clarke had to know how to handle the enemy. Joyce Maddison, Clarke's agent, noted that 'One of the things that was very good was that Ken seemed to have an excellent way of dealing with hecklers.' He didn't shrink from entering the most die-hard of Labour areas: 'People weren't rude, because he was always good natured. But he wouldn't just agree with somebody for a quiet life. If anybody said something that wasn't to his liking, he always had a charming way of letting them see that he didn't agree with them.' Maddison 'thought that was brilliant'.

Politics for Clarke, then, just as now, never became personal. The men's shop run by his Liberal opponent Reg Strauther was near the Conservative Club, and Clarke used to drop in for a cup of tea and a chat in the back room with his rival.

The campaign showed Clarke to be more than just an affable wordsmith as he stumped from eight in the morning until half-past ten at night. It also showed the generational gap he represented. His Labour opponent Bernard Taylor was an old-school politician, a parliamentary secretary at the Ministry of National Insurance, who had held the seat since a by-election in 1941. In Clarke's words: 'He'd become the MP only days after I was born, and he had a set speech about the old careworn hands of his mother. But on one occasion he jabbed his finger at me and proclaimed, "You said you would shut us out in the 1920s until grass grew on the headstocks." "Bernard," I replied, "I wasn't even *born* then."'

Unlike his older opponent, Clarke could see the political value of television. As an MP in 1971 he would sign an Early Day Motion calling for the experimental televising of parliamentary proceedings, and even in the 1960s he knew the value of the medium, challenging

Taylor to a television debate. Taylor, predictably, refused. This was more than the statutory challenge-and-rejection that takes place these days; it revealed the difference between a politician in the old mould and a rising young man. In refusing, Taylor complained about his previous experience of the medium, with Granada Television during the 1959 general election: 'I left Mansfield at about 1 p.m. and did not get back until about 9 p.m. I was on the screen for about a minute.'[5] This time Granada offered to double the screen time available to each candidate, but Taylor felt he was better off spending the time in his constituency. He blamed the mass media for the paucity of the audience at his speeches: 'Radio and television are playing havoc with not only public meetings but also churches, chapels, cinemas and public houses.'

While his opponent concentrated on the housing issue and the cost of living, Clarke argued that voters should ask themselves three key questions: Why did Labour want to nationalise steel? Why would they nationalise building land, and what would that improve? And why ban the nuclear deterrent which, he said, had given Britain a seat at international negotiations? The only possible explanation for these Labour policies, he concluded, was 'doctrinaire reasons'. As early as 1964, then, Clarke refused to accept the merit of any overall political doctrine, whether from the Left or the Right. In this vein he also expressed his early social concerns, praising 'the very real achievements of the Conservatives in improving and expanding the social services and welfare generally'.

Clarke expounded in Mansfield his belief in the free market and in the encouragement of individual enterprise. He told an audience at Pleasley Hill that he advocated shops where customers could buy stocks and shares. This, he said, would probably be the subject of his private member's bill, if he was able to introduce one (when it came to it, it wasn't; licensing hours took priority). 'We have set up betting shops which work fairly well,' he declared – partly from first-hand knowledge, as he had patronised them at Cambridge. 'And there is no reason why, if people are allowed to gamble . . . they should not be allowed to spend in a more sensible way by investing in stocks and shares and buying themselves a stake in the country.'[6]

Mansfield remained unimpressed. On 16 October, sandwiched between the Town Clerk and Reg Strauther, and wearing a knitted waistcoat cardigan under his jacket, Clarke learned his fate; he had mustered just over 10,000 votes, and Bernard Taylor had been re-elected with a 19,000 majority.

It had nevertheless been a good campaign for Clarke, and he was praised by Bernard Taylor for a clean fight. 'Mr Clarke is a newcomer,' he told the waiting crowds. 'Mr Strauther has got his roots here. But whether we have been strangers or friends we can part this morning as the best of friends, with no hard feelings, no malice and, I hope, no envy.'

Despite his defeat, Clarke had reinvigorated the Mansfield Tories with his energy and enthusiasm. Spurred by his example, they brought out their first year-book, a slim blue volume which features, among the advertisements paid for by the local petrol stations, soft drinks firms and insurance brokers, photographs of the Mansfield association's worthies. There, among the careworn features of a local alderman and the borough council candidates, and springing from a different generation, is a barely recognisable Kenneth Clarke: thin and tidy, and looking only just old enough to have left school.

On 20 November, a month after the general election, Clarke threw a party at the Rufford Arms Hotel to thank all the party workers who had helped in his campaign. He and Gillian had married three weeks after the election, and the local party chairman, Tim Martin, presented the couple with a set of Denby ware as a wedding present. During the evening Clarke's agent revealed to the Conservative throng that he had accepted an invitation to continue as the party's candidate, as he was honour-bound to do. It was time to put down political roots in the area.

Despite the undertaking he had given to the Mansfield Conservatives, Clarke was still on the look-out for a better seat. It seemed that the ideal one had come up in Birmingham, where he was working as a barrister. Midway between the general elections of 1964 and 1966, Clarke came into Tim Martin's downstairs office in the association's headquarters on Midworth Street and revealed that he had applied to be the candidate for Edgbaston and had been short-listed. Martin has told no one of this incident apart from his wife until now, and he took the decision then not to tell his executive. He knew that Clarke had broken his word by applying for the seat, and he knew too that he could keep hold of his candidate by refusing him permission to be interviewed. He wondered whether it was fair to stand in the way of this ambitious young man, but also whether he could square it with his association if Clarke was selected. Martin recalls:

> He knew he was asking a favour. If I'd said 'no' he wouldn't have gone. But I thought here we'd got someone who was going to make his mark and if I could be part and parcel of his selection for higher things I'd be very proud. So I said, now you slip off and if you don't get it I'll tell no one, but if you do get it I'll stand the rub with my executive.

Fortunately for Tim Martin, Birmingham's Tories preferred Jill Knight. The fates had decreed that Clarke would fight Mansfield at the next general election.

Three times more, however, electoral serendipity was to give Clarke's career a gentle push. The first stroke of luck lay in the election result of October 1964, a Labour parliamentary majority of four, which made a second general election inevitable sooner rather than later; this allowed him to quit his debt to the Mansfield Tories within only two years. The second break came with a chance speech which put Clarke firmly before the eyes of a wider political audience. And the third piece of good fortune lay in the result of the 1966 election, with its sweeping majority for Harold Wilson. It tipped out of Parliament the county's most prominent MP, leaving a prize seat ready and waiting for a younger man.

Clarke fought the 1966 election in Mansfield as he had fought the previous one, with good humour and enthusiasm. This time he was up against 'Don' Concannon, whose prospects of winning the seat were a great deal more settled than his name. John Dennis Concannon was a pit inspector and a local councillor, known confusingly to the newspapers as John, to his family as Dennis, but to everyone else as Don, because during a branch election at Rufford Colliery a union official had chalked his name wrongly on the blackboard used for marking votes.

Concannon was struck by both Clarke's ability and his charm. During the campaign the two met by accident one Saturday on their way to watch Mansfield Town play, combining the chance to watch football with the opportunity of canvassing the crowd. It seemed natural to the two men to walk to the ground together, despite the rival rosettes they sported. Concannon sensed the crowd's amazement at seeing the two political opponents walking to the match together: 'We both had to take some ribald comments. I had a load of pamphlets in may hand, and he had a load in his, so we went on dishing them out together as we walked along.'

This time Clarke had a record to attack, rather than one to defend: eighteen months of Harold Wilson's government. He did so by concentrating on speaking at indoor meetings, where he found he attracted greater support than on the stump. He talked of hospital waiting lists, which he declared were far too long; he attacked Labour for reducing prescription charges – the money was better spent on new hospitals and more pay for nurses, he said; more schools should be built, and the coal industry should be protected against short-term fluctuations in the fuel market. This was Welfare State Man at work; the Conservatives needed to 'help those who are still in need in our society'.

It was on this subject of society that Clarke came closest to outlining his political creed. He told Young Conservatives at Toton in Nottinghamshire that he wanted to make it clear 'to the people in the outside world who look upon us as the lunatic fringe' why they devoted so much time to politics: 'We are all of us engaged in active politics because we feel a deep concern about the public affairs of our country and, in particular, about the human problems of our society.'

Under Ted Heath's early leadership, which drew continuity from Macmillan but looked to the future to tackle Wilson on his own modernising ground, Clarke felt naturally at home. According to Nicholas Budgen, who watched much of Clarke's political development in the 1960s: 'He believes in efficiency, in modernising Britain and in many of the things that Ted Heath believes in . . . He's more a Conservative than he is a Tory.' The party, as Alan Watkins remarked in the *Spectator*, was no longer the party of the land or of big business, but was trying to become the party of the consumer. As he campaigned in Mansfield, Clarke's economic views reflected this desire to eliminate waste and encourage efficiency. Taxes should be reduced to encourage hard work and initiative; management should be improved through better education; restrictive practices in industry should be ended, and both the trade unions and 'archaic' industrial relations should be modernised.[7]

Clarke's second Mansfield campaign reached its climax, if such a one-sided battle could be deemed to have one, with the first ever joint meeting of its parliamentary candidates. It was a noisy affair, with shouts of 'Rubbish!' and 'Nonsense!' punctuating the speeches. Concannon turned up fifty-five minutes late and was barred from making his introductory address by the vicar, who was chairing the meeting in the civic hall. It made no difference to the election result; there was a recount, but only because the Liberal had lost his deposit, and when the result was finally announced to the crowd outside, Concannon's majority was just under 19,000. Clarke's vote went down, but by only thirty-four and his percentage of the poll went up marginally. While Mansfield's Tories were disappointed that he hadn't done better the second time around, Clarke put a brave face on it. With an overwhelming swing to Labour in the country at large, he claimed that Mansfield was one of half a dozen places which had shown a swing to the Tories. 'Labour are a thousand votes down,' he proclaimed. In fact, it wasn't true; the Labour vote was up marginally in percentage terms, although, like Clarke's, the numerical vote was down slightly, mainly because a Communist had stood.

Clarke had done his duty by Mansfield. It was time to begin the search for a safer seat and to build his legal career in Birmingham.

CHAPTER 4

Graduates on the Make

'What great cause is he identified with?'
'He's identified . . . with the great cause of cheering us all up.'
Arnold Bennett, *The Card*

For all Kenneth Clarke's many and varied interests, politics is the backbone of his life, and has been his motivating force, since his schooldays. His only other full-time job has been the law, and that was only as a means to an end, a way to support his family and to cushion the vagaries of political life. In any lengthy conversation with Clarke about his political career, the words 'the sack' will occur. He became a barrister, he says, 'because I assumed by political tradition that it would be easy to combine the two jobs. In fact they are both full-time occupations, and you are literally moonlighting.'

The law is nevertheless a perfect occupation for a man of Clarke's temperament. Lawyers are paid to express themselves in certainties, as well as to perform. Clarke's intellectual self-confidence, instilled at school and university, found the same expression in the court-room as it would at Westminister. 'I compare the Bar, and theatre, and politics, and the Church. To do any of the four, you need a temperament that allows you to tread the boards; there's an element of public performance.'[1] In time, his political opponents would charge that he brought a lawyer's approach to politics, that he was paid for his words, and not for his beliefs.

Clarke's legal career started in the summer of 1963, when he finally left Cambridge, with high prospects but little money. He presented himself at his bank in Eastwood, opposite the site of his father's first shop, and with some trepidation kept an appointment with his bank manager. His political entertaining at Cambridge had caught up with

him and he had run up what he calls 'a great overdraft'. He was forced
to confess to the bank manager that he 'didn't have a bean'. It was,
Clarke remembers, a dreaded interview, but the bank manager took
an enlightened view of the young man's prospects, observed his
crumpled appearance and offered to lend him more money in order
that he might go out and buy himself some decent clothes. So at the
bank's expense, Clarke bought a black jacket and striped trousers,
bowler hat, overcoat and umbrella: the outfit of a provincial barrister.
There was, inevitably, one further item on the shopping list: 'Sad to
say, he was particularly emphatic about footwear. He told me to go
and get a decent pair of good English handmade shoes.' The bank
manager, wisely, considered that he was more likely to get Barclays'
money back if his client started his life in chambers looking
respectable. However, having unfurled his umbrella once, Clarke
found it impossible to return it to its pencil-thin shape and so he
started his legal career in Birmingham looking like a youthful version
of Charlie Chaplin.

The pupil barrister had kept true to the calculation he made on
leaving school that he would head for the Birmingham Bar. The
chambers he joined, at 3 Fountain Court, are one of the city's oldest
sets and gave the new barrister a variety of legal work. The chambers
concentrate on criminal work; but some 40 per cent of the practice is
civil work, particularly personal injury cases for unions, because of a
good relationship with a local firm of solicitors which concentrates on
such cases. Clarke handled many of these compensation cases and won
a reputation for being a fair-minded, combative lawyer, and one with a
sense of humour.

When questioned about his career, Clarke tends to express himself
in anecdotes. This is partly because he finds life enjoyable and,
although self-confident and ambitious, is not averse to humorous self-
deprecation. It comes partly also from his knowledge of what
journalists need to write a story. Yet it appears, too, to be a defence
mechanism, a carapace against the outside world. It is not an act – this
is his natural ebullient character – but it also serves to protect him
from intrusion into his private thoughts.

Just as Clarke's friends in politics, outside his Cambridge circle, are
men who like a pint and a joke, so too his greatest friend in chambers
was David Jones, who shared his love of sport and good beer and his

sense of humour. The law could never be too serious when they were together in court. Once when Clarke and Jones were opposing each other at Coventry Crown Court a pair of handcuffs was produced as an exhibit. The judge retired to consider the case, leaving Clarke and Jones alone in court, with the handcuffs lying on the counsel's benches. The temptation was too strong for Clarke; he snapped the handcuffs on to his friend's left wrist. David Jones had never been in handcuffs before:

> I lost all circulation. Suddenly, the judge came back into court wanting some more information about the defendant, so I had to stick my left hand up the back of my gown to hide it. My hand hurt so much I had to keep flexing it, and there was this chink, chink, chink. Then the judge asked a question, and Ken started to snigger. Normally he can keep a straight face – but he kept hearing this chink, chink, chink, and he couldn't stop laughing.

David Jones was to wreak his revenge in a way he never intended. One Monday the pair were at Warwick Crown Court dealing with a large group of teenagers who had been 'joy-riding'. Clarke was prosecuting, Jones defending, and both of them found the case excruciatingly boring. The teenagers all pleaded guilty; the facts were the same in each case; and the paperwork was mountainous. As he ploughed through his opening submission, Clarke lost his concentration. One of the defendants had stolen a Ford Granada from Meriden, but Clarke, without realising it, told the court that the youth had stolen a Ford Meriden from Granada. Jones, highly amused, passed Clarke a note claiming that the police wanted it brought to the court's attention that there was a warrant from the Spanish police for the arrest of his defendant:

> I never thought he'd take it seriously. But for Ken, who was bored silly over this case, the whole day had suddenly livened up and he triumphantly announced the news to the court. The poor defendant, who hadn't been beyond Coventry in his life, didn't know what was going on, and I thought – that's my career gone. The police sergeant was by now looking round desperately, wondering which colleague had dumped this on him, and he

asked Ken for more details. Ken was halfway through telling him when he finally twigged what had gone on. He had to tell the court he'd had his leg pulled.

The two young barristers were extremely competitive. The image today of Clarke is of a man who never takes exercise, unless it is to raise a glass of beer or wine. But in those Birmingham days he and Jones used regularly to run a couple of miles through the woods in the south of the city, before going on to the local snooker club. Although they promised each other that they wouldn't race, as they neared the end of the run the pace would quicken, until finally it became an all-out sprint for home. The two only gave up jogging when they took so long to recover from their sprint that they missed their first frame of snooker. 'Our wives insisted,' says Clarke. 'They thought we were going to kill ourselves.'

Clarke impressed his new legal colleagues with his energy and enthusiasm, even after he became an MP. In the mid-1970s, when he was an opposition spokesman on social security, his standard way of life was to get up early in Birmingham, go to court at half-past ten until the end of the day, travel down to London for a ten o'clock vote and return to Birmingham on the midnight train. The former head of his chambers, Derek Stanley, remembers that Clarke 'had a very clear mind. He could dictate a whole pile of letters, read a brief, go to the County Court – and then catch a train to London. It was an absolutely punishing routine.' Twice Clarke fell asleep on the return journey and failed to wake up at New Street Station, ending up in Wolverhampton in the small hours. The first time he managed to get a taxi. The second time he had to sleep in the waiting room at Wolverhampton Station, using his blue barrister's bag as a pillow. 'The glittering prizes of politics and the law!' he thought to himself as he waited for the early-morning train to take him back to Birmingham and the start of another day in the courts.

By 1979 Clarke had had enough of this lifestyle. If Mrs Thatcher had failed to give him a job in government, he would have kept up the law but moved his practice to London. In fact, he became a junior transport minister and took silk 'as an insurance policy. Had we lost the election, had I been sacked I would have gone back and practised as a QC.'

During those early days in Birmingham, Clarke's way of life put immense pressure on his young family. While her husband was leading his peripatetic existence, Gillian Clarke had her hands full bringing up their two young children – Kenneth (again), who was born in October 1965, and Susan, born in November 1968. She also helped his search for a parliamentary seat and ran an Oxfam shop which opened near their home in Moseley. Clarke is fully aware of what he calls 'the down side of being a politician': 'It places a disproportionate burden on your family, which can cause distinct problems. You don't lead an ordinary family life, largely because of the hours you spend away. We used to joke about Gillian being a one-parent family.' His wife agrees with his analysis: 'Family life in Ken's early days in Parliament was obviously rather unusual, though many fathers in those days who commuted some distance to work saw little more of their children than he did. We responded by making the most of our holidays, and by being fairly firm about keeping Sunday free of political engagements.'

Their daughter Susan found there was a price to pay, and in her late teens she rebelled. This protest took the form of shaving and dying her hair, sporting a three-inch panther tattoo on her back and keeping a pet rat called Esmerelda. She was pictured in the flat she shared with her boyfriend, Ben, in a tabloid newspaper during a Tory Party conference when Clarke was Health Secretary. 'Both Ben and I are rebels. We want to function as individuals with identities of our own,' she was quoted as saying. 'My dad's terrific. He understands it's a big strain the way people expect me to live up to his standards. I was sick of being Kenneth Clarke's daughter.' Clarke, for all his affability and gregariousness, is at heart a private man, protective of his family, and he was very upset. His friend the MP Jim Lester still remembers 'the shock when he saw the headlines – "Cabinet minister's daughter in squat". She was going through a rebellious phase, but Ken didn't go spare over it, and it all settled down.' Susan later qualified to become a nurse, and her brother Kenneth works in a bank.

Clarke's wife, Gillian, has always made it clear that she wanted to be seen as a person in her own right as her husband pursued his career, and to that end she remained firmly out of the limelight while he climbed the political ladder. She has helped him with constituency work endlessly since he was first elected – commuting by train from

Birmingham to his Nottinghamshire seat, as she doesn't drive – but she prefers to stay at the Midlands end of the operation. She is still, however, a political animal, a ward secretary in her husband's constituency association and a sounding-board for him; as Mrs Clarke explains:

> Detailed and departmental issues tend to stay in the office – after all, Ken does come home to relax, often after a ten- or eleven-hour day. But we do discuss general issues, often those outside his general department. I also sometimes act as channel of communication when friends, neighbours and party workers are obviously concerned about a particular element of government, but not in any formal way.

Although they share a liking for small cigars, the Clarkes appear in many ways to be opposites. She is academic and fiercely private, more so even than Norma Major, while he enjoys the daily cut-and-thrust of public life. She is High Church and fiercely questions the right of the Church of England to permit the ordination of women priests, whereas he is not religious. Clarke's university friend, the Nottingham solicitor Martin Suthers, believes that 'Ken just lets her get on with it. You wouldn't find him in church unless it was the funeral of the chairman of Rushcliffe Borough Council or something!' Mrs Clarke also enjoys pursuits like architectural and flower photography, quilt-making and cooking, while her husband enjoys soccer, snooker and jazz. 'My wife is wholly interested in medieval music, Renaissance music, early classical music – Mozart, Handel, all that kind thing,' Clarke comments. 'I think I enjoy her music more than she enjoys mine. I quite like her stuff – no lover of jazz dislikes Bach. I also go to opera but I infuriate my opera-buff friends – I go because it's a good night out.'

Mrs Clarke's wide variety of interests are far removed from the academic career she might have followed. To quote John Barnes, a friend of the couple since their Cambridge days: 'Gillian set her career on one side, as many women did in the 1950s and 1960s. Her own interests have made up for that.' Mrs Clarke's quilts are certainly time-consuming in their intricacy; one, made for the royal wedding of Charles and Diana, had a bridal wreath in the centre, surrounded by

Tudor roses and oak leaves, with borders of a specially printed wedding fabric.

For his part, Clarke's main interest at home is his collection of political memorabilia and biographies. Outside the home, he and Gillian share a common interest in exploration. Clarke dislikes going on holiday to the same place twice, so a typical family holiday will see them trekking to remote spots to go 'monument-bashing', as they put it: a week at Easter, and a longer summer holiday. Such times are sacrosanct, even if a political crisis is brewing. 'More often than not, Gill will be flat on the ground, looking at an orchid, while Ken has his binoculars out to study a Scandinavian warbler,' John Barnes says.

When in November 1993 Kenneth Clarke held up his Budget box for the first time outside No. 11, it was for many television viewers the first they had seen of Gillian Clarke. She has aged, and is going grey, while her husband appears younger than his age. Unkind voices declared that she looked like his mother. From this have followed suggestions that their marriage cannot be a solid one – although this 'really is an extraordinary suggestion to anyone who knows them well,' according to John Barnes: 'They are extremely relaxed together, even if Gill will sometimes purse her lips if Ken makes a particularly outrageous remark and then grin or make an apt retort.'

In September 1993 the *Mail on Sunday* questioned the state of their relationship, claiming that Mrs Clarke had only twice stayed at her husband's official residence, Dorneywood, while his political adviser, 'happily married' Tessa Keswick, had acted as a 'stand-in'. A month later, on 6 October, at Jeffrey Archer's party on the third floor of the Imperial Hotel in Blackpool, Clarke came face to face with the *Mail on Sunday*'s editor Jonathan Holborow and tore him off a strip. 'The air was blue,' reported one seasoned journalist.

In the midst of the febrile political atmosphere engendered by John Major's 'back to basics' campaign, launched in late 1993, Clarke's friends and political colleagues raised the subject of his marriage unprompted. One of his former advisers describes seeing

female officials hung up on him, looking all dewy-eyed at him. But he doesn't even notice them, even if they're pretty. He's never looked at them or made one remark. It's extraordinary. I just don't think he notices other people. He's very self-centred. I don't mean he's selfish, but he's very self-contained – and so is his wife.

John Gummer concurs: 'He's the Cabinet minister I'd be most surprised about if people started scandal stories about him morally or sexually. I'd know it wasn't true – it just isn't him. He's a very strong character in that sense. He doesn't put himself in those positions.'

With his wife's support at home, Clarke managed to handle his busy Birmingham life of legal work, family and politics; but it was sometimes a close-run thing. Once, after he had become an MP, his legal duties clashed embarrassingly with his politics. In February 1972 he was asked by the NUM to defend two miners who were charged at Cannock magistrates' court with using threatening behaviour on a picket line outside Cannock Computer Centre. As Clarke arrived at court, he found that it was surrounded by hundreds of striking miners and police. It was not natural territory for a Tory MP:

> I was a bit alarmed when I was given the case, but the rule of the Bar is the cab-rank principle: you do it. So I went in and met the clients, and then had a quiet word with the solicitor. I said to him, these guys do know I'm a Conservative MP, don't they? He went off to speak to the NUM agent, who went pale and fired me from the case.

Clarke then applied for an adjournment, explaining that he felt it could be prejudicial to the miners if he acted for them. The presiding magistrate agreed to stay the case for seven days, declaring that the Bench 'would not wish to do anything that would add any fuel to the fire'. Three days later, as publicity surrounding the case grew, Clarke was forced to issue a statement, reflecting that he had not acted unilaterally in withdrawing from the case, because it would have been unprofessional conduct, but that the miners 'in a friendly discussion made it quite clear that they didn't want to be represented by a Tory MP'.

Despite his frenetic lifestyle, Birmingham gave shape to Clarke's political thinking, adding practical experience to the combination of working-class common sense and privileged education provided by Nottingham and Cambridge in turn. His legal work showed him vividly the acute problems of inner-city life in the Midlands, and he formulated specific answers in response. It suited his character so to do.

Clarke is not an ideologue or a man for all-embracing political theories, but rather a holder of firm views. He has never put forward ideological arguments for his brand of Conservatism, except perhaps on Europe. 'European involvement should be the guiding light of our international policy,' he wrote in 1965.[2] In general there have been no tracts, no polemics, no analysis of the overall future shape of Toryism. (In this he is not alone; it is the exception rather than the rule to be a philosopher-king within any political party.) Instead, there have been pamphlets dealing with unglamorous problems, such as the National Health Service, regional government, immigration and regional policy within Europe.

This was not, initially, Clarke's intention. After they went down from Cambridge, three of the Union musketeers promised each other they would try to write a book together, formulating their view of Conservative policy; they were Clarke, Leon Brittan and John Gummer. But the practicalities of everyday life overcame their eagerness to philosophise. Brittan and Gummer lived in London, Clarke in Birmingham, so they arranged to meet a third of the way north of the capital, on the basis that getting out of London was harder than getting out of Birmingham. 'We kept trying to find a suitable venue where we could settle down, but there'd be mishaps,' Brittan recalls. 'So needless to say, the book was never written.'

Birmingham gave Clarke no substitute philosophy for the one he failed to write, but it did provide a piecemeal insight into Britain's problems. There he also found a local platform on which to display his ambition and try out his views: the Birmingham Bow Group, which he ran, as research secretary, with Nicholas Budgen. Clarke sees that it was a way of keeping in touch with politics: 'Before that, I'd joined my local ward branch, but it was a waste of time; it was full of people three times my age all talking about organising whist drives. The Bow Group was a place we could go and listen to speakers or write portentous pamphlets.'

The Birmingham Bow Group had a fluctuating membership of between twenty-five and thirty. 'We were all graduates on the make,' according to Budgen. They held dinners, meetings and conferences, either in each other's homes or in a local hotel. As at Cambridge, important speakers came from London, including the recently deposed Douglas-Home. It was a way of stoking one's personal ambition within the Tory Party. Says Budgen: 'I think we most arrogantly regarded ourselves as the future leaders of the nation and that we were moving inexorably to the recognition which would probably come to us.'

The philosophy of the Bow Group had been outlined a decade earlier, in 1957, by a young lawyer named Geoffrey Howe, when he welcomed Harold Macmillan to the Constitutional Club to launch its new quarterly magazine, *Crossbow*.[3] The core tenets which inspired *Crossbow* were a market economy, a social conscience and a multi-racial Commonwealth, which implied a Tory Party which was against racial discrimination. Within that broad framework, Clarke's Bow Group pamphlets were based on his direct experience of the particular problems of living in Birmingham. National politics were seen firmly and pragmatically through Midlands eyes, through the effect that government policy was having on life in the second city.

The 1962 Commonweath Immigrants Act had stimulated an increased flow of immigrants, keen to enter Britain before controls were imposed. Those already in the country sent for their spouses and families, creating for the first time permanently settled Indian and Pakistani communities here.[4] In Birmingham the Bow Group could see the problem at first hand. One of the heaviest concentrations of immigrants, and an area where racial tensions seemed to be at their worst, was in the Black Country. In 1963 over 100,000 people in Birmingham out of a population of just over a million had been born overseas.

To address the problem, Clarke wrote a sixty-page pamphlet, called *Immigration, Race and Politics*, helped by Nicholas Budgen and the vice-chairman of the Birmingham Bow Group, John Lenton. They found that most people, including the police, appeared to be racially prejudiced but also that immigration had aggravated the social problems of the poorer conurbations – slum housing, poor schools and inadequate hospitals. Society, Clarke argued, had to make a choice between integration and segregation: 'For Conservatives there can be only one solution. The basic principle of British Conservatism is that individuals should be given the opportunity to make the best of their talents and potentials.'[5]

But Clarke and his team came to a surprisingly interventionist conclusion. They decided that, to retain 'the Englishness of our schools', immigrant children should be bused to schools where there would be fewer of them. Similarly, to spread the racial mix more evenly, the government should refuse mortgages to immigrants if they outnumbered white people in any given area. Finally, the pamphleteers proposed a five-year moratorium on immigration.

Some newspaper columnists have suggested that this pamphlet shows Clarke to have been illiberal on racial issues. But busing, for example, was considered a liberal policy, most notably in the United States, in the 1960s; and allowing for the spirit of the times, the pamphlet was a radical analysis of the problem, especially the criticism of the police. If the group's conclusions were extreme (and they appear the more so almost thirty years on), then its analysis was ahead of its time; a year later Labour's Political and Economic Planning report on discrimination in Britain would confirm the scale of the problem, and the Race Relations Act of 1968 would outlaw major forms of discrimination. Clarke argues that he has held liberal views on race relations throughout his life, advocating ethnic monitoring by employers to enhance equal opportunities when he was employment minister, and later, as Home Secretary, appointing the first non-white chairman of the Commission for Racial Equality. He says now that the pamphlet 'obviously turned out to contain a mixed collection of views'.

The second pamphlet of which Clarke was co-author, called simply *Regional Government*, is of import because it shows an early scepticism about the competence of local government, which would be a theme throughout Clarke's political career. It also shows a desire on the part of the future Chancellor to raise taxes to pay for a new and improved system of local administration. Again, this is no philosophical work, but a response to a national debate about local authorities and to the particular problems of the Midlands.

Clarke and three of his Bow Group colleagues considered that local government was in an appalling state, partly because local authorities were 'moribund' but also because central government was overriding their autonomy.[6] What was needed, they suggested, was the creation of seven new Regional Parliaments, to strengthen democracy in their areas and reduce the workload at Westminster. To pay for this new tier of government, Clarke proposed a regional employment tax, levying about £1 per week per employed person, which would raise about £1,000 million a year. There would also be an extra tax on planning permission, possibly levied on the size of the development.

These proposed reforms were predicated on the administrative failings of local government; the pamphlet talks of 'unnecessary conflict and waste' in local authorities overwhelmed by their task. The young barrister looked upon the works of local politicians and despaired. Local government, he declared, suffered from 'fundamental defects' which could not be cured simply by tinkering with its boundaries.

At this stage in his career, Clarke still saw the need for reinvigorated local government, albeit at regional level. Later on, as he despaired ever more strongly over the quality of local politicians, his critics would claim that he saw no need for local government at all. Clarke's dislike of local councils was to be a thread running through his career. But he has had no direct experience of local government; he has held no elected post except at Westminster. His close friend and fellow Nottingham MP Jim Lester believes this is why Clarke has little time for much of local government: 'I suppose it's because of his background in politics. Mine was to come through virtually every sort of local authority, from a parish to a district to a county council; whereas Ken came straight in virtually from university into government.'

Another clue comes from Clarke's writings. In a rare article for *Crossbow* he argued that the Tories' provincial constituency associations contained many people who were more interested in the mechanics of getting out the vote than in discussing policy.[7] Most of the party workers were in his opinion simply committee members, fund-raisers or those prepared to help with the chores. A candidate for a council seat would dutifully attend wine-and-cheese evenings in order to gain press attention, without there being a single political meeting a year.

Clarke compared the inadequacies of local parties to those of local government. The solution, he felt, was to form political groups within local associations to advise Conservative councillors on policy. This might draw in people interested in politics who lacked the time to serve on councils, and they could also give political backbone to the Conservative associations. His conclusions were pessimistic: 'It is no more than a hope that the Conservative Party in the provinces might become a more political party than it is at present.'

It is hard not to see here the high-flying barrister and early candidate for office, fresh out of the university debating chamber, disappointed at the gulf between the politicians he had met as a student and those he was meeting on the ground. Local politics, viewed from above rather than experienced directly, impressed him only with its limitations. This was a view he would take with him to Westminster and into the Cabinet. Within six years, as an MP, he would be persuading the government to reduce the number of rural councillors in areas of low population; and as Education Secretary, and then Home Secretary, he would introduce reforms aimed at raising standards by reducing the power of local authorities over schools and the police.

To put his ideas into practice, however, Clarke, the veteran of two Mansfield campaigns, still had to find himself a decent seat.

In the summer of 1962 a young man had walked confidently into the Bulwell office of the Conservative agent for North Nottingham and offered to help. The offer was of limited use. He was, he said, willing to address meetings on political matters; but as it was the height of summer and an election was two years away, the agent reflected wisely that the Nottingham public's appetite for political speeches was hardly overwhelming. The young man was Clarke; the agent, Roger Stewart; and they have now worked in harness in Rushcliffe for over a quarter of a century.

Clarke failed to find himself a public platform in those early days, but in 1966, as candidate for Mansfield, he was taken up on his offer to speak, and he was to be rewarded handsomely. The Conservative candidate for nearby Rushcliffe, Nottinghamshire's southernmost constituency, was Sir Martin Redmayne, who had represented the seat for sixteen years and was now the opposition spokesman on agriculture. Sir Martin, who had fought for the Sherwood Foresters in the Second World War, was an old-style politician. 'Television is a queer medium,' he told his constituents in 1965, a statement which befitted a man who public pronouncements were few and far between. For thirteen of his sixteen years at Westminster he enjoyed the monastic silence of the Whips' Office, and in public he was reluctant to press the flesh, preferring the political camaraderie at Westminster to glad-handing the voters. His style of campaigning reflected his reserve. During the week, when Parliament was sitting, he stayed at his London flat, coming up to Nottingham only at weekends. During an election, to the puzzlement of his party workers, he simply reversed the process, electioneering in Rushcliffe for five days but disappearing at weekends back to London.

So it was not altogether surprising that one Sunday during the 1966 general election campaign he preferred the delights of Knightsbridge to the pleasure of addressing an audience at the Sutton Bonington School of Agriculture. Clarke took his place and held forth confidently in the question-and-answer session which followed his speech. Watching him perform were members of the local branch of the Conservative Association, including Norman Beeby, who within a year would chair a selection panel to choose Sir Martin's successor: 'I lived next door to the college so I went along to listen to this young man. I was struck by his confidence as a speaker and how good he was at answering questions on a whole range of issues.' It was to be a decisive ingredient in Clarke's success in gaining a secure seat.

Sir Martin Redmayne's majority in Rushcliffe was always slim. None the less, he had held on in 1964 with more than 2,500 votes to spare, and it was something of a shock to Tory voters in the region when he lost the seat in 1966. The Liberals, standing for the first time since 1950, ate into the Tory vote to such an extent that Labour's Tony Gardner, a college lecturer fighting the constituency for the first time, scraped home after a recount by 380 votes. Sir Martin, who was later ennobled in the Dissolution Honours List, was moved to call it 'a slightly disappointing moment for me'. Within a year of this defeat the search was on for a younger, less reserved candidate who might wrest back the seat.

On Friday 2 December 1966, 130 members of the central council of the Rushcliffe Conservative Association met to consider more than sixty candidates who had applied for the seat. The selection procedure was tortuous. There are more than thirty branches in the association and each was allowed to choose members to help select the new candidate. All were allowed a say, including the coffee club. Eventually fourteen names emerged for the round of interviews; they included Clarke, Ivan Lawrence, Tom Boardman and a 31-year-old scheduling consultant from Burton-on-Trent, David Penfold, a borough councillor who had fought Nottingham West at the previous election.

It was only the second time in seventeen years that the selection committee had met to choose a candidate and they decided to short-list the two young local hopefuls with campaign experience, Clarke and Penfold. Their names went forward to a two-hour meeting of the association's central council in Beeston, where a record ninety members came to take part in the proceedings. It was not a smooth meeting. Some of them felt they should have been presented with a longer short list, so in order to keep the peace the dissenters were told they could abstain if they wished and that their abstentions would count; the winning candidate had to gain at least 50 per cent of the votes of everybody there.

The two candidates were asked to speak on future Tory policy and then to answer questions from the audience. They were left in no doubt that Clarke was his own man. He was asked for his views on capital punishment and he spoke out strongly against it, which was against the sentiment of the meeting. He was also asked whether he would come and live in the constituency, and he said no; he had put down roots in Birmingham, where his children were at school. Mrs Clarke, too, was not going to make false promises: 'My main memory is of the murmur of approval when I was asked about my possible participation in constituency affairs. I replied that it would always depend on satisfactory arrangements for baby-sitting.' In the end, Clarke's confidence and easy speaking manner convinced his questioners; he won by a large majority, with only two or three abstentions. Norman Beeby, who remembered the skilful way Clarke had handled the audience at Sutton Bonington, was again impressed: 'It was his attitude, his knowledge and his confidence. He was able to answer questions on almost any political issue, almost without thinking about it. He looked like someone who could win the seat for us.' Clarke's apprenticeship in Mansfield had served its purpose.

The new candidate's name duly went forward to a public adoption meeting at Roundhill School in Beeston, where he was acclaimed by an audience of several hundred, including his old Mansfield chairman, Tim Martin. Martin had, at Clarke's request, provided a testimonial letter for the selection committee: 'One of the proudest moments of my life was to sit in the front row of the audience, with all the top brass on the stage. The chairman read out my letter word for word. I'd never felt so proud in all my life.' Mansfield had repaid its dues.

The Rushcliffe Tories had picked a very different man to succeed the elderly Lord Redmayne. Clarke was young: a veteran of two general elections, but still only twenty-six; a believer in words by the yard, not a silent Westminster operator; an enthusiastic campaigner; a Macleodite who looked forward, not a Home supporter who looked back. In short, he was a man determined to win back an eminently winnable seat and to carve a Westminster career.

Like many marginal seats, Rushcliffe was then barely a coherent area. In those days, it spread across miles of green belt and farmland, but also across mining villages and the urban district on the edge of the City of Nottingham, which was its largest part. The first step for the new Conservative team hunting votes in this disparate sprawl was to build up the association's organisation and to find ways of attracting publicity in the main local papers of the constituency. A former Nottingham newspaper editor, Bernard Malkinson, remembers meeting Clarke early on in his career: 'I told him there's no politics or religion in my newspaper, but if it's news it gets printed. And he said thank you for telling it straight.' Clarke's campaign team worked out the circulations of papers like the *Beeston Gazette* and the *Loughborough Echo* and then concentrated their efforts accordingly. Clarke's agent, Roger Stewart, considers that they were rigorous in their approach: 'We used to have a system whereby we'd measure the column inches in all our local papers to see how much Gardner had got and how much Clarke had got. We used to produce weekly accounts – our aim was to equal the sitting MP.' It meant an endless round of coffee mornings, suppers and even beauty contests. The man who had shut the door against women in the Cambridge Union had a kiss planted on him by Miss UK, and found himself judging the 'Miss Rushcliffe Young Conservative' competition. It worked; the local papers sent their photographers to picture Clarke as he posed with the five finalists.

Westminster visitors helped Clarke nurture the constituency: Heathmen like Peter Walker and Tony Barber, and Margaret Thatcher too. One Friday at the end of October 1969 Clarke greeted the latter, now shadow Education Secretary, at a small village hall in Attenborough. They smiled, shook hands and made speeches which showed that, while they were fighting for the same cause, a Tory government with Ted Heath as Prime Minister, their political approach was a study in contrasts. Mrs Thatcher ground through a complex explanation of why the Bank Rate was higher under Labour, compared it in minute detail to the reduction of purchase tax under the Tories, and quoted a barrage of statistics to attack the balance-of-payments deficit. For Clarke, on the other hand, the 'really great issue' was Europe, and in particular the public's new-found doubt about the Common Market, which he blamed on the Labour government's faltering leadership. It was not a meeting of minds in style or substance.

Both parties sent the biggest names they could to Rushcliffe for the 1970 general election campaign. The Tories knew they had to win the seat to regain power and despatched their deputy leader, Reginald Maudling, the transport spokesman, Michael Heseltine, the shadow trade minister, Keith Joseph, and the shadow minister of power, Sir John Eden. For Labour, Prime Minister Harold Wilson made a ten-minute visit, and his deputy, George Brown, came too. Neither visit was an unalloyed success. Wilson's train was delayed by a storm which damaged signalling equipment and he was an hour late; Brown was heckled by Young Conservatives in Beeston, and as they left he called after them, 'Goodnight, children.' They replied, 'Goodnight, father.'

By contrast, the Tory campaign seemed to be working smoothly. There were 100,000 leaflets to be handed out, 45,000 letters to be sent and 40,000 houses to be canvassed. Clarke and his team wore special badges, not just rosettes, to spread the name of the new candidate across the length and breadth of Rushcliffe. He campaigned not just on prices and the balance of payments, which he felt would decide the election, but on his own belief in an efficient Britain which could provide for its poor: 'Bureaucracy and waste have grown to ridiculous proportions in Whitehall. A competent government can cut costs without damaging social services at all.'[8]

The swing to Ted Heath in the 1970 election came as no surprise to the campaigners of Rushcliffe. As in many constituencies that the Tories won, its canvass returns had defied the national opinion polls throughout the campaign. Clarke and his team were canvassing in Chilwell on the Saturday before polling day when the news came through that the gap had closed between Heath and Wilson, and it reinforced their belief that they were going to win handsomely. When the votes were counted at Bramcote Hills Secondary Modern School on Friday 19 June 1970 Clarke had a majority of more than six thousand, the largest since 1955 when the constituency's boundaries had been changed. He celebrated with a pint of beer at the Rushcliffe constituency headquarters. Just seven years out of Cambridge, Kenneth Clarke had become an MP. He had achieved his ambition of reaching Parliament by his self-imposed deadline with unerring accuracy; the State Opening of Parliament was held on 2 July – the date of his thirtieth birthday.

CHAPTER 5

Glittering Prizes

But the privilege and pleasure
That we treasure beyond measure
Is to run on little errands for the
Ministers of State.
              W. S. Gilbert, *The Gondoliers*

Clarke's baptism at Westminster reflected the upbringing which had shaped him both politically and personally. Politically, he stayed true to the European hopes he had first nurtured at Cambridge, and to his Macleodite background. Personally, he was a self-confident performer in the chamber and gregarious outside it, a friend of party colleagues and opposition MPs alike. His party made full use of his character. Clarke's ability to get on with the Labour opposition would help keep Ted Heath's European dream alive.

Clarke was still calculating his personal way ahead. On entering Parliament for the first time, he determined to avoid the politics of the law. Home Office speeches were not for him. He did not want to become typecast as just another Conservative lawyer who might, in the fullness of time, become a government law officer. For Clarke, politics was too broad a subject to travel down such a narrow legal road. Later, in a career slowed down by Mrs Thatcher, he would be tempted to take this very route. But for now he was eager to keep his politics and his practice separate.

Clarke made his maiden speech almost immediately in the Queen's Speech debate on education. Like his Bow Group pamphlets, his first utterances to Parliament, on 8 July 1970, were firmly rooted in his local experience. By a twist of fate, he addressed himself to the very woman who would keep him out of the Cabinet for longer than his talent dictated, and for longer than he would have expected under Heath.

Clarke's speech rested on an appeal to the new Education Secretary, Margaret Thatcher, to permit diversity of schooling in his constituency. The Conservative local authority had built what he called an excellent comprehensive school, to replace run-down buildings. But, conversely, the previous Labour administration had built another comprehensive school on three different sites, forcing pupils to travel several miles between them by bus. Clarke accused the Labour government of creating the mess in the name of educational uniformity.[1] From his first day in Parliament, therefore, Clarke showed that he was at heart a pragmatist, in the sense that he brought with him few hard-and-fast political theories. He asked Mrs Thatcher to issue her guidance on non-doctrinal grounds. Ironically, he went on to praise her speech that afternoon for its flexibility and common sense: 'Although it may catch the notice of the education Press a little less often, it makes far more sense to look at individual cases and to consider them carefully before plunging into changes which may seem on the face of them to have some doctrinaire attractions.'

Cambridge had prepared Clarke well for his Westminster career, and he was aware of it. He likened Parliament to the Cambridge Union: 'It seemed very much the same in layout, except the Union is shabbier.'[2] Something else was familiar: his style. As at the High School, so at Westminster, he swayed as he talked. In Parliament, however, the microphone picked up his voice at a variety of different levels. 'I shall have to speak to attention,' he said, injecting his usual brand of humour into the proceedings. Late one night, in front of six MPs, he raised the subject of a fowlpest outbreak at farms in his constituency. He contrasted the strength of public concern whenever there was an outbreak of foot-and-mouth disease with the lack of interest in fowlpest: 'Whether cattle evoke greater public sympathy than chickens I do not know. Perhaps there is something about the eyes.'[3]

Clarke made rapid progress in this Parliament. His comparison with the Cambridge Union was valid; he was back in the old club, among the right people. This time, his Bow Group membership served him well. Geoffrey Howe, now ensconced in a safe seat after an earlier defeat at Bebington, had become Solicitor-General in the Heath government. Howe had helped the Birmingham Bow Group come into existence and knew Clarke as a like-minded politician, regarding him as 'a kindred spirit'. He chose Clarke to be his parliamentary private secretary or PPS. The job thrust Clarke into the centre of the battle for the Heath government's two pillars of legislation, the Industrial Relations Act, which was to collapse humiliatingly around its ears, and the European Communities Act, which stands as Heath's memorial to his three and a half years in office. Clarke could not have wished for a more active start at Westminster.

The Industrial Relations Bill had been promised by the Tories ever since Ted Heath took over as leader. The events of 1970 had confirmed the party's determination – more days were lost through strikes than at any time since 1926 – and the government felt that this was its main mandate from the electorate.[4] With the passage of time, the bill's provisions seem modest, but it appeared then that they provided nothing less than the 'revolution so quiet and yet so total' which Heath had promised upon entering Downing Street. Older, wiser heads warned the new young breed of Heathmen that it might not prove to be practical politics. 'I became deeply immersed in the whole thing,' Clarke recollects. 'I sat through it all, and delayed going on my holidays until it was finished. I made piles and piles of notes on clauses as it went through.'

The bill's main aim was to reduce the number of strikes, especially unofficial ones. It proposed that the law should enforce agreements between management and unions, with the crucial exception that the two sides, if they both agreed, could exempt themselves from its provisions. A new national Industrial Relations Court was established to enforce the Act and hear cases of unfair industrial practices. It had the power to lift a strike by imposing a sixty-day cooling-off period, and order secret ballots of union membership. The closed shop was banned.

Clarke's role was a modest one and yet central. As Howe's PPS he performed a vital service for his mentor, liaising with backbenchers as the bill ate up over a hundred hours of parliamentary time. According to Howe: 'There was no doubt about his identification with what we were trying to do. It was very much part of mainstream thinking for our generation and our group of people.' This was the most bitterly fought legislation of the Heath government, with sixty-three success- ive divisions at the end of the report stage. Outside Parliament, the unions defied the law, led by the dockers and then the railway workers. When 30,000 dockers went on strike to support three colleagues who had ignored an order from the Industrial Relations Court to stop picketing, the Official Solicitor searched for and found a loophole enabling him to quash the court's decision.

Clarke identified himself wholly with the Industrial Relations Act. It fitted his vision of a Britain where individuals could thrive, untrammelled by vested interests. He condemned a one-day strike held against the bill in December 1970, saying it had been organised by people who 'believe themselves to be defending a traditional trade union freedom – to be the only organised group above the law in this country'.[5] In time, under a new leader, Clarke's attitude to union power hardened further, as he faced disputes at the Transport Department and at Health. The closed shop, still unopened more than ten years later, would provide him with an issue with which to cement his Cabinet position. But other Heathite policies he was identified with would serve him less well under Mrs Thatcher.

Geoffrey Howe's other main task was the legislation to take Britain into the European Community, a task which took fifty-three days of parliamentary debate. Clarke was again a keen supporter, responsible for helping Howe through some three hundred hours of duty on the floor of the House. Because MPs were not put under a guillotine it required tactical subtlety to know how to keep the procedure moving, with many Tory MPs indifferent to the legislation or even put off by Heath's heavy-handed pressure. There were long debates which had to be speeded through without giving the impression that MPs were being railroaded. 'Ken was very important in terms of telling people when to speak and when not to speak,' remembers Howe. 'We had people like John Gummer on the backbenches who could be turned on or off like a fruit machine. Ken was quite good at doing that.' But Clarke's role was to prove even more vital.

By the time the European Communities Bill had reached its final stages, Clarke was in the Whips' Office. No sooner had Heath, against his better judgement, been persuaded that the Tory Party should have a free vote on Europe than the Labour Party was then put under a whip to vote against the bill. Suddenly, Heath's pro-Europe majority had disappeared. During the ensuing parliamentary battles, Clarke was among those who 'had to work out how many rebels we had on a particular issue, and how the devil we could get it through'. As a new and relatively unknown member of the Whips' Office, he was chosen to form an unlikely alliance with Labour Party supporters of Roy Jenkins who wanted the bill to succeed. Each day he liaised with the Labour MP John Roper, who was the unofficial whip for the Jenkinsites:

> We might not have got into the Community if we hadn't had an unofficial arrangement in which I was the go-between. I would meet John each day and discuss with him how many Jenkinsites should fail to turn up that evening. We'd have to negotiate it, because they all had trouble with their constituency associations. I'd suggest the number we needed to match the number of Conservative rebels we knew we were going to have that night. The nearest we got to losing the European Communities Bill was when John and I made a slight error and the majority went down to three or four.

Geoffrey Howe was excited by Europe as few others were, but Clarke matched his enthusiasm. He spoke at a vast pro-Common-Market rally held in Trafalgar Square, and in May 1971 he argued in the Commons that its debate on the terms of British entry had to be speeded up.[6] He also asked Heath if he would visit France to try to increase the support of voters there in the country's referendum on Britain's entry. Later, as a whip, Clarke was drafted into the government team dealing with Britain's participation in the European Community. He also became a member of the Council of Europe, the Western European Union and the North Atlantic Assembly, spending two or three days a month at meetings on the Continent. Heath's Tory Party was a natural home for Clarke precisely because of the Prime Minister's European commitment. In John Gummer's view: 'Ken was wedded to a kind of common-sense Tory view of life which was pretty down-to-earth, and Ted Heath tended to surround himself with grandees who were left of centre in a rather patronising way. Ken never belonged to that. The crucial connection was Europe.'

The Conservative Party generally demonstrates loyalty, until it decides to be disloyal, when it becomes ruthless. Until that point, it dines on the problem. From the Carlton Club, the venue for the 1922 rebellion, to the wartime Tory Reform Committee and the high-flyers of the Blue Chip club of 1979, private dining clubs have chewed on good food and à la carte political dissent behind closed doors. Clarke's own position within Heath's party was marked by his membership of a club which he joined shortly after reaching Parliament in 1970. Nick's Diner was a club for like-minded politicians who were nervous about Heath's apparent drift to the right when he first took office. It had its roots in 'Selsdon Man' and it took its inspiration, literally and philosophically, from Iain Macleod.

'Selsdon Man' had been Harold Wilson's description of Ted Heath in January 1970, when Heath had held a conference of his shadow Cabinet colleagues at Selsdon Park. In reality, the weekend appears to have produced little in the way of new policies, but the newspapers convinced themselves that Heath had swung to the right, particularly on law and order and immigration. Wilson's clever turn of phrase rapidly invested in Heath a unity of purpose which was unwarranted. It also worried the Macleodite Left of the Conservative Party.

Macleod's death, so soon after he became Chancellor, robbed Heath of his most senior lieutenant and compounded the Left's worries. Clarke is one of many to whom this seemed a great blow to the government:

> I think he would have been a great Chancellor and I think it caused quite a weakness for us, although I don't know how well he would have continued to get on with Ted. But the fact is the government eventually fell by political misjudgement, and Iain was a political heavyweight whose judgement was good. Someone with his political influence might just have pulled Heath back from disaster.

After Macleod's death, his PPS, Nicholas Scott, found himself without a job but with the time to think about Heath's apparent rightward drift. By the end of 1970 he was also nervous that Heath might be pushed off his commitment to Europe by the Labour opposition and the truculence of his own backbenchers. So Scott invited sixteen fellow MPs to join his dining club, which was named after a Chelsea restaurant, to discuss their political views. There were three criteria that the chosen sixteen had to fulfil: they had to be young, congenial and sympathetic to 'One Nation' Toryism. It was a gentlemen's dining club, and political friction was not welcomed: discourse among friends, certainly, but not tooth-and-claw debate with the unenlightened. As each month the sixteen met in dining-room B in the House of Commons to talk about the government's progress, the whips suspected a deep-laid plot to reduce the government's modest majority.

The nucleus of the MPs who joined Nick's Diner was a group of philosophically like-minded friends from the early 1960s; and many of the MPs who were invited to join had been contemporaries at Oxbridge and active in the Federation of University Conservative and Unionist Associations and the Bow Group. For Clarke this was a continuation of the political clubs which had helped shape his beliefs. He joined, as did Hugh Dykes, Alan Haselhurst, David Knox and David Madel. One member of Nick's Diner declared that Enoch Powell had called them 'Macmillan's children'.[7] But they were more Macleod's children. Barney Hayhoe, now Lord Hayhoe, entered Parliament at the same time as Clarke: 'Ken was like Iain Macleod. He could be right-wing on some issues, but he showed a concern for social issues. And he had the same ability to be sharply critical in debate without being personally vituperative or wounding.'

Clarke's liberal credentials were making themselves felt. In his first month in Parliament he was among twenty-nine Conservative MPs who tabled a motion condemning apartheid and effectively criticising Sir Alec Douglas-Home's decision, as Foreign Secretary, to resume arms supplies to South Africa. Nicholas Scott recalls that Clarke was

> already tremendously committed socially to the Macleodite approach to life. Despite the fact that he carries into politics the adversarial, combative approach of the court-room, underneath he's very sensible, understanding the need for social cohesion. What he doesn't like is vested interest groups, people defending their own interests.

Nearly twenty years after he joined Nick's Diner, Clarke would reflect upon the nature of the club. As a guest of honour at a dinner to mark the fortieth anniversary of the Young Conservatives, Clarke remarked in the course of his speech that he found it something of a paradox that

Nick Scott and other ministers in Mrs Thatcher's government had found it necessary, as junior MPs, to establish a dining club to stop the Heath government becoming too right-wing: 'What happened was that under Ted it was quite obvious that everyone in Nick's Diner was very rapidly going to be in the government. And under Margaret Thatcher none of Nick's Diner were going to be in the government, apart from Barney Hayhoe and myself, who were both tolerated.'

Clarke was now making striking progress under Heath. Not only had he put his feet upon the first rung of promotion by acting as Sir Geoffrey Howe's PPS, but he was also making a good impression in the chamber. His views on the inadequacies of local government, threading back to his Bow Group days, persuaded the Home Office to change its Local Government Bill. Clarke pointed out that sparsely populated rural areas did not need or deserve to have as many as three councillors, elected annually. The government agreed, and non-metropolitan district councils were also allowed to opt for single-member wards. Clarke was delighted, declaring that 'this will ensure proper local representation and a minimum of electioneering politics at district levels'.[8] The pamphleteer against local government waste, the candidate who viewed with distaste the feebleness of local politics, had scored a modest victory and it did not go unnoticed.

In April 1972, at the age of thirty-one, Clarke became the youngest member of the Heath government, chosen by the Chief Whip, Francis Pym, to join his team as an assistant whip. On the day the news was announced Clarke was appearing in a Factory Acts case for a union at Hereford County Court. His new job meant he was a paid member of the government, and so he had to give up practising the law. Only once more would he return to the Bar – between 1974 and 1979, during Labour's interregnum.

For more than two decades Clarke has been a member of every Tory government. It has been a long journey – slower than many because of the party's change of direction under Mrs Thatcher – during which he has adapted and survived. But in the Whips' Office in the 1970s Clarke's political personality was already wearing thin with his more right-wing colleagues. While Clarke is genuinely liked by most of his political colleagues and even by his opponents, exceptions are to be found on the right wing of his party, among those who harbour suspicions about his lack of political commitment and his barrister's

approach to politics. As Cecil Parkinson, who served in the Whips'
Office with Clarke, remembers:

> He always liked to take the contrary view. He always wanted to
> argue. If the prevailing view was one thing, you had the feeling
> that he'd take the opposite just for the hell of it – and enjoy it. He
> gives this impression of being benign and very hail-fellow-well-
> met but in fact he's rather a contrary, quirky individual who
> really is quite chippy. He always, always, seems to find it
> necessary to contradict people. He just enjoys being the odd man
> out. It's his *métier*.

There was to be another cause of the Right's distaste for Clarke. For
Mrs Thatcher and her acolytes, the defining moment of the Heath
government was its U-turn on industrial policy, the reversal of the
very policy on which it had been elected. His entire government was,
in her eyes and with hindsight, tainted by this issue. Clarke fully
supported Heath's change in policy.

In January 1972 unemployment reached one million and the
Cabinet feared for the social consequences. From then on, the
government stood policy on its head, with the rescue of Upper Clyde
Shipbuilders, Anthony Barber's tax-cutting Budget, which aimed to
cut unemployment, and the Industry Act, which laid out vast schemes
for assistance. Clarke was fully behind the move, although he now
recants:

> I remember that at the time, in the Whips' Office, I was strongly
> in favour of the U-turn. We were convinced that intolerable
> social pressures would build up if unemployment went over one
> million. I think I began to have doubts about the subsequent
> policy as it went on and certainly now, with hindsight, I regard it
> as a serious mistake.

Only the fittest would survive under Thatcherite natural selection.
Clarke would gradually adapt his economic views as the habitat
changed around him.

Clarke did become partly convinced of some of the new Thatcherite
policies; but his change of opinion was also a consequence of his

refusal to stick to a doctrinal point of view. For example, he opposed the Heath government's incomes policy, which was imposed when lengthy talks with the unions over voluntary restraint broke down, but this was not a hard-and-fast position for Clarke: 'I am afraid that my views on incomes policy were always out of fashion throughout the 1970s. I tended to favour them when we didn't have them and to be against them when they were introduced. I came down to settled views in opposition to incomes policies in the early 1980s.'

Despite the political problems of the Heath government, Clarke had made rapid progress. After 1975, however, with his leader's political demise and Mrs Thatcher's ascent, his progress would seem far more pedestrian. Yet, while Clarke was still riding high at Westminster, there was a battle looming in Rushcliffe.

The boundary redistributions brought in by the Heath government created both an opportunity and a problem for Clarke in Nottingham-shire. One seat, Norman Fowler's Nottingham South constituency, disappeared; a new seat, Beeston, was created from the rump of the Rushcliffe seat; and Rushcliffe itself was made into one of the safest seats in the land.

The boundary commissioners had looked upon Rushcliffe's MP and smiled, ejecting Labour voters by their thousand and replacing them, wherever they could, with Tories. They took the middle-class enclave of West Bridgford out of Norman Fowler's old seat and the Bingham rural district out of Philip Holland's seat at Carlton. Clarke would be fighting the mirror image of Mansfield at the next election. He was guaranteed to win by at least 15,000 votes, while a Labour candidate, trying to make a name for himself, would have to try to make a dent in this little *Tory* outpost.

There was just one problem: Clarke was not guaranteed selection. Although the seat still bore the name of his constituency, it was an entirely new creation, and a fresh selection process had to be put in place. The contest was evenly balanced. Norman Fowler could expect the support of West Bridgford, while the South Basford area of the old Rushcliffe constituency would support Clarke. That made the votes of Bingham vital. The friends and rivals from Cambridge days were now locked in battle for survival at Westminster, and they pressed for a quick selection process to give the defeated candidate time to find another seat. Both used the MP's ultimate weapon: local publicity. 'The contest gave rise to fairly regular appearances in the *Nottingham Evening Post* for both of them,' Clarke's agent Roger Stewart drily remarks.

Clarke had kept a high profile locally since becoming an MP. One issue close to his heart was the state of Britain's motorways. As befitted a man who divided his time between Birmingham, Nottingham and London, driving at least three times a week to his constituency, he campaigned ceaselessly for the M1 to be made safer. He also tried to persuade Mrs Thatcher when she was Education Secretary to rid Nottinghamshire of its Victorian primary schools, and campaigned for refuse tips to be moved from a local colliery site. All three efforts were rewarded with generous local publicity. Later, Clarke stepped in when a local firm complained that it couldn't get the right kind of apples to cover in toffee. The difficulty, he explained to a bemused minister at the Department of Trade and Industry, was that many types of apple were quite unsuitable for toffee-apple manufacture because they wrinkled with the application of hot toffee.

When the Rushcliffe selection committee met on 31 January 1972 it knew Clarke to be an assiduous MP. He faced stiff competition, and not just from Norman Fowler. 'Some of my friends also applied for the seat,' Clarke remembers. 'But they wrote to me to apologise for doing it.' His name went on to the short list with those of Fowler, Tony Newton and Peter Temple-Morris. Leon Brittan and Nigel Lawson both failed to make the final round.

The four candidates still left in the race were questioned by 120 local activists, drawn from all the association's branches, at Nottingham's West Park Pavilion. Peter Temple-Morris won loud applause for declaring himself in favour of capital punishment; Clarke once more voiced his opposition. The candidates were then asked if they would live in the constituency. All of them said yes – except Clarke. Nevertheless he won comfortably on the first ballot. Cambridge man had beaten Cambridge man, and Norman Fowler had to take himself off around the circuit of other likely seats.

These events summed up the sometimes contradictory impulses which ran through the differing personalities who made up the Cambridge mafia. Magnet-like, they frequently stuck together, but at times their polarity would be reversed. They were not just bound together by the friendship of like-minded men who had stared into the future together at university, they were also rivals and competitors throughout their political careers. Clarke believes that 'the contest actually made Norman Fowler and me closer friends than we had previously been. Norman sometimes overstates the extent to which we were friendly at Cambridge, although we knew each other well there.' From the battle for Rushcliffe, therefore, came an alliance which would serve Clarke well; but it would be the only time in the next decade that he felt more successful than his friend, who re-entered Parliament in 1974 as MP for Sutton Coldfield.

Clarke now had one of the safest seats in the land. Until the next election he also had the new Beeston constituency to nurse, in conjunction with its Conservative candidate, Jim Lester, a local politician who became one of his closest friends. 'I now have a constituency and a half,' said Clarke. 'I hope I can produce the effort and a half to succeed at the next general election.' He was being a touch disingenuous. He could have stayed in bed for the duration of the next campaign and still won comfortably. Through skill and serendipity, he had that precious political commodity, a seat for life. As the youngest member of the Heath government, without a marginal seat to nurture, he could look forward to a rapid rise to the top. The glittering prizes appeared within reach, after all, despite those nights at Wolverhampton Station.

At the start of 1974, Clarke was made Lord Commissioner of the Treasury, a full whip, in the reshuffle which put Lord Carrington in charge of Energy. It was a job that suited his talents as a communicator between the government and its troops. But Clarke's new government job lasted little more than a month, as Heath battled against the miners' pay claim and the three-day week. The two elections of 1974, and Heath's departure the following year, turned Clarke's political world upside-down. His constituency majority was never less than 17,000 in those two elections, but his ministerial chances, once so promising, were subject to the whim of a new leader whose political persuasions would evolve into a creed very different from his own. Clarke's dilemma was that he had seen Heath's demise coming and, Cassandra-like, had been powerless to prevent it: 'One of the things that went wrong with the Heath government, in my opinion, was that Ted as he went on began to take less and less notice of his political colleagues, began to get closer and closer to the civil servant William Armstrong, who was always dubbed the second Prime Minister.'

In 1973 Clarke had warned Jim Prior, the Leader of the House and deputy chairman of the party, that a miners' strike was likely that winter:

> In my constituency, people working in the coal mines were leaving to take other jobs in the autumn, but were not selling their pit packs, which was a sure sign that they contemplated returning in due course. All the gossip was that the winter was going to see a serious strike. But Jim Prior expressed near-total disbelief that we faced any risk.

When the strike duly materialised, Clarke was loud in his objection to the calling of a general election on a single issue. 'I did not think that the government would be able to explain how an election victory would alter the situation we were in. I think posing the question "Who governs Britain?" undermined the authority of the Heath government.' One night Heath dined with the Whips' Office to hear their views, but the supporters and opponents of an early election divided equally – eight on each side. Only Sir Walter Clegg was more vociferous than Clarke in his objections. Together, they combined to enrage Heath's PPS, Timothy Kitson, because the whole exercise had been staged to persuade a reluctant Heath to go to the country. 'It produced this passionate evening', Clarke remembers, 'at the end of which we put Ted off from calling an election for two or three days, but not for much longer.'

When Harold Wilson returned to power in February 1974 at the head of a minority government, Clarke resumed his legal career. To his consternation, after two and a half years' absence, a fellow barrister greeted him in the robing room by asking him if he'd been away on a long case.

For nearly a year in opposition, during the last period of Ted Heath's party leadership, Clarke combined the Birmingham Bar with his new role as pensions spokesman under his mentor Sir Geoffrey Howe. Clarke had always been interested in social policy. It was a way of expressing his view that Conservatism could be about caring, for he still considered himself to be 'a very left-wing Tory'. This interest, expressed at the Llandudno party conference of 1962, and shown again to his party workers on the Mansfield campaign trail, had led to many speeches on the subject in the House of Commons; and at the end of 1972 he had changed his duties in the Whips' Office from employment and the law to education and social security. It was an expertise which would aid Clarke's rise enormously, making him stand out among the 1970 intake: 'It probably helped my career in that the number of MPs on either side who were prepared to speak on social security was quite small. It's so technical; there were few people prepared to take part in debates on the subject, or who knew anything about it – so you could always get called.' Along with Nicholas Edwards and Robert Maclennan, Clarke was the mainstay of any pensions debate until he became a whip. So when the Tories were consigned to opposition in 1974, he was a natural choice to be shadow spokesman on the subject.

Clarke had hesitated briefly before accepting his new post because of his revived law career. His new job would mean hard work and the detail of which his critics say he is not capable. He was replacing a walking lexicon on the subject, Paul Dean. The subject would require all Clarke's abilities to master a brief. On one occasion he asked the Department of Health and Social Security what National Insurance contributions a person with two jobs, one as an employee and the other self-employed, would have to pay. The reply he received from Brian O'Malley, the minister of state in the department, ran as follows:

Sections 1 (7), sections 2 (2), sections 3 (1), sections 5 (1), sections 5 (2) of the Social Security Act, 1973, now amended to update to 1974 terms the 1972 illustrated figures in the Act, show that, in respect of such a person, clause one primary and secondary contributions will be payable on all his earnings with respect of an employed earners' employment if the earnings exceed the lower earnings limit of £11 per week up to the upper earnings limit of £79. And that unless he can obtain exception on grounds of lower earnings he will be liable for a weekly class 2 contribution as a self-employed earner, plus class 4 contributions if it is profits or gains chargeable to income tax and case 1 or 2 of schedule D exceed £1,600 a year.

In short, pensions legislation was highly technical.

For some years the parties had agreed that the Beveridge system of National Insurance, which provided flat-rate pensions for flat-rate contributions, put too great a burden on the poor. Various governments of different political hues had tried to change the system without success, and each new government had effectively undone its predecessor's work without putting anything in its stead. In 1969 Richard Crossman, as Secretary of State for Social Services, had produced an earnings-related scheme; in 1973 his successor Sir Keith Joseph replaced it with a two-tier system, comprising the flat-rate state pension with an earnings-related pension on top, both to be paid for by earnings-related contributions. Under this scheme, which Sir Keith admitted was modest and limited in its scope, every employee had to qualify for the second pension, either by belonging to an approved private pension scheme or by becoming a member of the inferior State Reserve Scheme.

The Labour Party had pledged itself to undo this measure, calling it a sop to the insurance industry because it set the standards of the approved private schemes too low and made the Reserve Scheme less attractive still.[9] One of the problems was that the level of payments from the Reserve Scheme was determined by the performance of its investments. Labour duly committed itself to the repeal of this 'inadequate and unjust' scheme and it became one of Barbara Castle's major tasks. She had less than a year to abolish the Joseph legacy before it came into effect. Clarke was one of her main antagonists across the despatch box, even though Sir Geoffrey Howe had agreed in principle to accept her legislation. Clarke recalls 'making a terrific meal of it': 'I argued the toss for a bigger role for the private sector and for better terms for opting out. I reckon I was a considerable expert on the level that Tony Newton and John Major subsequently became.'

Clarke had a simple tactic for dealing with Barbara Castle in the Commons – he tried to make her lose her temper: 'She had two tones of voice. One was her concerned tone, when she was a bit boring, but if you provoked her she became a real spitfire. This was far more fun and actually she used to make a mess of it far more often when she lost her temper.' One of his tricks was to refer to the Castle legislation as 'the O'Malley pensions bill'. Brian O'Malley, who tragically died from a brain haemorrhage during the reading of the bill, became a friend of

Clarke's and tried to stop him provoking Mrs Castle, because it only made her interfere with his work. 'I know what the Tories are up to,' wrote Mrs Castle. 'They want to maintain the "ogre" image of me . . . in his winding-up speech Kenneth Clarke even went to the lengths of talking about the "O'Malley Bill".'[10] The tactic nevertheless struck home. Barbara Castle wrote later: 'I was immensely gratified when, replying to me in the debate, Kenneth Clarke instinctively referred to the legislation as the "Castle Bill".'

As befitted the son of a small shopkeeper, Clarke won a name for himself as the champion of the self-employed, hounding Barbara Castle over the cost of her new earnings-related rates, which he calculated would cost a worker on £3,500 a year an extra £3 a week. Clarke prophesied a revolt by small businessmen and he came up with an eclectic list to back his claim; those who would suffer most, he said, were window dressers, the professions, translators and parsons. There was one other group most at risk – people like his father: 'On top of the rate increases and personal taxation increases these changes threaten ruin for small shopkeepers.'[11]

In the final stages of the new Social Security Bill, Clarke was given the task of leading for the opposition, scoring a political triumph which seemed to put him even more firmly on a future ministerial ladder. He forced an amendment enabling pensioners to earn £20 a week, and £50 in two years' time, without jeopardising their pensions. With nine rebel Labour MPs voting with the Tories, Clarke managed to force through his concession by fifteen votes. The Commons, he said, 'had battered some common sense into the government'.

Clarke made his mark as social security spokesman most notably in committee, where the cut-and-thrust was if anything sharper than in the chamber and where he could deploy his barrister's mind. The impression he made on the Labour front-bencher Michael Meacher, who spent nine months in Barbara Castle's team, was that 'he was quite cocky, but he was extremely articulate. He could respond very rapidly on his feet in a rational and thoughtful manner – he would dismiss any intervention and sweep on. He was a strong performer.' In 1975 Clarke was teamed with Normal Fowler, who was made head of the opposition social services team, but Clarke sometimes outshone him. Barbara Castle remarks that, when she was forced to postpone her child benefits scheme, 'the debate went well. Norman Fowler was moderation itself and Kenneth Clarke's more effective and more critical speech came too late – to an empty House – to have any effect.'[12]

Parliament was for Clarke, in a sense, just an extension of his court work and his career in the Cambridge debating chamber. He was good with words, never lost for them, a professional wordsmith – and this would lead later to the charge that, while he could pick up a brief and more than hold his own, his mastery of detail was tenuous. He would be described as better at the despatch box than at the red boxes. There is a story about him that, confronted with a pile of red boxes to take home one weekend, he ordered his driver: 'Take two of those – any two.' Famously, Clarke once declared that he had not read the Maastricht Treaty. Clarke's friends say in his defence that his command of detail can be remarkable. But it is precisely that – a *command* of detail, rather than a love of it; he prides himself on needing to read a document only once to remember the salient points. Tim Eggar, who worked under Clarke at the Education Department, suspects that 'his view of the role of a secretary of state is that basically a secretary of state who gets too bogged down in detail is not actually doing his job. Whenever he had to master the detail he would, but I suspect the answer is that he's a details man when he has to be but he doesn't see it as the be-all-and-end-all.'

Being pensions spokesman proved that Clarke could master the detail if he had to. Indeed, so expert was he that the whips were reluctant to move him, and it took the intervention of his friend Jim Lester to persuade them to relent. But Clarke was at heart a debater, a House of Commons man, preferring the argument itself – the chance to provoke Mrs Castle because it was 'fun'. Jim Lester contrasts him with John Major:

> John Major's a details man, but Ken isn't in that sense, although in pensions you've got to be detailed to that degree. I've seen him at midnight get hold of a brief and whoosh! concentrate on it solidly. When he was doing committee stage work he could make a forty-minute speech without looking at a piece of paper. That's why he does so well in the House of Commons, because he's got the knowledge in his head.

Kenneth Clarke had come a long way in his first five years in Parliament. He had secured his seat, honed his debating skills, put his foot upon the first rung of government and sharpened his chances of reaching the higher ranks of the party ahead of any of his contemporaries. But the prizes were to stay tantalisingly out of reach. The male club which had sustained him since his Cambridge days was about to admit a woman.

CHAPTER 6

The Counter-Revolution

*'Dying for an idea' . . . sounds well enough, but why not let the idea die
instead of you?*

Percy Wyndham Lewis, *The Art of Being Ruled*

At 4 p.m. on Tuesday 4 February 1975, in an upstairs committee room
of the House of Commons, Kenneth Clarke's political ascent came to a
sudden halt. As the emollient voice of Edward du Cann gravely
intoned the results of the first round of voting for the Tory leadership,
it became clear that the normal rules of the political club in which
Clarke had been brought up had been suspended; astoundingly,
Margaret Thatcher had beaten Ted Heath by eleven votes. The club's
membership had been thrown open to admit a woman, and one who
seemed harsh and unyielding.

All the old nostrums had gone, banished for ever. Heath had his
faults, even his closest supporters admitted, but he represented the
party in which Clarke had grown up. The Cambridge Union, FUCUA
and Westminster itself: all had been points of contact between Clarke
and his deposed leader. Modern, efficient, pro-European, a Conservative with a social conscience – these were epithets which could apply to
Clarke as well as to Heath. In a straight fight with Finchley Woman,
Clarke instinctively backed Heath. Indeed, so public was Clarke's
support for Heath that the Thatcher campaign did not even bother to
canvass him: 'I was surprised nobody had tried me out. I couldn't
think why it was. But by chance I was sharing a room at the Commons
with Norman Tebbit and I didn't realise how close he was to her. Of
course, in conversation with him in the room I'd said on more than one
occasion that there was no way I'd vote for her.'

Heath had lost three elections out of four. His rule had ended in

95

the débâcle of the three-day week, with his attempt to constrain the unions emasculated and his industrial policy in tatters. Further, he was personally awkward, gauche in handling his relations with backbenchers, and they had decided they could stand no more. Even Norman Fowler, who voted for Heath in the first round, initially had tried, with Norman Lamont, to persuade Keith Joseph to run. 'The shortest campaign in history,' he now reflects ruefully. Clarke, however, felt strongly that Mrs Thatcher's political instincts were not to be trusted: 'I thought she had an approach to politics which was too right-wing, too hard core.' Looking back, he is unsure why he didn't vote for William Whitelaw in the second round: 'I just thought his style wouldn't lend itself to being a modern Prime Minister.'

In the eye of the storm created by Mrs Thatcher's first-round success, Clarke and his friends searched for a new version of the old order which had been swept away. They gathered in Sir Geoffrey Howe's house in Vauxhall to try to persuade him to run in the second ballot. The group reflected the very continuity for which they were searching; as well as the younger Cambridge troika of Clarke, Fowler and Leon Brittan, there were the older Tony Buck, the MP for Colchester, and Peter Temple-Morris, both of whom also went to Cambridge. They met more in despair than hope. No ready band of Howe supporters was willing to take up arms, and it was already clear that Mrs Thatcher was unstoppable. Howe was reluctant to throw his hat into the ring. 'His wife didn't want him to run,' explains Clarke, 'but we persuaded him. We knew perfectly well we had no chance of winning, but I regarded it as an intelligent man's abstention. I argued that he combined right-wing economics with left-wing social policy, the old Bow Group combination to which I always say I adhere.'

To abstain in a leadership contest, mentally if not in practice, was a sign that Clarke and his political friends did not know where the party was heading in their new, disoriented world. At the same time, they could hope to gain a strong shadow Cabinet presence if their candidate did well. Howe scraped only nineteen votes but duly won his reward; Mrs Thatcher made him shadow Chancellor. Many of his supporters, including Clarke, remained on the front benches.

When Mrs Thatcher won the second round of voting, and was elected leader, the little group of Howe supporters arranged a subdued gathering in the House of Commons. Leon Brittan held a marginal seat (Cleveland and Whitby, which he had won the previous February) and thought the outcome was disastrous for anyone in his position. Clarke, too, was upset. He cannot recall speaking out against his new leader, but Norman Fowler remembers him declaring that 'the counter-revolution starts here'. Little was known about Mrs Thatcher's policies, but the Howe group suspected enough to be appalled. They saw her as a right-wing politician with views which seemed difficult to sell to the nation, and she lacked foreign affairs experience, which disturbed this band of pro-European activists. 'There was a feeling that this was a pretty strange step to take,' Sir Norman Fowler recalls. 'Was Margaret's middle-class London voice the voice that was actually going to win the nation over? I suppose we felt it was all a bit of a throwback in a curious way. It wasn't the modern Conservative Party – it sounded like a different party altogether.'

Clarke and his friends regarded Mrs Thatcher with foreboding mainly because they no longer had any political compass-bearings to guide them along the way that had been charted for them since university. In fact, there no longer seemed to be a map at all. There was no clear indication of what the new leader offered politically, other than her ability not to be Ted Heath; indeed, Airey Neave, her campaign manager, had tried to persuade Willie Whitelaw to run before turning to her. The only sign that Mrs Thatcher contemplated a new, radical direction came in an article she wrote for the *Daily Telegraph*, which had asked all three first-round candidates to set out their stall. 'One of the reasons for our electoral failure', she stated, 'is that people believe that too many Conservatives have become socialists already.' Even so, there was no striking ideological divide between the candidates, no clear-cut choice between what they stood for. It was, as the political commentator Hugo Young put it, 'the first truly astounding achievement of a fairly routine career'[1] – brought about by a peasants' revolt.

The problem for Clarke was that he wasn't a peasant. He was a courtier who had hopes of preferment under the *ancien régime*. This need not have been a problem; many of the insiders were kept on, and many of them adjusted to the new political realities, although a few were cast out and never admitted again. Clarke's view is that 'I was obviously doing all right in my parliamentary career up till then. I'd only been in the House six years and I was on the front bench. So I suppose I felt that any change of leader created a moment of uncertainty, particularly if you'd just been campaigning for some other candidate. I had to wait and see.' It would be a long wait.

At first there seemed little to worry about. Clarke was kept on as pensions spokesman, under Norman Fowler. He dealt with the shock of Mrs Thatcher's victory, as he would deal with the many disappointments which would come his way under her leadership, by getting on with his work and not dissenting publicly. For Sir Leon Brittan the experience was similar: 'It wasn't a dilemma, but it was a situation to which you had to accommodate yourself. I don't think he [Clarke] said or did what he didn't believe in, but there is such a thing as keeping your head down to an extent.'

So Clarke gave Mrs Thatcher his guarded loyalty. He told his constituents shortly after her election that she had the job of shaping the opposition into a sharp, intelligent alternative to the government. This left open the question of whether she was up to it. And he expressed, albeit in the mildest of code, the worry that Finchley Woman was not the leader the Midlands might follow. The 'new look' Tory Party, he said, had to do more than just express middle-class grievances. It had to set out its case for a prosperous, free society 'and show it can be run with compassion and concern for those who need help'.[2]

For her part, Mrs Thatcher did not warm to her junior spokesman. They were political opposites in all but the certainty with which they expressed themselves, despite their shared Midlands upbringing and their early days in common above a parental shop. Clarke was a Westminster insider who had never thrown off his Midlands roots, whereas Mrs Thatcher's whole political career had been a journey away from Grantham. Not for Clarke the elegant pin-stripes, immaculate shirts and perfectly coiffed hair of Mrs Thatcher's close friend and ally Cecil Parkinson. Nicholas Budgen describes Clarke as being 'very unlike Parkinson and other people who have moved away from their class background. He's not in any way inconvenienced or abashed by people from different backgrounds. He's genuinely satisfied and comfortable in the provinces, socially secure and not at all pretentious.' For Mrs Thatcher, Clarke was too blokeish, too hard to define as a human being and too easy to define politically as a Heathite.

In time, his debating abilities would save him, but he would not be admitted to the inner circle. Sir Bernard Ingham, who served as Mrs Thatcher's chief press officer, believes that 'Clarke was always suspect politically as far as Mrs Thatcher was concerned, but he was by no means suspect intellectually, as a parliamentary performer, or even, you might say, as a rough-house man. He was seen to have many political qualities, but not necessarily the right ones.'

The charge against Clarke from some quarters, however, is that he accepted the new order too willingly, placing preferment above belief. This appears unjust, if only because his brand of politics places pragmatism above doctrine. Clarke is not an ideological politician, so he was not ideological in his acceptance or rejection of Mrs Thatcher's policies. He made up his mind as he went along. Thatcherism was to take him into economic territory he had not considered; once there, he accepted some aspects (notably privatisation) and rejected others (monetarism, in its purest form). 'The argument I always use about Margaret,' Clarke declares, 'and I apply it to the party as well as to myself, is that she gave us the courage of our convictions.'

Clarke's Macleodite mixture of right- and left-wing views helped him adjust his political sights. With few predetermined positions, he had the advantage of being able to adapt to his new surroundings. On some issues he naturally came to adopt the shape and colour of a Thatcherite creature (for example, on union reform). On other, social issues he stood out without camouflage in the Thatcher jungle, but the vibrant colours of his rhetoric disguised his liberal markings. Throughout her long leadership, Clarke survived because of his political skills in the Commons and because his political upbringing gave him such flexibility. He did not change his character, because he did not have to; he simply accented his own tough side which, in the eyes of his new leader, might redress the balance of his other, less acceptable views. He was a political amphibian, capable of living in the sea or on dry land, even if Mrs Thatcher saw water as his natural habitat.

Almost immediately, however, Clarke was dubbed a 'deft band-wagon jumper' (by Andrew Roth's *Parliamentary Profiles*) for launching, soon after Mrs Thatcher's accession, a fierce attack on 'the army of scroungers' who were claiming benefits to which they were not entitled. But Clarke had always expressed strong views on fraudulent pension and social security payments. As a backbencher he had tried to obtain assurances from the Heath government that it was taking steps to deal with abuse of the social security system, and he went before the Public Accounts Committee to raise the issue. There was no right-wing or left-wing agenda within the party on the subject. Clarke wanted to free the money for those who needed it. In John Gummer's opinion, 'He has real understanding that there are people out there who need very real help, but also a pretty hard-headed view about cheating. It's all part of not wanting to have the wool pulled over his eyes. If that happens, you let down the people who do need help. I think that comes very deeply from his own childhood.'

It was, then, merely the continuation of an old theme when Clarke continued his attacks after Mrs Thatcher became leader, a sign of his Macleodite instincts. 'The line I used to take and I still take', he argues,

> is that the system failed to benefit quite a lot of people it should have helped – for example, I supported the introduction of child benefit. On the other hand, some people abused the system. So we had a system which was all wrong because it wasn't meeting the needs of people who ought to be assisted, but it was also far too easily fiddled by people who knew how to play the system.

Under a strident new leader, of course, a streak of toughness patently did not go amiss.

There were, nevertheless, early problems between Clarke and Mrs Thatcher. He was chafing at the bit, anxious not to be typecast as the pensions expert. Two years were long enough: 'My interests were broader than that. So I had the nerve to go along to Margaret and say I'd like to be moved. She ticked me off and said no – *she'd* done four and a half years on pensions. It was a ludicrous thing for me to do. She said if you don't want to do it, someone else will. She could easily have sacked me altogether.' Mrs Thatcher was to relent, but only in a way which made her suspicions about him clear. She told Clarke that he had spent too long thinking up ways in which he could *spend* money; it was time he had some contact with creating it. So she sent him to join the industry team, initially under the leadership of John Biffen, whose promotion to the inner circle was a direct consequence of Heath's defeat. Clarke, at thirty-six, was still the third youngest member of the front-bench team, after Norman Lamont, who was thirty-four, and Malcolm Rifkind, who was spokesman on Scotland at thirty.

Clarke had a cavalier approach to opposition. He was not a philosopher. Debate was political food enough for him, and if the party was in opposition, a prospect he considered would inevitably happen from time to time, then he had a living to earn at the Bar. Being in opposition was not for him the time to reflect on the future of Conservatism, or even the time to formulate specific policies. It was merely the opportunity to biff and bash the government of the day, enjoying the performance rather than the substance. John Biffen observes that

> Clarke was very relaxed about his great industrial responsibilities. I don't think he was particularly well informed, but he was happy to pick up the brief and have a go. He was not terribly happy at having a quiet, calm detailed discussion among politicians of goodwill to see where the common ground could be secured. I think he enjoyed being agressive.

Norman Lamont was also a member of this team, and Biffen remembers the contrast between the two, which would later underscore their very different periods as Chancellor of the Exchequer:

> Kenneth Clarke was more relaxed; Norman was rather more tense and looking for points to score. It was a difference of temperament almost all explained by their dress. Whereas Norman Lamont would be immaculately turned out, as if he'd just drifted down from Rothschild's, Ken Clarke wore those appalling Hush Puppies and certainly was not up to Savile Row standards. Somehow or other it symbolised the rather different approaches.

Though not of Clarke's political persuasion, John Biffen had the elegant good humour to tolerate his junior spokesman's energetic approach to politics and to life in general. So varied were Clarke's enthusiasms that his colleagues found it difficult to judge whether political ambition ruled his life or his life ruled and circumscribed his ambition. He was still a passionate football supporter, still an habitué of Ronnie Scott's jazz club, still a man to have a pint with in Annie's Bar or the Kremlin, the two Commons watering-holes where draught Federation bitter could be quaffed. According to Biffen: 'His rather boyish look may have disarmed some people into thinking that he was really a bit of a lad. But just because you go off and sink a few pints at Ronnie Scott's wouldn't conceal from me that politics for Clarke is the whole of his existence.' However, Clarke's former ministerial colleague Lord Hayhoe disagrees: 'If one evening there was the option of going to Ronnie Scott's because there was some new group or performer there or going to an important but dull dinner which furthered his political future, you knew which Ken would choose every time. I saw him as a fellow soul, as someone who didn't think life was all politics.'

The truth is that politics was and remains Clarke's life, if necessary to the exclusion of all his other interests, save his family. The interests complement his career but are in no sense a substitute for it. He was ambitious, then as now, but it was not something which ate into him and corroded him. He was, above all, self-confident and secure within himself. His upbringing and his education had determined that. In opposition, with three years before Labour might go to the country, it was simply not his style to sit around thinking deep and glorious thoughts about an industrial policy which might be put into practice if the Tories were to win the next general election. One former minister who worked with him comments: 'There's no introspection – he doesn't think deeply about anything. He goes to work, does his job, then doesn't think about it till he goes into work tomorrow.' Clarke does think about his politics, but he is a problem-solver and a performer, not a philosopher.

That role had fallen to someone else: Sir Keith Joseph, whose tortured manner and ascetic soul had about as much in common with Clarke's rumbustious nature as a monk has with a boxer. They were about to be paired together. In November 1976 Mrs Thatcher appointed Joseph as her industry spokesman, when John Biffen dropped out, pleading he was exhausted by his work. It was, from Clarke's position, an unfortunate move which was to damage his prospects. 'Temperamentally they were miles apart,' explains Sir

Norman Fowler. 'Keith was very tense, and Ken was anything but that. Secondly, Ken actually had to make a living and so he was going backwards and forwards to Birmingham all the time. And thirdly his view of opposition was very much unlike Keith's view of opposition.'

Unlike for Clarke, the whole point of opposition for Joseph – indeed, the whole point of overthrowing Ted Heath – was to think, think and think again about the future of the party he loved. Mrs Thatcher's leadership victory might have started as a peasants' revolt, but it was to become an ideological revolution. Clarke praises Joseph's personal acts of kindness towards him but says that 'Frankly, I didn't share his views on a lot of things. He didn't always make his mind up in a hurry – and when he did, he changed it.'

So while Clarke pursued his law career, or cheerfully attacked the government across the despatch box, Joseph began to articulate the new way forward. He argued that the main political parties were 'stranded on the middle ground' which had moved continuously to the left under its own dynamic, producing a collectivist consensus. He began to expound the economic and political beliefs which were to become known as Thatcherism,[3] touring the country to promote his case that there was a new 'common ground' to be found – one which the Tories must make their own. The revolution depended, above all else, on economic rectitude. 'What I believe', he argued, 'is that if we get the money supply wrong, too high or too low, nothing will come right. Monetary control is a pre-essential for everything else we need and want to do.'[4] Government spending, in Joseph's view, was a major cause of unemployment. More was being spent on education and health than ever before, he said, but all it created was a dangerous level of dependency.

For all the rhetoric, the early Thatcher programme was modest, summed up by two documents, *The Right Approach* and *The Right Approach to the Economy*. There was much here that a Bow Grouper like Clarke could welcome, but also much with which he might disagree. That was only natural; *The Right Approach* was a compromise between the differing views of Keith Joseph, Geoffrey Howe and Jim Prior; *The Right Approach to the Economy* was more specific, demanding control of the money supply and lower taxes. Overall, the two documents clearly called into question the shape of the welfare state and the degree of state intervention which might help the poorer members of society. But they represented something of a balancing act, and there was little tangible to oppose, even if Clarke had wanted to put his head above the parapet, which he didn't. Nor, however, did he go out of his way to appease his new leader.

While Keith Joseph was applying himself to the rigours of rewriting Tory Party philosophy, Clarke had been pursuing a very different, and more basic, line of thought. He had come eighth in the ballot for private members' bills, and his choice of legislation was not, as he had once suggested to the voters of Mansfield it might be, the introduction of share shops, but the liberalisation of pub opening hours. 'When he was on holiday with us in Cornwall,' John Barnes remembers, 'he always thought it nonsense that the children had to go into the garden when we went into the pub.'

The 1972 Erroll Committee report on liquor licensing had advocated more flexibility in pubs and extended hours, and Clarke decided to promote some of these measures in his bill. He did not want to force publicans to stay open longer, but to let them to serve drinks between ten o'clock in the morning and midnight if they so wanted. Children would also be allowed into pubs, if the magistrates approved. Clarke had the support of the British Tourist Authority and the Consumers' Council, but he ran straight into the opposition of the anti-drink lobby, who treated his reforms as an attempt to turn children into drunks.

Clarke shrugged off their attacks, describing the licensing laws an unnecessarily complex and out of date. Not only were they much overdue for reform, he said, but they were regarded by overseas visitors as comic. His Licensing Amendment Bill demonstrated his liberal social side: 'At the moment we have a daft situation where you can take children into a pub car park or into a room without a bar, regardless of its suitability. It's ridiculous pretending that children should be unaware of alcohol until they are 18. It may take away some of the mystique.'[5] The anti-drink lobby had friends in the Tory Party, however, and a filibuster by Sir Bernard Braine prevented the Commons from reaching a vote on the bill when it emerged from its committee stage. Clarke signed off in typical style: 'I don't feel like doing what the government is doing with its devolution measures – flogging a dead horse.' More than fifteen years later he was to get his own back, changing the law when he was Home Secretary. But of all the bills he could have chosen, this was probably the one least designed to catch the eye of a leader who was the daughter of a strict Methodist.

Under the watchful eye of Sir Keith Joseph, while others carried out the new survey on the party's future direction, Clarke contented himself with doing what he did best: taking a single issue and harrying the government with it, notably when he revealed that it had been operating a black list of firms suspected of breaking its pay policy. While he might wish for the past and fear for the future under Mrs Thatcher, he was professional enough not to let it show. He neither helped the political ship steer its new course nor threw himself overboard. Lord Hayhoe believes that 'Maggie and those around her wouldn't have seen him as anything other than an able figure in the party who didn't quite share their values. There were others who were more willing to swing themselves in line and get on the coat-tails of Margaret.' Thatcherism was still evolving, the tenets of its creed still in the hands of her lieutenants; and it suited Clarke, in opposition, to keep his distance from it. As Norman Fowler says: 'Ken took the view that no one in their right mind actually set out too much detail of what they were going to do, because the only thing that might happen would be that people would come and shoot you down for your ideas. So you didn't put forward a great menu of detailed policies.'

Europe was still an abiding interest. Clarke spoke from the back benches, as he was entitled to do in opposition, to argue for direct elections to the European Parliament, along with Hugh Dykes, another ex-CUCA chairman. But he found to his dismay that there were few opportunities to speak in the Commons, because the minister he was shadowing, the Swansea MP Alan Williams, dealt mainly in written answers, affording Clarke little chance to reply in the chamber itself. He recalls: 'I got involved in lots of debates about worker co-operatives – quite disproportionately so. I tried to take a view on industry that was reasonably pragmatic, more pragmatic than Keith Joseph, who was at that stage in his deeply ideological state – so I was not entirely on the same wavelength.'

Clarke's few speeches during this period showed the gap between his policy expectations and the ideological rethink which was coming the party's way. The Labour government had commissioned a report by its industrial adviser, Sir Don Ryder, on the ailing car giant British Leyland. Ryder's report argued that the firm was essential to Britain's economic base, and he proposed a massive investment programme of £2,800 million from public funds over the next seven years.[6] The government had accepted his proposals, acquiring a major shareholding in the company through the National Enterprise Board. To Clarke this was an example of bad and expensive political decisions being taken for no useful long-term purpose.[7] Nationalisation, he argued, had made the problems of the car, steel and shipbuilding industries worse: 'The government has bought them in order to try to avoid difficult changes being made in them and has poured public money into all three to subsidise them in their present state. A Conservative government will inherit them as three giant wrecks.'[8] Later, as a Cabinet minister, Clarke would himself suggest and organise the sale of British Steel. But in the late 1970s privatisation was far from his mind: 'Like most people in 1979, I thought you can't privatise things. I felt the whole word is ugly, the mixed economy is here to stay. My view then would have been, well, it's very desirable but of course we'll never do this.'

Even on the subject of union reform, a cause closer to his heart, Clarke was cautious. Keith Joseph argued that solving the union problem was the key to Britain's recovery.[9] Clarke did not dissent. The collapse of the Labour government's 'social contract' with the unions and the Winter of Discontent of 1978–9 were proof enough of that. For a man who had denounced trade union might since his Cambridge days, and even at school, the state of Britain in the late 1970s was no more than the visible proof of his long-held beliefs: 'Some attempt must now be made to set sensible limits on industrial action so that individual sections of the public do not take it in turns to inflict misery on each other by withdrawing their labour.'[10]

The problem with the unions, for Clarke, was the old one: the power of a vested interest, wielded by leaders who were often elected for life, and who did not necessarily reflect the views of their members. When the lorry drivers' strike was settled with a 15 per cent pay rise, in the last winter of the Labour government, it was for Clarke 'a complete victory for extreme militant Trades Union action . . . The lorry drivers acted as if they believed might was right and they will think the settlement justifies that view – as the coal miners did.'[11]

Union leaders, Clarke claimed, would not allow people to stand on their own two feet; they had 'pursued a ferocious persecution of responsible members who merely wish to work'.[12]

Despite such views, Clarke wanted to move slowly against the unions. When later in the first Thatcher government there was a dispute between advocates of Prior's softly-softly approach to union reform and supporters of the more aggressive plans of Norman Tebbit, Clarke sided with Prior:

> I was very much in the Prior camp. I though this had to be done gently. I was always against abolishing Neddy [the National Economic Development Council] because, however useless it was, and we all thought it was useless, I thought you had to have a forum to meet trade union leaders, and have a dialogue with them. Being in office, and for the first time having to deal with union leaders face to face, my views did harden. Things were just ungovernable if you didn't alter the relationship with the trade unions.

On the night of 28 March 1979 Clarke and his friend Jim Lester were to be found in Soho celebrating over a few pints of beer at Ronnie Scott's jazz club. The defeat of the Labour government that night in a confidence debate had precipitated a general election which, it already seemed clear, would put the Tories back into office. The Winter of Discontent had saved Mrs Thatcher from discontent within a party which had seen Labour rising in the polls, and her personal popularity slipping behind that of James Callaghan and even Ted Heath.

Entering the 1979 election campaign in confident spirit, Clarke likened Jim Callaghan's government to the singer in 'Ol' Man River', who was tired of living but scared of dying. Clarke had emerged from Mrs Thatcher's take-over with his Commons reputation intact and was for the first time attracting a reputation in the national press. During the campaign the *Financial Times* stated glowingly:

> Clarke is one of the young men in the party who is going places. He may not be as flamboyant as the Boysons, Biffens and Taylors, but he has already been earmarked for advancement . . . In the past two decades, unlike earlier times, many a Cabinet

Minister has emerged from the anonymity of the Whips' Office, including Edward Heath, Francis Pym, Ted Short and countless others.[13]

This was not a list which was likely to recommend itself to his new leader – and it didn't.

CHAPTER 7

At the Sultan's Court

I never wanted to pin myself down so that anyone could say, 'This is Mingus.' I don't ever want to be caught in one groove.

Charlie Mingus (jazz bassist)

The Conservative victory in the 1979 general election brought only bitter disappointment for Clarke. In opposition two or three years previously, Mrs Thatcher had promised him that she would make him a minister of state. But Sir Keith Joseph flatly refused to have Clarke in his team, and while Mrs Thatcher might have been prepared to argue her corner for someone who was obviously sympathetic to her cause, Clarke was not such a politician. The contrast between his evident abilities, so warmly acknowledged by the *Financial Times*, and his prospects was sharp. The clash between his outgoing personality and the internalised intellectualism of Keith Joseph had proved his undoing.

On the other hand, Norman Fowler was admired by Mrs Thatcher where Kenneth Clarke was not. This was partly because he had tried to persuade Keith Joseph to run against Ted Heath for the leadership, so he was not so tainted by his connection with Ted Heath. But Fowler was also instinctively closer to Thatcher. 'Norman has a political mind that's almost Japanese,' remarks one former minister who has worked for both Fowler and Clarke. 'He looks at it from all sides. Ken Clarke would take a knife and if the patient bled to death – so what?' Fowler was made Minister of Transport, while Clarke waited for a call which never came. When the Chief Whip, Michael Jopling, gave Fowler a list of five names from which he could choose his second in command, Fowler was surprised to see Clarke's name on the piece of paper: 'I was amazed to find that Ken was on the list – I'd assumed he was going to the Department of Trade and Industry. Obviously his partnership with Keith Joseph hadn't worked out.' He offered Clarke the job at Transport.

It was a marriage which was to last five years, at Transport and at Health, a political pairing of caution and boldness, the school prefect and the playground bully. The Home Office minister Charles Wardle, who worked for the pair at Health, says: 'Norman's great skill was a skill for those times – he was extraordinarily cautious. He had antennae that looked round corners. Ken could play his shots perfectly cheerfully, confident of his own judgement, so it was a different style, a different approach.'

Friends of both Fowler and Clarke argue that the partnership reflected credit on both of them: 'Clearly Ken is a lot brighter than Norman,' explains one. 'But he didn't under-value Norman's common sense and presentational qualities. And Norman didn't feel upstaged by Ken even though people kept saying the one who's really bright is Ken Clarke. He specifically wanted Ken with him even though he must have realised that Ken, in certain respects at least, outshone him.'

Mrs Thatcher's readiness to promote Norman Fowler, rather than Clarke, also reflected on her. One Cabinet minister of the time, who belonged to Mrs Thatcher's inner circle, recollects that 'Norman Fowler nearly always used to send Ken Clarke to do the statements in the House of Commons, and as I sat there in Cabinet I reflected that it was a curious way in which politics works. It was as unfair as life is unfair that Ken Clarke should be carrying the bags of Norman Fowler.'

Clarke was at first not pleased with his lowly position. He says that Norman Lamont, who was also upset at missing out on a better job, went to see Joseph to ask why the two of them had been overlooked. According to Clarke: 'Keith Joseph more or less said we weren't good enough yet – you've got to learn how to do it. So I was disappointed but, looking back, that was silly. If I had somebody of my age making similar noises now I would be slightly amused at this keen young guy, frightfully miffed that he had been given a job below his true importance.'

When Fowler phoned his friend to ask him to join his team, he says he found Clarke to be less than his usual cheery self. It took Clarke some time to come out of his gloom, and he confided his unhappiness to Leon Brittan. Brittan recalls: 'He wondered whether anything else was going to happen. He came to stay with us in Yorkshire and we went for a walk and had a discussion to that effect. I encouraged him and said I'm sure it will, because sheer quality will out.'

There was a financial price to pay, as well as a political one, for not being 'one of us'. Norman Fowler was allowed to attend Cabinet meetings but he was not, strictly speaking, a member of the Cabinet – because Mrs Thatcher had already appointed the maximum number of twenty-two ministers. As he was not formally a secretary of state, his number two could not be appointed at minister-of-state-level but would have to be a humble parliamentary under-secretary on £6,000 a year. Looking back, Clarke calls the pay 'genuinely pathetic':

It had become a tiny amount of money. I'd had the same problem in 1974 – we lost that election in the nick of time because I was able to go back to the Bar and earn some money! Now I seriously wondered whether I could afford it if I wasn't made a minister of state. I had dinner before the election with Norman Tebbit and we both agreed we could not afford to become parliamentary under-secretaries. After the election that's what we both became.

On the other hand, Clarke had been given the chance to work in a large department, some 12,000-strong, as one of only two ministers controlling a budget of £2,000 million. Buoyed by the support of his closest friends, he set out to make the most of his new brief. In many ways it was tailor made for him. In opposition, Norman Fowler had been given a free hand to rewrite the Tories' transport policy. It remained only to put it into effect. Clarke did it with aplomb. John Major, a new entrant to the Commons in 1979, remembers being impressed: 'He seemed to me to be extremely efficient, extremely able, very friendly and under-promoted. I compared his attributes at the time with many people who were ministers of state and I thought he was a more skilful and able politician than them.'

The last Conservative transport minister to make any impact had been Ernest Marples in the 1960s, and there had been no Tory transport legislation since 1964. Fowler had used his time in opposition to set out his new policy in a document called *The Right*

Track. The aim was to try to put the needs of the customer and taxpayer ahead of those of the transport owners. To that end, only essential railway services were to attract state support; bypasses and economically important roads to the ports were given priority; restrictions were to be removed from coach and bus services to encourage competition; and the National Freight Corporation was to be opened up to private investment.

The policy was laid before Clarke and he could do what he enjoyed doing best: selling it to the Commons. Clarke clocked up more than a hundred hours in the committee stage of the Transport Bill alone. 'If you gave him a committee to do he loved it,' Sir Norman Fowler remembers. 'Because it was barristerial to some extent – you picked up your brief and you did it. He's extremely good at understanding the detail and he's extremely good at arguing. It would be his boast that he could master his brief very rapidly indeed. What he likes is the cut-and-thrust of debate.' By the time Clarke left Transport, not one but two new under-secretaries, Reginald Eyre and Lynda Chalker, were appointed to succeed him.

Despite the workload Clarke's relationship with Fowler worked well. John Barnes recalls:

Once we were on holiday in a place which had no phone, when a despatch rider arrived with a red box. Ken said, 'Oh, hell', and tossed it into the back of the car, saying that it was too bad of Norman to expect him to work over Easter. When we got to the pub for lunch, he said he'd better have a look. All that was in the box was a bottle of champagne and a cheery note from Norman saying, 'Enjoy your leave.'

Clarke sold the new Transport Bill with enthusiasm, claiming the government's radical changes in the bus services were designed to encourage 'the Freddie Lakers' of the transport industry. It matched his ideas about efficiency and trade unions: 'Trade unions representing those who work in the transport industry are entitled to be consulted. But transport industries do not exist for the sole purpose of providing business for the operators and work for their employees.'[1] Indeed, Clarke's views on unions were beginning to harden: 'I saw what an iron grip the railway trade unions had over the running of British Rail, how every policy decision bar none was totally determined by whether or not the unions would agree to it. And I saw how utterly unreasonable Ray Buckton of ASLEF appeared to be. So I'm afraid the iron did rather enter my soul.' The iron was to do him no harm as he sought to catch the eye of the Iron Lady herself.

Clarke was, however, less enthusiastic about some of Fowler's other ideas. The National Freight Corporation's future had been outlined in the Conservative manifesto and it duly became the government's first privatisation in the 1980 Transport Act. 'It was farcical how as a junior minister I was often called upon to take what were regarded as political decisions about which depots ran particular lorry services, the future of Pickfords, all this sort of thing,' Clarke remarks. 'My officials certainly thought it was my job to second-guess all these details of how we ran a parcels service. And this completely useless lorry company turned practically overnight into a hugely successful company.'

Clarke was not an immediate convert to wholesale privatisation. The 1981 Transport Act allowed private investment in British Rail's subsidiary companies and effectively denationalised the British Transport Docks Board. Clarke was not convinced. Norman Fowler recalls that he was 'a bit cautious at times' and Clarke accepts the point:

> I had always believed in free-market economics but I combined it with what I thought was sensible pragmatism – the R. A. Butler art of the possible. When Nick Ridley first started advocating that you took great state industries out of state control I think most people regarded it as completely mad. When we first started privatising, the main aim was to get private-sector capital into industries previously deprived of it. I was never sold on rolling back the frontiers of the state, all this stuff. But as time went on, I became persuaded that not only did you get rid of all the politics out of it, and put private capital in, but you raised the performance of the company. But if you'd asked me that in 1979, I would have regarded it as all a bit ideological.

Clarke was given his own empire within the Transport Department – where Fowler took rail, he took roads, one of his enthusiasms. They divided up the ports between them, Fowler taking the problem ports of London and Liverpool, with Clarke doing the rest. Clarke considers that he 'learned his trade' a lot at Transport:

> Norman had this funny way of running it: we had meetings together all the time, so the whole department was run by the two of us and the Permanent Secretary. On top of that, the road programme was in a complete mess – it had all been cut back by Labour, and there were endless High Court challenges to road schemes all over the place. So I became totally immersed in my department, seeking to get it all moving again.

Yet some of this must have been humdrum work for an MP who had been a member of the Heath government at only thirty-one.

It was now ten years since Clarke had entered Parliament, and the Rushcliffe Conservative Association presented him with a copy of the *Country Life* book of *Britain in the Seventies* to mark the anniversary. He had spent two years in the Heath government, followed by five years as a front-bench spokesman, and he was entitled to ask himself whether he had made the progress that was his due. For all the enthusiasm he put into his work at Transport, some of it must have been a numbing experience. 'During a visit to the Transport and Road Research Laboratory', proclaims one of Clarke's press releases from the time, 'in which he saw a demonstration of the experimental safety motorcycle, Kenneth Clarke, Parliamentary Secretary for Transport, said: "Ordinary disc brakes which are increasingly being fitted to motorcycles lose efficiency in the wet. The sintered brake pad which has been developed at TRRL maintains full efficiency." '[2] It may have been a burning issue for motorbike enthusiasts, but it was hardly the heady stuff of politics. Equally, was Clarke going to make his name by assuring MPs that motorists would be allowed to drive backwards without fastening their seat belts under the Road Traffic (Seat Belt) Bill?

Clarke had an antidote to the problem he faced. He decided to found another dining club, to replace the loss of Nick's Diner, which, as a member of the government, he could no longer attend. With like-minded colleagues, such as Tom King, Barney Hayhoe, Douglas Hurd and Malcolm Rifkind, Clarke named the club half-jokingly after the Birmingham street where he lived.

The Amesbury Club was for junior ministers only, to help them see over the mountain of paperwork on their desks in order that they might peer into the distant valley of government deeds below. It was Nick's Diner by another name, except that just as ministers were barred from Nick's Diner, so backbenchers were barred from the Amesbury Club. To quote Tom King:

> When you went into government you left all these dining groups and therefore you missed the chance to talk together. What tends to happen as a minister is that you're much less in government, and the conduct of party policy is much more a political thing between backbenchers and the Chief Whip, while ministers are much busier getting on with their departmental duties.

They met every fortnight in one of the Commons dining-rooms, usually C or D, which can hold up to eighteen people. Most of the ministers had been in either Nick's Diner or the One Nation group. Unlike the Conservative Party this was a club which Mrs Thatcher could not gatecrash; membership was by invitation only. Lord Hayhoe describes it as 'the coming together of a group of people who were happy dining with each other and tended to have similar views'. If the club wasn't politically 'wet', it was distinctly 'damp', and its members included many who might venture the opinion that 'life was awful under Margaret'.

Clarke was essentially the convener of the group; the administration was done initially by his secretary, and later by Lynda Chalker. While he wasn't an out-and-out critic of the Thatcher government, he was showing clearly where he stood within it. Clarke also became a patron of the Tory Reform Group. But he was effectively a 'hard wet', as John Biffen puts it, too trenchant in his views to be sodden, too opposed to the Tory grandees who surrounded Ted Heath to join the anti-Thatcher club. Clarke reflects that 'the landed interest who were the leading figures in the wet faction were not of my persuasion. Ian Gilmour rather epitomised that section of the left-wing Conservatives who didn't think we should ever do anything which annoyed anybody.'

Clarke remained publicly discreet about his leader and her policies, even though his friends say his wife detested Mrs Thatcher. He neither trimmed nor launched the counter-revolution he had pro-claimed. He dealt with Mrs Thatcher's leadership as he dealt with all political problems, practically and pragmatically. Some aspects of her leadership were to be welcomed, others not; he would not make himself a single-issue man and perish upon his belief: 'Every minister must have some nights when he goes home and is boiling with rage, and says to himself, that's it, I'm going to resign. But you wake up in the morning and you're not. I never seriously agonised about whether I was going to resign under Margaret, except at the very end.'

Clarke kept such moments to himself, although he now concedes that in 1981 he was certain that the Tories would not win the next general election, and was even unsure whether the party would hold together. 'There's no trace of it in Nigel Lawson's book, but even the most fervent monetarist must have been concerned as to whether it was going to come right,' Clarke declares. Yet while he would willingly have a pint in the bars and pubs around the Commons, the beer never loosened his tongue; he never gossiped or moaned publicly about Mrs Thatcher's policy or his prospects. 'He was very professional about that. I never heard him complain,' says Lord Parkinson. 'He was very patient about it.'

The Falklands War was central to Mrs Thatcher's second election victory, that of 1983, and for once Clarke did question government policy in public: 'I remember that I couldn't believe we were going to war in the South Atlantic. I'm now used to the fact that events in politics get almost surreal at times. Like most people, it slowly dawned on me after the Task Force had been sent that we were about to go to war. I wasn't against it but I was nervous about it.' At one point Mrs Thatcher brought together a group of junior ministers to keep them in touch with events. Only two of them tackled her about the Task Force – Timothy Raison and Clarke: 'The point I was making was that it was six thousand miles away and there was no air cover. If we have an aircraft carrier sunk, I said to her, that's it, it's disaster. *It's all an enormous risk, Prime Minister*, I said. And she fixed me with a stare and said, *Kenneth, politics is about taking risks*.'

Between 1979 and May 1983 eight ministers were sacked or resigned from the Cabinet, and sixteen junior ministers suffered the same fate, including Clarke's close friend Jim Lester. Clarke, despite his scepticism about the values of Thatcherism, was not one of them. His choice was simple: to stay in government and hope, as Leon Brittan had put it, that 'quality will out', or to become a voice in the wilderness. He chose to stay. Leon Brittan argues that Clarke, for all his pragmatism, did not put preferment above belief: 'There are some people who don't have views at all and will just support what the traffic will bear. That's not true of Ken. He was always a strong supporter of the National Health Service, though he wanted to reform it, and dead against abolishing the welfare state – he won't have any truck with that. So there's quite a continuity of thought.'

There were two crucial turning-points for liberals like Clarke under Mrs Thatcher's leadership: the Budget of 1981, which cut the public-sector borrowing requirement by £3,500 million and increased personal taxation; and the Lawson cuts of 1983, which made a sweeping £500 million reduction in public spending. Each event could have been designed as a litmus test of 'wetness'.

Clarke says he was 'very startled' by the 1981 Budget, although when he himself became Chancellor and needed to put up taxes he called it 'the finest Budget of the 1980s'. 'It was the increases in taxation and the threat they posed to economic recovery which alarmed me,' he remembers. He criticised the Budget at the time: 'I was, of course, very much a "wet" in our first years in government. In retrospect, Geoffrey was right and his critics were wrong.'

The Lawson cuts of 1983 were even harder for Clarke to swallow, as indeed they were for Norman Fowler. As Chancellor, Nigel Lawson was faced with a huge public-sector pay award which the government had promised to honour, the costs of a deepening recession and increased spending on defence and on law and order. To get the public finances back into shape he demanded a £128 million cut at Health, exceeded only by savings of £230 million at Defence. The *Daily Mail* and *Daily Mirror* both suggested that Fowler and Clarke might resign in protest, although Clarke says that was not his intent. Ever since his speech to the 1962 party conference in Llandudno, in Mansfield, Rushcliffe and Parliament Clarke had stressed the need for the welfare state, albeit an efficient one:

I was very angry about the cuts – especially the way it was done. We were suddenly told one day, and you had no time to prepare or sell it. I disapproved of dramatic gestures of that kind and I blamed the 'Lawson cuts' for the climate of political debate which lasted thereafter, when were accused of cutting back on spending on the health service at a time when current spending was actually increasing in real terms. We never quite shook it off.

Clarke supported the move to reduce taxation but, like Fowler, he wanted a balanced approach.[3] In the end, income tax was reduced, and the health budget went up, as did spending on social security.

Nor was Clarke a monetarist, at least in the sense that the early Thatcher government used the word. 'I have always been open about the fact that I have never been a monetarist in that sense,' he says:

> I had always shared Reggie Maudling's view that the money supply was difficult to measure and difficult to control. I think the overemphasis on chasing monetary targets such as sterling M3 as the overriding determinant of policy was eccentric. I was never entirely, however, a so-called Keynesian in the sense in which that term was misused in the 1970s and 1980s. Keynes was a considerable expert on monetary policy and I have always believed, as I do now, that a judicious combination of fiscal and monetary policy is required.

In this sense, Clarke is very much a product of the late 1950s and early 1960s, when both monetary and fiscal measures were used to manage the economy.

Protean politicians have suitably pragmatic monetary theories, but Clarke does not side with theorists of any description. In none of his jobs at Health, Education or the Treasury would he subscribe to any overarching philosophy except his own political common sense. For, unlike the Thatcherites, Clarke has a somewhat pessimistic view of the value of politicians, as John Gummer explains:

> People who were 'dry' in Mrs Thatcher's terms accepted a theoretical, philosophic view, which Ken wouldn't do because he never was that sort of person. And in a sense it's because he's a very traditionalist Tory in a Hailsham-like sense. He doesn't think politics can solve everything. He doesn't think like

socialists and Thatcherite theoreticians, that if you get the politics right everything will be all right, that they have the panacea.

In the political arena of the House of Commons, meanwhile, Clarke came through his time at Transport with his reputation enhanced. His debating style and his relaxed manner were winning him friends. The former party vice-chairman Sir David Trippier recalls that as a junior MP he went to seek Clarke to plead for a motorway sign for his new constituency, Rossendale, which like Clarke's constituency was a figment of the boundary commissioners' imagination, rather than a place on the map:

> Ken turned to this civil servant and said, 'How much would this sign cost if we put on the main town, Rawtenstall?' And the chap, straight out of *Yes, Minister*, said, well, actually, it will cost more than the average motorway sign because there are too many letters! We both laughed and Ken said, 'I'll tick the box; you've got your sign.'

But Mrs Thatcher was not prepared to tick the box for Kenneth Clarke's advancement. As her programme became more radical, so she considered him with even less favour as not being 'one of us'. Norman Fowler believes he spent 'hours and hours' trying to persuade her of Clarke's merits, with no success – although he was still able to perform another rescue act on his friend's career.

Fowler had been in line to be party chairman; it was a choice between him, Cecil Parkinson and Norman Tebbit. When Parkinson won the job, Fowler was switched to the Department of Health and Social Security as secretary of state in the reshuffle of September 1981. His political antennae told him that an NHS pay strike was approaching fast. He also thought that his team was not strong enough to deal with it; specifically, he considered that his health minister, Dr Gerard Vaughan, would not be a robust defender of the department's faith in any forthcoming dispute. Fowler wanted Clarke.

The problem was that, while Vaughan did not enjoy a reputation for decisiveness, he was staunch supporter of Mrs Thatcher and enjoyed access to her. To replace 'one of us' with a damp Kenneth Clarke, Mrs

Thatcher would need much convincing, and she was not yet convinced: 'There was much humming and haaing,' remembers Fowler. But in politics, timing is everything – and unbeknown to him, his timing had been perfect. The consumer affairs minister, Sally Oppenheim, had just been to see Mrs Thatcher to say she wanted to stand down. So Mrs Thatcher, who generally allowed Fowler the freedom to pick his own team, agreed to the switch, with Vaughan taking Oppenheim's job, and Clarke rejoining Fowler at the DHSS.

Fowler never regretted his decision. When the threatened pay strike became a reality, 'We'd send in Ken as a tank and then I would smooth it down. As a partnership it worked extraordinarily well. He was intellectually good; he was tough, the sort of bloke you wanted around in a dispute. It proved to be exactly the right judgement.' But Clarke was still carrying Fowler's bags – so much so that there was a joke in the DHSS that if anyone had put early money on Clarke rising to the top, they would now be worried about it. 'It was called a steady rise,' comments one insider, 'but it was very slow.'

Alexander Fleming House, the old home of the DHSS, is a grimy 1960s office block which lies lost in the sea of traffic that washes its never-ending way around the Elephant and Castle roundabout in south-east London. If the planners had been looking for a more unhealthy place to site the Health Department they would have had difficulty, and it enjoyed a miserable reputation among some employees in Whitehall.

Clarke nevertheless entered the lead-polluted atmosphere of south-east London willingly, even if it was again as number two to Fowler. The political duo was aided by the department's Permanent Secretary, Sir Kenneth Stowe. 'It was a bit like the court of a sultan,' remembers one official. 'Norman Fowler would cry, "Send for the two Kens!" Stowe and Clarke would be plucked from whatever they were doing to a great Crowned Heads of Europe meeting – which, because of Fowler's caution, would decide nothing.'

Several battles lay ahead of the new team. The health budget had reached more than £15 billion, and Fowler decided to try to trim it, first by forcing health authorities to put out to tender their ancillary services, such as cleaning, catering and laundry. Clarke firmly backed this move, though it enraged the unions and the Labour Party. They argued that the new operators would show a weaker commitment to the NHS than their predecessors. Fowler also decided to cut five thousand jobs from the NHS, saving some £40 million a year. Second, he reduced the drugs bill by £100 million by listing branded drugs which could no longer be prescribed, forcing doctors to use cheaper generic substitutes, a measure on which Clarke was very keen. Third, Fowler appointed Roy Griffiths, the chief executive of Sainsbury's, to lead an inquiry into the management of the health service. In each of these areas Clarke would step into rows which he would remember when he became Secretary of State for Health in his own right five years later:

> When I first went as a minister to the Department of Health . . . there was an absence of any clear objective other than struggling to cope with demand. There was a total inability to hold anyone to account for their performance. There was more time given to placating the trade unions and the big lobbies than heeding the voice of the patients. There was an almost total lack of information on such basic matters as the quantity and quality of output or the breakdown of costs.[4]

The main dispute was the one Fowler had feared, and the one for which he had requested the Clarke tank. Clarke had been there for just four days when the strike started: 'We used to do the soft-guy/hard-guy routine in a rather foolish sort of way. But it was a pretty vicious dispute – the whole health service was on strike for a very long time, longer even than the coal strike in the 1920s. It got very tense.' The tough Macleodite side of Clarke would be his passport to the Cabinet.

The Clarke tank performed its armour-plated role as forcefully as Fowler had expected, trundling inexorably towards the enemy strongholds, to fire shells at the union lines. A 12 per cent pay claim? *Crump*: 'ludicrously unrealistic'. A three-day health strike? *Crump*: 'callous'. The unions had rejected the government offer? *Crump*: 'they've fiddled the figures'. A health workers' demonstration? *Crump*: 'they were larking about'.

Tanks, though hard to destroy, sometimes have difficulty finding their range, and when in trouble they suffer from a lack of manoeuvrability. Some of the Clarke shells landed on his own side, while others hit their target but succeeded only in spreading the conflagration. Also, being heavy, impractical machines, tanks rumble around noisily and expensively unless they have a battle to fight. They prove their value only when they are under fire or when they have a target to aim at. Clarke sometimes gave the impression he was spoiling for a fight. 'I seem to move from one hot seat to another,' he said soon after taking up his new job, adding: 'I much prefer crises. It sounds perverse, but the one thing that I wouldn't like in government would be a dull job where nothing particular was happening.'[5]

Much would happen to him at Health. One of his first tasks, in 1982, was to tour hospitals at the centre of the strike:

Norman was persuaded by officials that in the hard-pressed areas morale was flagging among the managers and that somebody had to go and visit them. That was me. I was sent off on what was called a 'hot-spot tour'. Needless to say, in the silly season in August, which I've often suffered from, this became the first high-profile appearance of K. Clarke and it became a real hot-spot tour because it got the unions going. Each visit got livelier than the last as more and more national journalists followed this disastrous tour. It was all Norman's idea, not mine – God knows what it did for the morale of the managers.

The tour began peacefully enough in Doncaster, but at Liverpool's Walton Hospital in August Clarke was surrounded by jeering protesters, and it took the police at least five minutes before they were able to rescue him. Some of the demonstrators thrust pay slips at him, to show that their take-home pay was less than £50 a week. Clarke was hit on the head with a rolled-up newspaper but otherwise managed to escape unscathed. It was the worst reception he had ever received, although he took it calmly, reflecting that ministers were usually pelted with eggs (Michael Heseltine been greeted thus on a recent visit to Merseyside). 'It was the nearest thing to being in the middle of a riot I've been in. The police got me into the grounds but pickets were streaming in from all directions and the police didn't know which door to get me into. We rushed across to a door which was blocked by a television crew and it all got out of hand.'

After Clarke's visit to the hospital was over, he had to run the gauntlet of demonstrators again, and he responded to the physical violence by calling the demonstrations 'daft, silly, schoolboy stuff'. It may have been understandable in the circumstances, but nothing could have been more calculated to irritate the unions, or give them cause to look outraged. One union divisional officer was moved to remark that they were going to 'give that man a bloody nose'.

Later in his career, this phenomenon would be repeated, with Clarke losing patience when what he saw as vested interests blocked progress – whether at Health, Education or the Home Office. On each occasion, his negotiating style and his trenchant manner would lead to a heightening of feeling between the two sides. But his being threatened with a bloody nose was not typical, and Clarke never saw the battle in personal terms. Indeed, even his fiercest opponents of the last decade speak warmly of his personal qualities. Roger Poole, who would clash with him over the ambulance crews' dispute seven years later, considers him to be 'the one human being in the Cabinet. He's wrong about lots of things, terribly wrong – but at least he's got a human face.'

Sometimes Clarke's love of disputation, and his admitted attraction to a crisis, would pitch him into a predicament from which he would struggle to escape. This happened when he gave an interview to the *Daily Telegraph* about the course of the health strike, while Norman Fowler was on holiday. The *Telegraph* reported that Clarke was prepared to put troops into the hospitals if the level of patient care fell any further – for example, if the hospitals could no longer provide a basic level of care for accident victims or emergencies. Clarke maintains he was misinterpreted:

I was asked what's going to happen if people die, are you going to let the service collapse? So I said portentously, 'We would not allow that to happen.' Then the reporter asked, will you put the troops in? I think I made some solemn remark along the lines of, 'We will do whatever is necessary to keep the services going.' This was headlined by the *Telegraph* as 'Tanks in, says Clarke', or words to that effect. The Home Secretary, who was Willie, got frightfully concerned and said only *he* had the right to order in the military.

The timing could not have been worse. Clarke was flying out the next day on a curtailed family holiday and the press were on his tail. He arranged to meet Fowler, who was on his way back from a four-day break in France, in the lounge at Bordeaux airport. 'It was the only time I've ever seen Ken slightly hot and bothered,' remembers Norman Fowler. 'He was pursued on to the airfield by the press and it was only because the captain of the plane refused them entrance that they didn't actually get on board with him.' Clarke admits he was fairly 'churned up by the experience – I wasn't so used to controversy in those days. I gave Norman the most hair-raising account of what it was going to be like when he got back.'

Whatever the truth behind the *Daily Telegraph* interview, it showed the side of Clarke that had bothered Mrs Thatcher. Although she came in time to respect him, her fear was that if she ever gave him his own department he would be too difficult to handle and would charge at every issue on the table, ending up, Tigger-like, with the tablecloth wrapped over his head. Even a sensitive issue, such as whether to close Tadworth Court Children's Hospital to save a million pounds a year, seemed to produce a tablecloth response, with *Hospital Doctor* magazine claiming that the visiting Clarke had declared that there were more horses grazing in the hospital's fields than there were patients in the wards.

At the same time, Mrs Thatcher could not but admire Clarke's toughness. The Trades Union Congress day of action in support of the health workers – Wednesday 22 September 1982 – saw 60,000 demonstrators taking to the streets of London – and yet, within weeks, Clarke was confidently making his case for staff cuts in the NHS. Objections from the nurses were dismissed sweepingly: 'They are a trade union and they don't like the idea of their membership numbers going down at all.'[6] It was back to a much-loved theme; the health service unions had 'a vested interest in the continued waste of resources' and were trying to frighten the public into believing the NHS couldn't achieve greater efficiency, which Clarke firmly believed it could. One insider at the Health Department ascribed Clarke's toughness to his need to balance his liberalism and attract Mrs Thatcher's attention: 'It's hard to see Ken as a liberal. He's always aware of that role. So he puts up a barrage of thuggery to balance that liberalism. It can be brutal, frank and nasty.' In this way protean politicians can survive without doing any damage to their long-held views.

Meanwhile Clarke was dealing with highly complex legislation in the Commons, such as the Mental Health Bill which laid down the extent to which treatment could be given without consent to patients who were compulsorily detained, the terms of their detention and the ability of tribunals to review the basis on which they were held. Clarke was also given a higher-profile role in developing new relationships between private medicine and the NHS. All of these were intricate jobs, carried out deftly, according to his friends, but which his critics, like Michael Meacher, say he approached with inadequate preparation: 'He doesn't give the impression of someone who reads his briefs methodically and studies his papers closely.' Clarke certainly did not seem overenthusiastic about the administrative side of his department. One former minister recalls that he spent the first four months after Clarke's departure signing letters which began: 'Thank you for your letter. I'm very sorry you haven't had a reply earlier.' Clarke himself says that he was effectively running the health service while Norman Fowler launched his social security review, so answering letters was not his main priority.

Clarke insists that the devil lies in the detail. But his self-confidence makes him a relaxed minister who makes up his mind quickly. In conversation, he prefers the sweeping phrase or anecdote to a dry recitation of statistics. By contrast, Norman Fowler was renowned for his hesitancy. One official drove with him from the Elephant and Castle to the House, where Fowler was due to make a statement, only to find he was still agonising in the car over what to say. Lord Glenarthur, who joined the department as a parliamentary under-secretary in 1983, sums up the difference of approach of the two men: 'Norman would go into very great detail about everything and we had very long meetings with officials where he'd test the water, but Kenneth had a slightly more laid-back attitude towards it all. He may appear to cuff it when he came to a view, but that view was very often based on very sound instincts.'

Those instincts are the crucial factor in Clarke's political make-up. Like most politicians, he relies on them heavily, but he also has the confidence to act on them, Indeed, if Clarke's friends have a criticism of him, it is that he is the apotheosis of common sense, that he sometimes believes in the value of his own common sense too much and that he makes up his mind too quickly. 'He can be taken off his conclusions, but he does jump,' comments a former Cabinet ally. Sometimes this will lead to extraordinary results. In 1986 the government launched its AIDS campaign after a special Cabinet committee had been set up to co-ordinate Britain's response to the onset of the disease. But in the early days of the illness, as it first began to enter the country and scientists began to report their findings, Clarke was sceptical of their claims. Indeed, generally Clarke seems to display a scepticism about matters outside the confines of his direct experience or knowledge. His friend Sir David Trippier, who was Clarke's PPS at Health, calls him 'a bit of a flat-earther'. Accordingly, when Clarke became the Secretary of State for Health, he told everyone that scientific warnings about the dangers of cholesterol were nonsense. To quote one of his ministerial colleagues: 'He thought it was a load of claptrap. He doesn't like having the wool pulled over his eyes.'

Later in his career, Clarke would debunk space scientists and educationalists in similar vein. 'He's got a healthy disrespect for experts,' John Gummer says, 'and people who masquerade as being right when all they mean is that it's their theory. I think he overdoes it in some areas. But being a minister is about that. It's about saying, I don't think that's true, prove it to me. He takes that to a wonderfully extreme limit.'

Clarke once told his friends that there are two seemingly endless moments in a political career: the first when you're waiting to get into a ministerial job, and the second when you've been a minister for a while and you're hoping to get into the Cabinet. Both stages of his career had taken far longer than he could have expected when he first joined Ted Heath's government, and by now he was tempted to follow a new political route, one he had eschewed on first entering Parliament. In 1983 the Attorney-General, Sir Michael Havers, approached Clarke about becoming Solicitor-General in the place of Sir Ian Percival, who had decided to retire at the next election. 'It's another route,' Clarke told his friend David Trippier. Trippier was appalled at the prospect of the party losing Clarke's debating skills: 'So I sat there and said it *is* another route, and it's not necessarily the kiss of death. But I said it's not you. Just then, the phone rang, and it was Clarke's wife, Gill, with the same message.' Clarke decided to play a long game and take his chances under Margaret Thatcher's leadership.

By the end of 1983 there were signs that his patience might pay off. 'As always, AS ALWAYS, Heseltine and that podgy life-insurance-risk Kenneth Clarke are approvingly tipped,' wrote Alan Clark in his diaries.[7] In the New Year's Honours List of 1984 Clarke became a Privy Counsellor. His combative performances were winning him praise from Tory MPs, and from right-wing newspapers. Eighty-seven of the new intake of Tory MPs who won their seats in the 1983 election were questioned by *The Times* about who would be the most suitable successor to Mrs Thatcher.[8] Thirty-two of them voted for Norman Tebbit, the Trade and Industry Secretary, with Defence Secretary Michael Heseltine in second place. But a third of them backed Clarke as the next-generation leader. Two weeks later the *Sun* picked up on the news with a '*Sun* special on the Tories' rising star . . . The miner's son who could be PM – Ken's the right lad to watch'.[9]

The problem for Clarke was that his rise had taken fifteen years.

By that time, if I'm honest, I was getting rather itchy feet about why I wasn't in the Cabinet. No names, no pack drill, but people who I did *not* think were as effective as me as a minister were in the Cabinet. Again, if I'm being totally honest, I thought I hadn't done a bad job as health minister. Once Norman was doing his social security review I did single-handedly the Health Secretary's job and all the casework of a minister of state as well. Until I became Chancellor of the Exchequer, I have never worked so hard in all my life. So I was getting a bit impatient as to why I hadn't made it.

As each reshuffle had approached, Norman Fowler always pressed his friend's case, to no avail. In David Trippier's opinion:

Ken's very friendly with everybody, but he had an unusual relationship with Mrs Thatcher. Once Margaret was giving him quite a tirade about how we should stand firm on this, that and the other, be tough with the budgets, and so on – and Ken's attention began to wander. He started to stare at an invisible spot on the ceiling. He was sitting right next to her, so she touched his knee and when he looked round she said, 'I know you think it's boring but it's my job as Prime Minister to go on like this.' And he couldn't help but laugh.

Such were Clarke's parliamentary performances, however, that Mrs Thatcher could ignore him no longer, even though she was more anxious to bring on the younger ministers of the Right. There were no truly Thatcherite candidates of comparable talent. Lord Howe agrees that 'Ken Clarke was more left of centre than Margaret's natural instincts would allow, but he had abilities which in effect made him unstoppable.' Yet Mrs Thatcher retained the suspicion that Clarke would be hard to handle if he was given senior office, that he would be too difficult to control. As Sir Norman Fowler observes: 'She didn't particularly like Ken. She reluctantly admired him. She regarded him as a bit bouncy and cocky. She admired his intellectual strength but she didn't remotely regard him as sympathetic to her.' So in the reshuffle of September 1985, although Clarke finally entered the Cabinet, he was given a Gilbert and Sullivan title and no department of his own. He was to be Paymaster-General, which meant nothing, and the Commons spokesman for Lord Young, which meant something, if not much more. He became known as 'Lord Young's representative on Earth'. Nevertheless he had, at last, made it. After breaking the news to Clarke at No. 10, Mrs Thatcher turned to Norman Fowler and said wryly: 'There! You must be pleased.'

CHAPTER 8

The Odd Couple

He's a man way out there in the blue, riding on a smile and a shoeshine.
And when they start not smiling back – that's an earthquake . . . A
salesman is got to dream, boy. It comes with the territory.
                    Arthur Miller, *Death of a Salesman*

David Young and Kenneth Clarke made an unlikely couple – the Lord
Suit and Mr Crumpled of British politics. On the one hand, the
unelected businessman with a dapper line in double-breasted jackets
and a somewhat tangential hold on the realities of political life. On the
other, the young veteran of seven general election campaigns, a
consummate Westminster operator who had no experience of
business and who looked as if he dressed from his wife's Oxfam shop.

Lord Young was a truly Thatcherite creation, where Clarke was
not: a businessman who had run the Manpower Services Commission
and who owed his fast-track entry into politics to Keith Joseph, the
man who had effectively slowed down Kenneth Clarke's career. Only
six years earlier, while Clarke had been hoping for ministerial office
after nearly a decade in Parliament, Young had had his eye on more
modest preferment: to go to the Department of Trade and Industry as
a humble civil servant.

Young became Keith Joseph's political adviser at the DTI, initially
on a part-time, unpaid basis. Where the relationship between Clarke
and Joseph had withered, that between Young and Joseph fructified.
Joseph now took to handing out prescribed reading to his eager
colleagues – a dozen books from Adam Smith to de Tocqueville, and
even some by himself. Clarke had ignored Joseph's ideological rethink
of the mid-1970s; Young was no great political reader but he was a
believer.

Young's progress thereafter was as rapid as Clarke's was slow. From

129

Joseph's side at Trade and Industry, and with Norman Tebbit's help, he bounced into the Manpower Services Commission as chairman, and thence rapidly into the Cabinet with a peerage. While Clarke had no inkling of his imminent invitation to join the top table, Young knew exactly what to expect; Mrs Thatcher had told him of his new job as Employment Secretary several days before the reshuffle happened.

What Lord Young didn't know was that he and Clarke were to be harnessed together. 'It was an absolute bombshell for both of us,' recalls Young. Clarke agrees: 'We had hardly spoken to each other before, so each of us was a totally unknown quantity to the other. It could have been very difficult.' They shook hands for the first time at 10 Downing Street on the day of the reshuffle, and so began a curious working relationship which was to last for three years.

For Clarke, after nearly six years outside Margaret Thatcher's Cabinet, it was a moment of mixed emotions; he had finally made it to the Cabinet table, only to be paired with one of the Prime Minister's placemen: 'The happy day had dawned, but if I'm being honest it was a slight disappointment that I wasn't getting my own department. I was told you're both junior members of the Cabinet, but one of you has got to be in charge and it's David. We were sharing the department but he was the senior one if it ever came to disagreements.' Clarke's first reaction was to telephone a backbench friend and ask for help. 'I just don't have any feel for the job,' he declared. He was also worried about how he could work with his new colleague.

Young was as far removed from Clarke's background as it was possible to be. Clarke had spent his life in the Midlands, whereas Young was from the East End of London; Clarke had little interest in material wealth, but Young had pursued it; Clarke had fought and won his way into Parliament after a brace of ritual bloodings in Mansfield, but Young had been hand-picked by the Prime Minister; Clarke had taken fifteen years to reach the Cabinet, while Young had reached it on his very first day at Westminster.

Whatever her feelings towards Clarke, it was an astute move by Mrs Thatcher to hand him to Young. Apart from the practicalities of running a department from the Lords, the precedents for outsiders moving straight into the Cabinet were not good; the last businessman to try, the Confederation of British Industry's former Director-General, John Davies, had suffered terribly in the Commons. Young, without political support, was likely to fare little better. Extraordinarily, he didn't even belong to the Conservative Party: 'I sat in my first Cabinet and suddenly thought, Christ! I'm not even a member of the party, and that afternoon I sent off a cheque.' Clarke would buttress Young considerably with his parliamentary pugnacity. 'A cynic might say that he provided a very considerable stiffening to Lord Young,' Bernard Ingham suggests, 'because Young certainly wasn't a party politician and he had some very curious ideas.'

For his part, Lord Young was meant to keep an eye on Clarke, because Mrs Thatcher had not appointed Clarke without misgivings. 'There are some people that it is better to bring in because they would cause more trouble outside,' she writes in her memoirs. 'Peter Walker and, to a lesser extent, Kenneth Clarke, are examples precisely because they fought their corner hard.'[1] Clarke's toughness had won its reward. But by not giving him a department of his own to run, Mrs Thatcher could keep him under her thumb. 'Margaret thought plainly that David, as a wholly reliable right-winger, could look after a wholly unreliable left-winger like me,' Clarke cheerfully concedes. He was in the Cabinet, but still not flying high. Others would soar higher, faster; on the same day that Clarke joined the Cabinet, thirteen years after he had first entered the government, John Major gained his first ministerial job, in the department Clarke had just left. Some of those who flew higher than Clarke, on the other hand, would go too near the sun, while he continued to rise.

Suprisingly, in view of its antecedents, the relationship between Young and Clarke ran into no great difficulty. Although Clarke was frustrated not to have his own department, the friends whose advice he sought pointed out that Young would be short of political skills, so that there was a clear role for him to play. Clarke remembers that 'It was a bit awkward in the first month or so. He knew the department because he'd been at the Manpower Services Commission, and I was on a learning curve.' There were also some ground rules to lay down. At first the department assumed Clarke was going to do the job Peter Morrison had done as a junior minister, namely the casework for the MSC. 'So I suppose I got a bit pompous and said *I* was in the *Cabinet*. Then I was told I had more ministerial correspondence to handle than all the other ministers in the department, and I said, "I'm not doing it on that scale, I'll do the Privy Counsellor stuff, I've paid my dues on ministerial correspondence." '

Within a short while, the new team seemed to gel. Lord Young says that the two combined well together 'because our instinctive attitudes about most things were exactly the same'. So while the new political couple were conjoined through a marriage made in Downing Street rather than in heaven, it was not an unholy alliance. Young, like Clarke, was no political philosopher but a man who saw specific problems and came up with specific solutions. And, unlike Keith Joseph, Young had an appetite for fun. He and Clarke accepted their differences with good humour: 'There were things about Ken I couldn't understand. For example, he'd go anywhere for a duty-free. He'd never go to the VIP suite at the airport – he always preferred to go to the main building because he could go and get his bottles there and he couldn't in the other place!'

At the same time, Clarke was once more incurring the wrath of the true believers. The then junior minister at the Department of Employment, Alan Clark, makes no secret of his distaste for his near-namesake in his diaries. Clark was a Thatcher acolyte, fervent in his admiration for her. He looked upon his colleague with disdain, partly because he felt Clarke had no fixed political purpose, unlike the leader he worshipped. Ill feeling between the two also arose out of a later incident over the game of Trivial Pursuit, which asked, 'Which minister thought that immigrants to Britain came from Bongo Bongo Land?' The answer should have been Alan Clark, but it said Kenneth Clarke instead. Clarke threatened to sue, through his Nottingham lawyer friend Martin Suthers, and the makers of the game apologised and made a donation to Gillian Clarke's favourite charity, Oxfam.

The whole episode annoyed Alan Clark: 'I mean, who does he think he is? If I wasn't irritated why should he be?' But he has also paid tribute to the ability of Clarke to take whatever brickbats are thrown at him: 'I was at a dinner with him recently, with some twenty other people, and he stood up and said that my *Diaries* were one of the best political reads of 1993. It was very handsome of him.'

If Clarke has a capacity to take criticism, another notable quality, as he entered the Cabinet, was his political discretion. David Trippier mentions that 'David Young couldn't wear Peter Bottomley. Peter can be a bit off the wall at times, and you'd say something to Ken about it, but he'd just say, have you seen the good side? Very rarely have I heard him criticise anyone. He's just like my mother.'

The challenge facing the newly created Cabinet duo was daunting. Unemployment was nearing the three and a quarter million mark, and Mrs Thatcher deemed the reduction of the jobless figure and the encouragement of enterprise to be the two main aims of the reshuffle. 'Unemployment was probably going to be fatal to the government,' Clarke remembers. 'The government was blamed firstly for three million unemployed and secondly for appearing not to care about it. We set the objective that unemployment had to be below three million by the time of the next general election, and to demonstrate that we had a policy, that we were doing something.' The Enterprise Years had descended upon the country with a glossy thud.

Lord Young decreed it was time to be positive about unemployment. He ushered in an era of self-help schemes and small-is-beautiful, an era when the government looked to small businesses to replace the thousands of manufacturing jobs which had disappeared in the recession, an era when the government decided it would no longer be defensive about unemployment but, instead, would sell its wares in the market-place. As the son of a small businessman, this appealed to Clarke. The pair duly came up with a variety of ingenious schemes to reduce the jobless total. All of them stemmed, essentially, from Lord Young's experience as a self-made businessman, from his belief that the economy was the sum of its many small parts. He was micro-man.

The first scheme to help the unemployed was actually promoted by Clarke, not Young, although its genesis lay abroad. The United States had shown that one way to deal with unemployment was to run 'job clubs', where unemployed people were given advice and help in applying for jobs if they turned up to the club at regular hours each day. Supporters of this policy within the Department of Employment were pushing for the go-ahead to introduce job clubs in Britain, but on his first day in office Young dismissed the scheme as dangerous and liable to political criticism from his own side. Clarke saw its apparent merits straight away. Within twenty-four hours he had persuaded Young to change his mind. Lord Young now says that 'In the course of time it turned out to be one of the very best self-help ideas of the decade . . . so much for my political instincts!'[2]

On Clarke's instinct, therefore, not Young's, a network was established which grew to span two hundred job clubs nationwide, providing free facilities, including telephones, typewriters, photo-copying and stationery for those who had been out of work for more than six months. It matched Clarke's belief that people should be given practical help to stand on their own two feet. He made no demands for more direct government involvement, unlike the wets on Mrs Thatcher's back benches.

The whole towering structure of Lord Young's later employment schemes was based upon this foundation stone. Young came up with the idea of asking in all the long-term unemployed for interview and combining the various schemes run by the department into one programme. In nine pilot areas around the country, jobless people who came in for an interview were offered a bewildering variety of choices: a place on the Community Programme, entry into a job club, a place on the new weekly course set up under the Enterprise Allowance Scheme, or a new programme which offered to supplement the wage of anyone who had been unemployed for more than a year and who was prepared to take a job at less than £80 a week.

As the success of this project grew, the nine areas initially selected expanded into twenty 'Task Force' projects. There were two great merits to all these schemes: first, they kept some people off the unemployment register; second, Lord Young hoped that people who were fiddling the system would drop out before their interview. Clarke also tried to make sure that the Task Forces helped the jobless to find work on urban regeneration projects, especially if they were unemployed black or Asian people. His point was that otherwise only the property developers would benefit. It was a theme he was to return to when he ran the whole of the government's inner-city policy himself.

Clarke was not only an enthusiastic supporter of Young's ideas, but a driving force behind them. They accorded with some of his central tenets – the drive against inefficiency and waste, the rights of the individual and the wrongs of local authorities. In front of a Tory Reform Group audience where he might have been expected to make coded criticisms, if he felt there were any to be made, he declared instead: 'This to me is what Government aid should be about, not throwing money at a problem in the vain hope that it will somehow go away, but working with local people to see how they themselves can overcome their own difficulties. It is a question of encouraging responsibility and involvement, not funding municipal socialism.'[3]

However, Clarke was prepared to indicate that the jobless issue was a more complex one than the Tory Party might allow. He refused to concede that there was a link between unemployment and rising crime, but he came closer to it than most of his Cabinet colleagues. Shortly after taking up his new post, he stated that 'the enforced idleness of many of our young contributes to the complex social problems of our cities'.[4] Later, at the Conservative Party conference in Blackpool, he told a Bow Group fringe meeting that unemployment, while not the cause of crime, made worse the pattern of criminality which was breaking out around the country. He also accepted, which more aggressive Tories did not, that it was foolish to suggest that there were many unwilling, idle people within the pool of unemployed who would not leap at the chance of a job if they could get one.

Even so, Clarke's solutions remained solidly Thatcherite; governments could not solve unemployment by greater spending:

The belief that a lasting answer for jobs lies in irresponsible, untargeted infrastructure spending is fanciful, fashionable nonsense. Much of the money would be spent, not on people, but on machines and material. By contrast, the £2 billion that this Government is spending this year alone on employment and training measures is directed towards individuals.[5]

Clarke did not join, even privately, those MPs who demanded more spending on new projects. He accused the six Tory and five Labour MPs who made up the Commons Select Committee on Employment of 'dodging difficult choices' by calling for a £3 billion programme to create work for the unemployed. 'David and I used to amuse each other by the fact that I often took a more hard-line view than he did on individual issues, but both of us were far more pragmatic than the outside world realised.'

Clarke appeared to be an easy convert to Lord Young's lingua franca. The word 'enterprise' was rarely absent from his lips; his speeches came to be peppered with phrases about the need to 'support enterprise' and to reward and encourage the enterprise of business-men, not politicians. So was Clarke convinced by the Enterprise Years? David Trippier thinks he was: 'He recognised that Lord Young had been there at the sharp end and knew a lot about business. And he saw that David had this enormous strength, which was public relations – he thought, my goodness me, if you want to get a message across, this is the way to do it.'

The Enterprise Years were never knowingly undersold. Lord Young had decided that the department's advertising was 'totally forgettable', with no unified style. So he decreed that it was to be brought together into one umbrella programme which would make the unemployed aware of the myriad of different schemes being set up on their behalf – and, in consequence, make the Department of Employment less like the Department of Unemployment.

Young once spent a whole day watching a 'beauty parade' of four selected advertising agencies for a £3 million campaign. One agency's audiovisual presentation was so powerful that it fused the depart-ment's equipment; none the less, it persuaded Young to hold twenty 'Action for Jobs' breakfasts around the country, to take the message to the people. 'At the time when Alan Clark in his memoirs says he was sitting bored out of his skull because there was nothing to do, David Young and I were having the time of our lives running all these job schemes,' Clarke remarks.

The Action for Jobs breakfasts began at eight o'clock in the morning and finished an hour later after a presentation which, Lord Young recounts proudly, used no fewer than 1,700 slides. David Trippier was among those who had to turn out for these breakfasts: 'It was like a ten-line whip. There was background music, and an Americanised form of presentation. Ken was struck by it all. The only problem was that he's rotten at getting up in the morning and he should have had a make-up artist!'

Clarke was certainly impressed by Lord Young's presentational ideas:

We had this tedious range of job-training and employment-creating schemes and we found that the people for whom they were designed knew nothing about them. Here we were with all these marvellously complicated schemes designed to help the unemployed and small businesses, but what was the bloody use if no one had ever heard of them? So we decided if these were going to work, they had to be marketed. We spent an awful lot of money to sell them hard and aggressively. I got genuinely enthused about all the things we could market.

By 1987 unemployment was firmly on a downward path. Despite opposition claims that the pair had effectively massaged the figures, they had delivered the political success Mrs Thatcher had demanded, defusing the issue in time for a general election. She wrote that 'happily the [1986] Bournemouth Conference coincided with increasing evidence of prosperity, not least the fall in unemployment . . . it gave us a lift in morale which, in retrospect, set us on course for winning the next election'.[6] Their critics suggested, however, that a few modest training schemes and clubs had been established instead of any long-term solution to the problem; there was, it was said, a more structural failure in the economy, and North Sea oil could have been used to finance a massive increase of investment in industry and infrastructure.

One of the leading dissidents of the time, Ian Gilmour, has written: 'The Thatcherites believed . . . that the only way to achieve low inflation and low unemployment was for the government to control the money supply, balance its books, cut income tax and allow market forces to work. That attitude always seemed to me to have an element of witch-doctory about it.'[7] Yet Clarke seems to have been convinced by at least some of the 'black magic':

My answer is that we provided both style and substance. The unemployment figures began to fall the moment we arrived, because the economy itself was improving, whereas poor old Tom King had been murdered month by month whenever the figures came out. But we did get the number of long-term unemployed down, so there was substance, and we were just consciously trying to add a bit of style to the presentation of it.

To make progress when you are a Cabinet minister with no department of your own is a hard task. All ministers need a power base, where they can formulate policy and impress the Prime Minister with the sharpness of their views on future developments, the smooth running of their department and their suitability for the next promotion. But for Clarke, whose Cabinet seat was held only in the long shadow of Lord Young, there was correspondingly little chance to impress. The success in bringing down unemployment was associated essentially with Lord Young; he was head of the department which had triumphed, the man who brought Mrs Thatcher solutions. If Clarke was to progress, he needed an issue to call his own.

The issue Clarke found was thoroughly consistent with the views which have coloured his political career. He came to speak about trade union power and local authority ineptitude in ever more bestial terms. 'The monster of excessive trade union power', he declared, 'is now caged by a sensible, modern, industrial relations laws, but it is not yet a domesticated beast.'[8]

Clarke had latched on to the idea of further union legislation within a month of joining the Cabinet. This both accorded with his long-held view that the unions abused their power and had the merit of appealing to his leader. The year-long miners' strike was fresh in people's minds, and Clarke wanted to plug the loophole in the law which allowed Arthur Scargill to hold the presidency of the National Union of Mineworkers for life. 'If Scargill and Todd think they can hold back the tide of democracy then they are as foolish as King Canute,' Clarke told the Commons. 'We have to stick to our task for the sake of our industry and our services, for the sake of jobs and above all for the benefit of individual trade unionists.'[9] It was a sign that the wet versus dry distinction of the early 1980s was hard to apply to Clarke as he cemented his Cabinet position, or that the very distinction had itself broken down, to be revived only in 1990 as the two factions became delineated, at least in the minds of Mrs Thatcher's supporters, in the battle over her fate.

Three times the Conservative government had brought in laws against the unions between 1980 and 1984, and three times it had raised the spectre of the Winter of Discontent to justify its action. There were by now more contemporary battles to fight; in addition to the recent miners' dispute, police and pickets were fighting at the new Wapping headquarters of Rupert Murdoch's News International, the Docklands fortress he had set up to break the print unions' stranglehold on his Fleet Street newspapers. Clarke's Green Paper on union reform reflected the nature of these two disputes as well as his own long-held beliefs. He claims that he has been 'as constant as the northern star' in his political views, and if the Green Paper was the product of expediency – in that it appealed to the Prime Minister and capitalised on the latest union unrest – then it was also the product of his belief that the use of organised union strength was wrong where it overrode the rights of individuals, or where he saw it as special pleading dressed up as principle. Clarke maintains that his thoughts were crystallised by the health strike of 1982:

> I saw how the whole system was dominated by sheer terror of COHSE and NUPE [the health unions], and how vehement they were in that strike. I think I've mellowed now. I never took Norman Willis terribly seriously, but his successor John Monks is the model of a modern trade unionist. If we'd had a bloke like him as General Secretary of the TUC then we'd never have had the trauma or the sort of trade union movement we then had.

For more than a year Clarke campaigned against the unions before he finally won the right to launch his Green Paper. The Wapping dispute made some ministers fear that the unions might be winning the propaganda battle against Murdoch's News International and, like Clarke, they were concerned that a groundswell of public opinion might threaten the existing union reforms. Clarke saw the danger clearly. He told a lunch of the parliamentary press gallery that the print unions were engaged in a losing battle to defend their 'notorious rackets', but conceded that Rupert Murdoch's lack of appeal contrasted unfavourably with that of the personable print union leader Brenda Dean.

The government felt that it was under more pressure from the trouble at Wapping than the outside world realised at the time, although it tried to adopt a pose of studied neutrality in the dispute. The unions alleged that Murdoch had set up a number of new companies so that picketing would be judged to be unlawful secondary action. Labour argued that this highlighted the iniquities of the government's trade union reforms, in particular the 1980 Act which had placed severe limits on secondary action. John Prescott, the shadow employment spokesman, put forward a bill of rights to replace the government's reforms. But Clarke took the lead in heading off the attack, labelling the Wapping dispute 'Custer's last stand' and blaming the trouble, not on the government's legislation, but on the 'pig-headedness' of the Labour movement.

Labour and the unions cemented their new alliance in the document *People at Work: New Rights and Responsibilities*. The government considered the threat from this pact to be very real – it had a vision of Neil Kinnock in Downing Street and the unions once more pre-eminent. The great Tory political phobia had returned, if it had ever been away: an aversion to the smell of beer and the taste of sandwiches. It could do Clarke no harm. In the forefront of this battle, he determined to put the case for further trade union reform to the audience least likely to welcome it: the Trades Union Congress itself. He was the first Cabinet minister to accept an invitation to the conference since Mrs Thatcher had won power in 1979. In one newspaper interview after another, Clarke went on the offensive, raising the spectre of the Winter of Discontent. People should fear the Labour Party's new understanding with the unions, he argued: 'They forget what it was like when the power was cut off. They forget what it was like when inflation galloped away because of Labour's spendthrift policies and union greed for more pay . . . They perhaps also forget that it was at the expense of the individual member that the trade union barons prospered.'[10]

When Clarke finally won the opportunity to bring in new laws, an election was approaching. Mrs Thatcher and her ministers became convinced that the public appetite for further union reform had not been blunted, and early in 1987 decided to give Clarke's campaign a higher profile. The reason was clear. The Tories considered there was considerable political capital to be gained out of the slogan 'handing the unions back to their members'. It could be translated either into legislation or, if there was not time, a manifesto commitment to put before the electorate. Three trade union acts, combined with the recession, had transformed Britain's industrial landscape and had served to remind the country of the failures of the last Labour government. For a party hoping for a third successive general election victory, there was a danger that it might have to be run purely on its own rather mixed track record, unless it revived once more memories of the ructions of the 1970s. The trade union leaders were convenient victims. They could be safely hung on the quarterdeck to encourage Tory voters, and their fate would remind Tory waverers, too, of the humbling of Ted Heath's government: the atavistic fear that lay behind the Thatcher years.

Clarke unveiled proposals to remove the remaining legal protection for the closed shop, to increase the rights of union members to defy strikes and to force all union leaders to stand for regular election. His Green Paper, prosaically entitled *Trade Unions and their Members*, also proposed the appointment of a commissioner for trade union affairs to handle members' complaints against the unions to which they belonged. He told the Commons that his Green Paper would have made considerable differences to the Wapping dispute. First, he said, any member of the print union SOGAT could have won an order stopping the union calling a strike until it had balloted all its members. Second, neither the National Union of Journalists nor the transport workers' union could have so easily taken action against members who crossed the picket lines. Labour called it a petty, miserable and vindictive attack on the rights of trade union members. But Clarke held his ground.

Clarke served his leader, and himself, well with his doughty union bashing. He may still have been seen as a moderate, firmly within the mainstream of the party, but he displayed a toughness and self-confidence, as well as an approachability, which made him popular at Westminster. His skills were widely recognised in the press. 'Clarke is not always at ease with the government's policies,' *The Times* pronounced. 'But the pragmatist and lawyer within him . . . understands the necessary art of compromise.'[11] He could enter the 1987 general election in the expectation of emerging with a department to himself. Yet it was not to be. Mrs Thatcher was still wary of her untypical minister – and she paired him once again with Lord Young, this time at the Department of Trade and Industry, with the title of Chancellor of the Duchy of Lancaster.

It was another in the long line of disappointments meted out to Clarke by his Prime Minister. Since 1979 he had served Norman Fowler twice and David Young once; now, in 1987, he was for the fourth time to be in someone else's shadow – despite the fact that in each department it was clear, even to his enemies, that he was the more talented minister. So what had gone wrong? For all his verbal talents, Clarke remained a difficult man for Mrs Thatcher to define. While he had provided the necessary political stiffening to Lord Young, he also showed an alarming independence of spirit, mind and even body. He was, for the Prime Minister, the minister who didn't quite fit in, politically or sartorially. Were those suede shoes the natural Clarke, or a studied attempt to stand out from the crowd? The former, according to Clarke: 'I didn't even notice I was wearing them . . . I just wore suede shoes because about thirty years ago everybody wore suede shoes.'[12] Once the manufacturers of Hush Puppies set him a new pair; but he prefers to wear out an old pair, because he finds it more comfortable.

For Mrs Thatcher, there was a broader question of Clarke's style. He had been an untidy sort of junior minister, the kind who threw his notes on to the floor of the House of Commons, which offended her campaign against litter (he stopped doing this when she actually got on her hands and knees and started to pick them up during a division). He appeared too easygoing, his enthusiastically good-humoured debating talents giving the impression that he wasn't quite serious about his politics, that he took greater pleasure in the performance than in policy. He even let on that among his political memorabilia he had a collection of political toby jugs at home including one of his leader 'with a very long nose', though this, he declared cheerfully, was balanced by a Ted Heath gurgling jug.

Besides, for a Prime Minister who had become known as a conviction politician, wasn't Clarke a bit too friendly with the other side? For all his verbal aggression, politics is for Clarke a battle which rarely spills over into personal abuse. Few of Clarke's Labour opponents actively dislike him. John Prescott, for example, says: 'He's a guy I could talk to and respect as a professional politician. His style is like mine – he takes a cigar, takes a drink, gives them two fingers if he doesn't agree with them. He doesn't just respect the established authority.'

Then, as far as Mrs Thatcher was concerned, did he have to be so blokeish? It wasn't just the well-publicised love of jazz and the trips to Ronnie Scott's, the Bass Clef or Dean Street (trips which, in fact, went into a steep decline when Clarke became a minister). It was also his love of beer, boxing and football. All could have been forgiven if he had been 'one of us', but he wasn't. According to Bernard Ingham, Mrs Thatcher never lost her suspicion that he was wet: 'In Mrs Thatcher's terms that has acquired a very precise meaning – and that is, he's too free with money.'

Clarke's friends describe him as an unselfconscious character who accordingly made no effort to change his image for his Prime Minister's benefit. Certainly, for a man who is ambitious, he took remarkably little care over his appearance. When David Trippier was his PPS at the Health Department in 1982 he frequently told Clarke to get his hair cut and also bought him a belt for his trousers:

> I was his Jeeves. His manner in the House was that his hair would continually flop forward over his eyes, so he had this mannerism of sweeping it back with his right hand. And he'd lost a bit of weight, which is a miracle for him, so he started hitching his pants up at the despatch box at the same time that he was sweeping his hair back, which is well nigh impossible. I said I can't stand this – so I gave him the belt. He took it but when I ceased to be his PPS he went downhill.

Indeed, when Clarke attempts to act in a studied, self-conscious manner, it seems so out of the ordinary to his friends that they soon undermine him. Jim Lester remembers that 'Once Ken had this new light-check suit on, and I said, "Good God, Ken, where did you get that from? You look like a bookie's runner!" He didn't say anything, but then his wife asked me, what have you been saying to Ken – you've wounded him.'

There is, nevertheless, something studied about Kenneth Clarke: his desire not just to debunk grandiose political theories but also to be his own man, an individual who is not lost within the uniform greyness of government, which is why the Hush Puppies suit him perfectly. They are a pair of shoes, so they are within the limits of what is acceptable in that they cover his socks and he is not actually parading around Whitehall and Westminster barefoot. But at the same time they shock a little. Cabinet ministers aren't meant to wear suede shoes with their regulation grey uniform. 'I just rather defiantly do my own thing,' Clarke concedes:

It only shows up nowadays in silly things, like my taste for jazz, like my taste for these filthy cigars, like the way I dress – although I do try to turn out looking reasonably like a Cabinet minister. The shoes are a slight act of defiance, because people began to be rude about them and if anything I began wearing suede shoes more often because I was getting advised to stop wearing them.

Clarke had also developed a new interest which made Mrs Thatcher and her supporters think he was a more complicated character than he let on. In the mid-1980s he took up bird-watching. His Nottingham friend Martin Suthers puts the interest down to a holiday in Cornwall, when Clarke looked out of a window and saw what he considered an unusual bird: 'He said, "Ooh, what's that bird? It's very attractive", and Gillian said, "Oh, come off it, Ken, it's a blue tit – you can see those in the garden in Moseley!" ' Bird-watching thence became an obsession, encouraged by holidays each year with Suthers and their mutual Cambridge friend John Barnes.

This bird-watching confused the picture even more for Mrs Thatcher and her favourites. Clarke had a hinterland to which he could retreat and which they could not comprehend. 'He's one of the lads,' says one former Cabinet minister, 'but the lads don't go off bird-watching. No, he's a much more complex character than his rather overweight, badly dressed, suede-shoed appearance suggests.' In short, Mrs Thatcher couldn't place him. His enthusiasms were too varied, and his politics too ambiguous, for such a single-minded Prime Minister.

Despite all this, Mrs Thatcher shared an identity of purpose with Clarke – a mutual iconoclasm. 'What Ken has in common with Margaret', suggests one minister, 'is a willingness to challenge the establishment. He does that with unerring accuracy.'

While Clarke and Thatcher accorded each other an increasing respect, based on admiration for each other's abilities, there was no personal chemistry. Clarke usually refers to Mrs Thatcher publicly as 'Margaret', but the use of her first name sounds formal when he says it. It is ostensibly friendly but distant at the same time. The relationship worked only in so far as the two of them had to tackle practical problems together.

As a junior Cabinet minister, Clarke continued to keep his thoughts about Mrs Thatcher to himself. A ministerial colleague describes him as having 'hordes of friends, but he always keeps his own counsel. It's not just political shrewdness; he's one of those self-contained men.' This, in many ways, is a key to Clarke's personality and success. He is gregarious, affable, naturally easy company. But he is also a private man who rarely shows his hand.

So Clarke was too talented for Mrs Thatcher to sack but too set in his own idiosyncratic ways and too self-reliant for her to trust entirely. In mid-1987 her own favourite was clear: John Moore, promoted in the reshuffle from Transport to the Department of Health and Social Security. At forty-nine he was only three years older than Clarke, indisputably dry, and with clothes which were considerably less creased.

CHAPTER 9

Dressing the Part

*Any man may be in good spirits and good temper when he's well dressed.
There an't much credit in that.*

Charles Dickens, *Martin Chuzzlewit*

On the night of her third consecutive election victory, on 11 June 1987, Mrs Thatcher paused on the staircase of Conservative Central Office in Smith Square to deliver a surprising message. Instead of striking a triumphalist note as she received the greetings of ecstatic party workers, she declared that 'we must do something about the inner cities'. Compassion and a caring society were now, apparently, going to be the watchwords of the third Thatcher term, unlikely as it seemed. But there was hard logic behind the apparent compassion; there had been a swing to Labour in the North of England, as well as in Scotland and Wales, and big cities like Manchester, Liverpool and Newcastle upon Tyne had elected not a single Conservative MP. 'It was a strange remark for her to make,' Clarke agrees. 'I don't think she meant what she was taken to mean at all. What she meant was they're the only bits left which the Labour Party is winning, we're going to win those next. But it was interpreted quite a different way.' On such threads political careers do hang. As the existing inner-cities minister, Clarke had been given a boost, and a chance to bring out the caring side of his politics.

First, however, an internal battle lay ahead. Over the next few months the famous commitment to the inner cities seemed as unlikely as it had first sounded as the Prime Minister dallied over who should co-ordinate the government's policy. The Department of the Environment, led by Nicholas Ridley, mounted a fierce rearguard action to keep the inner cities within its own empire. The row rumbled on right up to the party conference that autumn, with Ridley even suggesting that the speech on inner cities should be made by a 'neutral' minister so that Clarke might not be seen to be winning the battle.

For five months the infighting went on as Clarke held out for overall control of the £1 billion programme. Ridley led the battle against the DTI, pointing out that his department spent three times more on the inner cities, the bulk of it through the Manpower Services Commission. The row put David Trippier, who was his junior minister, in an awkward position because of his friendship with Clarke: 'It's fair to say that Nick was not besotted with Ken, and he knew we were as thick as thieves.' At one point Trippier was ordered by Ridley not to attend a Cabinet subcommittee because it was chaired by Clarke. As the arguments wore on and the weeks went by, the great reforming initiative so peremptorily launched by the Prime Minister looked as if it was running into the sand.

It was here that Clarke's good relations with Lord Young came to his rescue, epitomised by, of all things, an incident in their shared lavatory. One day, shortly after taking over at the DTI, Young was washing his face in the changing-room on the eighth floor of the Victoria Street building, when his ministerial colleague bowled in from a garden party wearing full morning dress and with a carrier bag in his hand. To Young's amusement, Clarke took his shirt out of the bag, where it had been rolled in a ball, and then his trousers, which were also rolled up in a ball with no apparent regard as to how they might crease. 'By the time he'd changed his clothes', Young recalls, '*he* looked as if he'd been rolled up in a ball.'

When the Prime Minister asked Young's advice on who should run the inner-cities programme he remembered this incident: ' "Prime Minister," I said, "there's only one suitable candidate." "Who's that?" she asked. And I replied, "Ken Clarke – because he looks like he lives in one!" And she burst out laughing and said yes!'

There were other reasons for Mrs Thatcher's decision. It heralded a shift away from the land reclamation schemes sponsored by the Department of the Environment, in favour of trying to create jobs and 'enterprise' in the inner cities. Besides, if the object of the exercise was to show compassion then the lordly disdain exhibited by the Environment Secretary, Nicholas Ridley, was not necessarily the best

Previous page *Kenneth Clarke at Mablethorpe, c. 1950* (© PATRICIA CHALMERS)

The home in Upper Dunstead Road

Kenneth Clarke Senior's watchmaker's shop at 25 Highbury Road now

And then (© PATRICIA CHALMERS)

Opposite top left *Family holidays with sister Pat at Mablethorpe, 1947* (© PATRICIA CHALMERS)

Opposite top right *With a favourite Mr Punch puppet* (© PATRICIA CHALMERS)

Opposite bottom *Jersey 1951: Pat, Kenneth, Doris, Michael and Kenneth Senior* (© PATRICIA CHALMERS)

Top *On holiday at Bridlington, c. 1950* (© PATRICIA CHALMERS)

Bottom *Round Bridlington bay aboard* The Yorkshireman, *c. 1950*
(© PATRICIA CHALMERS)

Top left *The Nottingham High School pupil, 1951–9* (© KENNETH CLARKE)

Top right *Homework in the back garden at Bulwell* (© PATRICIA CHALMERS)

Bottom *St Helier, c. 1956: closer to his father than his mother, his father had high hopes for Kenneth* (© PATRICIA CHALMERS)

Top left *Kenneth and Doris* (© PATRICIA CHALMERS)

Top right *Expo 1958* (© PATRICIA CHALMERS)

Bottom *A first glimpse of Europe, with High School friends in Spain, 1959; Kenneth Clarke is on the left* (© PATRICIA CHALMERS)

Top *The Cambridge Union Society Committee, 1963: Clarke sits in the front row on the left; behind him stands Norman Lamont, and third from the left in the back row is Michael Howard; David Frost sits third from the right in the front row*

Bottom *Mansfield man, the prospective candidate, 1964* (© KENNETH CLARKE)

Top *The ritual defeat, 1964, in Mansfield at the hands of Bernard Taylor (extreme right)*

Bottom *And again, in 1966, by 'Don' Concannon (left)*

Opposite *The Mansfield Conservative Association Yearbook, 1965.*

From our
Prospective Parliamentary Candidate

Mr. KENNETH CLARKE, M.A., LLB.

THE NEXT ELECTION MAY BE SOON

NO-ONE yet knows whether 1965 will be another Election Year, but the indications are that it may be, and it will certainly be in the national interest if another General Election is held. Mr. Wilson is holding on to power by the skin of his teeth, having already lost a by-election, and his Government seems unlikely to be able to last into another year. The Government is only avoiding defeat by inactivity. After its first six months of life it has not got one important achievement behind it. No major Bill has yet passed through Parliament and no important new policy in any field has yet emerged. The only projects that the Government seems to be considering introducing are its disastrous schemes for the nationalisation of Steel and Building Land. This period of stagnation in Westminster cannot continue. The country will soon be going to the Polls again to correct the mistake of October 1964.

my second in Mansfield and I am The 1964 result was, in my opinion, sfield Conservatives. In simple terms , (to use the language of the Opinion nservatives to the Socialists of just better than the national result, so Conservatives elsewhere. More im- ansfield, at a time when the Labour Election, actually went down. The up, and it was only the division of Liberals that stopped us cutting the rply.

rvention is a nuisance to us and is successfully fought off the challenge. Mansfield in any local or General bad third. We continue to get the lion's share of the move away from the Socialists and as that move grows in importance, so shall we.

Of course, the success or failure of the Association in 1965 will not depend on elections alone. It is in the continued success of the various regular activities of the Association that are its permanent strength. Personally, I particularly enjoy the supper meetings and I am very glad that they continue to thrive. But this is not to reduce the importance of all the other activities and the Women's Branches in Mansfield and Warsop, and the Young Conservatives show no signs of reducing the whole scope of their activities.

Our political progress in Mansfield will call for patience as well as for enthusiasm. We must look for steady step-by-step advance rather than miraculous over-night success. But the signs are that this steady advance is being achieved and that in 1965, whether we face the major challenge of a General Election or not, we shall continue to move nearer to our goal—a Conservative Council and a Conservative Member for Mansfield.

Top *An early Cabinet photograph? In fact it is Kenneth Clarke, his best man John Selwyn Gummer and, from the left, Peter Fullerton, Michael Howard, Leon Brittan, Christopher Mason and Norman Lamont*

Bottom left *Kenneth Clarke married Gillian Edwards in 1964*

Bottom right *Kenneth and Gillian, with Kenneth Junior (born 1965) and Sarah (born 1968)* (© KENNETH CLARKE)

Top *On the road to Parliament – the Conservative Party Conference at Brighton, 1969* (© KENNETH CLARKE)

Bottom left *Campaigning in Rushcliffe in the run-up to the 1970 General Election* (© KENNETH CLARKE)

Bottom right *Support from Tony Barber, Chairman of the Conservative Party, in the 1970 Election campaign* (© KENNETH CLARKE)

Above left *Speaking in Europe as a junior Whip in 1973* (© KENNETH CLARKE)

Above right *Helping Gillian Clarke's favourite charity: Nicholas Scott and Kenneth Clarke both come from the same wing of the Tory Party; both founded dining clubs in their own image and both looked to Iain Macleod for their inspiration* (© NICK FOGDEN/OXFAM)

Opposite top left *Campaigning against inflation under Labour, 1975* (© T. BAILEY FORMAN LIMITED)

Opposite top right *Under Secretary of State at the Ministry of Transport, 1982, here overseeing the conversion of a disused railway line into a cycle track* (© PRESS ASSOCIATION)

Opposite bottom *A rougher ride at Health followed, running the gauntlet at the Walton Hospital, Merseyside, 1982* (© LIVERPOOL DAILY POST AND ECHO)

Top *The Odd Couple: in the Cabinet at last but paired with David Young*
(© T. BAILEY FORMAN LIMITED)

Bottom left *The government's minister for inner cities: Lord Young recommended Clarke for the job 'because he looked as if he lived in one'*
(© T. BAILEY FORMAN LIMITED)

Bottom right *As Secretary of State for Health he brought a new approach to the job* (© PAUL SMITH/FEATURE FLASH)

...AS WE SEE IT, MR. CLARKE, IT MIGHT BE WISE TO LISTEN!

Top left and right *The ambulance crews' leader, Roger Poole, gave Clarke his roughest time in politics – and the doctors tried to land a few low blows too*

Bottom *Clarke became Chancellor of the Exchequer in May 1993 and presented his first Budget in November of that year* (© ADAM BUTLER/PRESS ASSOCIATION)

Overleaf *An ambition unfulfilled: Clarke, the jazz lover, has never found time to learn how to play the saxophone* (© T. BAILEY FORMAN LIMITED)

way to go about it. Clarke, with his liberal credentials, was a much more appropriate figure.

Clarke's role was to unify the different departmental programmes and to produce a White Paper for the spring of 1988, setting out the government's policies:

> It was one of the most frustrating jobs I've ever had, because I was meant to be co-ordinating government departments and the turf wars between them were hopeless. There was one Cabinet minister I couldn't sort out: Nick Ridley, who was much closer to Mrs Thatcher, felt his own empire was threatened, and his department was totally hostile to us. They regarded urban policy as their policy.

Clarke's aim was to build a force of businessmen who would take pride in their cities; interventionism was strictly limited to private enterprise, and the government should not get involved directly. More public money, he considered, was not the answer for the inner cities. What was needed was not grandiose schemes but the involvement of ordinary people:

> The one thing I tried to plug, and I think I had some success, was targeting help, going for micro-economics in set areas. I don't believe in the trickle-down approach. I don't believe that if the economy gets better, the problems of Toxteth or Peckham will merely melt away – they will remain islands out of touch with a prosperous society unless you do something about it.

The problems of the inner cities captured Clarke's imagination and took up a disproportionate amount of his time. Frequently he met small groups of people from blighted areas for hours on end. It encapsulated his overall political outlook, according to one of his former advisers:

> Yes, he'll help people, but only to help themselves. The DoE [Environment] spent millions of pounds on these high-profile projects, but it knew bugger all about the people who lived there, and within a week they were all pissing in the lifts again. Ken was

very down-to-earth about what he wanted to do. He spent the money on workshops and training.

Clarke argued that the problem of blight could not be seen in isolation. Local people had to be involved in regeneration. If a hotel was to be refurbished, local labour should be used; if houses were to be rebuilt, the residents themselves should be trained to do the work: 'They do not need the men from Whitehall or from the local town hall to tell them what to do. It is enormously important that people work out how to do things for themselves and that they believe that what they get by their own efforts is really theirs.'[1]

Some of Clarke's solutions came directly from the United States. In January 1988 he made a whirlwind visit to some of the inner cities of North America, stopping at some of the poorest neighbourhoods in Atlanta, Pittsburgh, Los Angeles and San Francisco. He was a minister in search of a big idea. 'If we can pick up one idea in a week we can take back with us, we're doing well,' he said.[2] It became clear to Clarke that the United States had successfully persuaded large, rich companies to invest in cities and that the vast regeneration projects costing billions of dollars which had been mounted were the result of co-operation between local and central government, private money and local people.

Clarke's aim was to get more private finance into the inner cities without giving the cash to the detested local councils. As early as November 1985 he had joined forces with Norman Tebbit to argue in Cabinet that left-wing councils should be bypassed when the government gave aid to the urban areas. He was struck by the role that North American chief executives played in improving their cities – from hiring consultants, to promoting a development plan, to spending their own money and organising recruitment and training:

The idea of the big company as a responsible, corporate citizen appealed to me – the idea that American companies saw it as a natural part of their obligation to get involved in the social problems of cities; the idea that you had to get companies in because, above all, what inner-city areas required was a prospect of jobs and training. The problems of inner cities were not the physical fabric, it wasn't all bulldozers and putting up new projects. The problem of the inner cities was the people, disillusioned, unskilled, out of touch with the labour market.

On this American trip, Clarke moved towards his own fusion of Thatcherism with a liberal social conscience, one he could now afford to express. The caring side of his Macleodite apprenticeship now came into the open. In a speech to the Atlanta business club Clarke praised the 'aggressively competitive Britain' created by Mrs Thatcher, but acknowledged that he would not be in his new job if Britain did not have substantial pockets of poverty that had yet to share the benefits. 'Clarke's task, if he is to break from the pack,' wrote *The Times*'s correspondent David Walker, 'is somehow to reach for a post-Thatcher synthesis in which caring capitalism fills those pockets.'

Walker proved to be prescient. Within a month Clarke made a speech to an audience of Young Conservatives which was the closest he came to outlining a political creed under Mrs Thatcher. He spoke both of the advantages of Thatcherism and of the need for compassion – of the importance of private enterprise, rather than state hand-outs, but also of the importance of a social conscience. It was his first clearly defined attempt to stake out his personal political ground: neither wet nor dry, neither Heathite nor truly Thatcherite, but a combination of the two. 'We still have to win the argument that successful free-market economics can be combined with care, compassion and good public services,' he said:

> Success in wealth creation can go hand in hand with a social conscience . . . it is utter nonsense to claim that a wealthier, more efficient society which offers more choice is automatically a heartless society. Our success is creating the best chance we have had since the war to tackle the problems of the inner cities, poverty, long-term unemployment and homelessness. I am a leveller. But unlike Mr Benn I want a levelling up in society . . . it is crucial that we improve standards in housing, in the NHS, and in our schools . . . For it is our belief in efficiency that allows us to put into practice our belief in justice.[3]

It was a fusion of business practice with concern for the welfare state. The government was put on notice not to ignore its new commitment to society. 'I'm now a fan of Margaret on economic and industrial policy,' Clarke concedes today. 'But she never had a proper feel for social policy. Not at all. She didn't have a clue about the inner cities.' As inner-cities minister, he could afford to show his hand.

Clarke's response was part wet, part dry: a commitment to the European tradition of the welfare state, with the American tradition of business success. From now on he consistently stressed the social concerns which that implied. He was later to declare: 'I'd like to combine North American get-up-and-go economics . . . with an up-to-date, efficient, cost-effective European-type welfare state.'[4] His critics, however, argued that he could not have his political cake and eat it; if he was truly committed to solving the problems of the underclass, he should put public money where his mouth was. On the one hand, they said, Clarke called for greater compassion and a caring society; on the other, he backed the 1988 Budget which reduced the basic rate of taxation by a further 2p on the grounds that 'it is necessary to encourage people to earn the wealth the country needs for personal prosperity and good public services'.

How could *cutting* tax help pay for better public services? Clarke's answer was Macleodite in its pragmatism; wealth-creation and efficiency were the answer. He considered government policy was too often judged solely on how much taxpayers' money was spent. The qualities which produced commercial success could improve public services too. The key was the attitude of ordinary people. It was pointless throwing money into a rebuilding project if all the labour was imported from outside. Instead he advocated a small-scale, micro-approach, much like Lord Young's employment ideas: 'It is individuals themselves who hold the key to regenerating the run-down parts of our cities. Indeed, to put it at its most simple, if we can succeed in changing the attitudes of inner-city residents to enterprise, work, choice and personal responsibility, I believe that in time we would have no inner-city problem at all.' Here Clarke brought together the two strands of his approach: 'The Government's drive in the inner cities demonstrates how commercial success and social conscience are not mutually exclusive.'[5] It enabled him to be tough on public spending, but compassionate with it.

Immediately after taking over at the DTI, Lord Young had declared year zero on the departmental budget; every penny had to be justified from scratch. Even so, Clarke impressed his colleague with his economic dryness. As part of this spending war, Young decided to abolish regional development grants, which gave businesses help towards the capital costs of new buildings if they were sited in assisted areas. Young knew them from his time as a businessman, and had been told by his friends in industry that they were regarded as a free hand-out. When he decided to abolish them, his officials were horrified. Young remembers their reaction and Clarke's instant response: 'You can't do that, they said – the Commons won't stand it. "Oh yes they will," said Ken. "I'll see to that." '

He did. Discretionary grants were introduced instead, with Clarke telling the House that it was not the *level* of expenditure in which he took comfort, but the fact that the government was now making more intelligent and sophisticated use of the money. This was how in part Clarke could reconcile his belief in the caring side of Conservatism with his apparent dryness on spending issues. If money was going to waste – and Clarke would argue, for example, that hand-outs to local authorities were wasteful – then the payments should be stopped.

Was this the same man who, in his Birmingham Bow Group days, had proposed a new tax to pay for an extra tier of government? Was this the man who had always been billed as wet on spending by Mrs Thatcher? Was she right, or was Lord Young? David Trippier explains: 'Ken has changed noticeably on spending. He started off as a wet in Transport, then moved through a period of rising damp, and then moved over to being as dry as dust.' Certainly, in 1987 Lord Young found him to be Saharan.

Young tells how his Permanent Secretary, Brian Hayes, 'thought he'd pull a fast one' by asking if he could finalise the DTI's budget with Clarke, because Young had a lunch engagement:

Of course, I knew immediately what they were thinking but I also knew Ken. So I said, I'm delighted, whatever he says is fine with me. And I came back after lunch to a shattered department. He just carved everything away. The thing people don't understand about Ken is that he is economically dry and socially wet. I think that's a very good combination.

The crucial question for any left-wing Tory survivor of the Thatcher years is this: if you are socially wet, is it possible to be economically dry? When Clarke finally won a department of his own in 1988, in an area close to his heart, Health, his colleagues say he was ruthless about demanding more public spending. According to Lord Parkinson: 'He never felt the slightest embarrassment about going for the optimum, but the very next breath he'd turn round and be very rough on any other people who were bidding for money. I don't think he's at all ideological, I think he's a total pragmatist. What he wants is right and what other people want is wasteful.' But Clarke's friends reply that he spends only on what he believes in and he saw the NHS as an essential welfare service. 'He is tough on public expenditure,' says Charles Wardle. 'He stands as little of the whole hypocritical nonsense of the Left as Margaret would stand, *but* he's unshakable in his view of a sound National Health Service and a sound state education system, from which he's benefited.'

Clarke himself believes he is dry on spending, despite his reservations about the 1981 and 1983 Budgets, and he is sure that is why the Chancellor, Nigel Lawson, chose him to be a member of the 'Star Chamber' in 1988, the body which used to adjudicate on spending disputes between the Treasury and other government departments. Clarke also likes to point out that Lawson's memoirs praise his performance: 'The most effective members in my day were, in their very different ways, Norman Tebbit and Kenneth Clarke.'[6]

On the other hand, as Health Secretary, Clarke succeeded in upping his own budget each year. In 1988 he won an extra £2.6 billion pounds to ease the impact of his health service reforms, and in 1990 he demanded an extra £2.76 billion. (Embarrassingly, a confidential Health Department memo was leaked, showing he had built in an £800 to £900 million negotiating margin.) Clarke cheerfully talks of the time when he 'was determined to argue long and late to try to blackmail my colleagues against a background of crisis in the health service'.[7] He was prepared to spend heavily in the areas he believed in, and not in others. In a sense, this made him, as Lord Parkinson has maintained, as opinionated in such matters as the Thatcherites, who drew lines in the sand in advance. 'He had a contempt for those who wanted increased expenditure for the *wrong reasons*,' believes David Mellor, who worked under Clarke at Health.

Clarke approached the question of public spending case by case, but he tried to make his views consistent through his continued demand for efficiency. He sought refuge in wanting a bigger bang for his buck, as he liked to put it. As Health Secretary he came under pressure from the opposition because the government's spending on the NHS, as a proportion of the nation's gross domestic product or GDP, was lower than it was in many other Western European countries. One day he looked out of his Health Department office window so that he could see the Treasury, turned to his colleague, David Mellor, and remarked: 'If I went over to the Treasury now, got a billion pounds in used fivers, burned them outside the Cenotaph and danced round them for an hour, I would at a stroke have increased the percentage of GDP devoted to health and done no good at all.' The two of them used to joke that they were the last Thatcherites left in Whitehall.

Equally at the DTI, Clarke was not keen to spend money on projects he wasn't interested in or did not understand. In his restricted role as Lord Young's representative on Earth, Clarke had none the less been given a whole galaxy to roam; he was the space minister. A more unlikely combination could scarcely be imagined. Clarke's scepticism had already led him to be dismissive of AIDS and would lead in future to his rejecting global warming as 'bunkum', to the horror of the then Environment Secretary, Chris Patten. Now, to the Treasury's delight, Clarke proved impervious to the entreaties of British space scientists for extra money.

The European Space Agency, to which Britain contributed £116 million a year, wanted to expand its operations to build the Columbus space laboratory and the Hermes mini-shuttle. Clarke refused to give any more money to the agency, privately comparing its manned space programme to 'an attempt to put a European dwarf on the moon'. One minister remembers Clarke telling him: 'I'm not wasting money on that intellectual élite.' Publicly, too, Clarke was rude; most people, he suggested, thought Hermes was a type of French scarf. If money was to be spent, it should be private money – a view not shared in the hi-tech corridors of Washington, Tokyo, Paris, Bonn or Rome.

The Times was furious about the decision. The research would have a far-reaching impact on the European economy in decades ahead, it declared; the economic spin-offs from contracts associated with the manned space programme would now be lost. 'Cocooned in a cloak of nonchalant indifference', Clarke had secured for Britain the mantle of Ned Ludd, it declared. The space minister was unmoved; the government later took a small stake in a modified Columbus project, and Clarke could claim some credit for the move to make it more commercially attractive. But he also rejected putting public money into the revolutionary British space-plane Hotol, which aimed to put satellites in orbit at a fraction of the cost of ordinary rockets.

While Clarke's 'nonchalant' approach to politics attracted criticism at times, in the Commons it was his greatest asset, and one which would make him invaluable to his party. One occasion that showed how his debating talents could rescue the government arose when he was thrown before a restless House expecting a statement on the sale of the Rover Car Group – a statement Clarke couldn't make because the deal had just fallen through.

When the ebullient new chairman of British Aerospace, Professor Roland Smith, first suggested to Lord Young that he would like to buy the Rover Group, it seemed, at a stroke, to solve many of the government's problems with the loss-making company. Rover's chief executive Graham Day had been demanding a £1 billion investment over a five-year period; the politicians might have reflected that nothing had changed much since the Labour government had been forced to rescue British Leyland in the 1970s. British Aerospace now offered an alternative, a take-over which could be dressed up as privatisation. It would require a huge injection of state cash, but it would be a once-and-for-all payment. Rover would be taken off a grateful government's hands.

Inevitably there were problems as the government and British Aerospace haggled over the Danegeld that the former had to pay to push the deal through. Young had kept Rover for himself when allocating the departmental affairs and he negotiated hard, reducing the cash injection to some £650 million and trying, at the same time, to placate the European Commission, which feared that its competition policy was going to be infringed.

On 12 July 1988 the deal was accepted by the British Aerospace board, and a statement to both Houses of Parliament was arranged for the next day. Young looked forward confidently to his moment of glory, dining at No. 10 with the Prime Minister and the visiting President of Turkey as his officials agreed the wording of the statement.

At the last minute, however, the deal ran into trouble. British Aerospace wanted to pull out, because of conditions laid down by the European Commission. Young was in a political fix. It was too late to scrap the statement to Parliament, yet he had nothing say. Hastily three different statements were drawn up, saying that the deal was on, that it was off, or that it was on but that there was a hitch. Only seconds before entering the chamber did Clarke find out which he was meant to present: the holding statement. It was a moment of liberation. Answering the questions which followed, he was no longer bound by facts handed down by his superior; he had to live off his wits. While Young floundered in the Lords, with nothing to say and little to invent, Clarke breezed through his ordeal with insouciant good humour.

First, Labour attacked his thirty-second statement:

Bryan Gould: '*Is not this brief and astonishing statement an embarrassing confession that the Government have got themselves into an unholy mess?*'
Clarke: '*My statement may have been surprisingly short, but it is not in the least embarrassing for me, my Right Honourable and noble friend the Secretary of State, or the Government.*'

Then it was turn of the Liberal Democrats' Truro MP:

Matthew Taylor: '*Is not the Minister looking as red today as would do credit to the Labour front benches?*'
Clarke: '*My florid complexion is a natural result of my healthy lifestyle. I agree that it contrasts somewhat with the pallor of the honourable Gentleman, who does not appear to get into the open air very much in the south-west of England.*'

Finally, Labour had another go:

Dennis Turner: '*Would it not be a good idea if the Chancellor of the Duchy of Lancaster were to nip off to his office to find out the up-to-date situation? He might then put us out of our misery. We shall keep the debate going while he is away.*'

Clarke: '*I agree entirely with that suggestion. I am dying to get back to my office to find out what is happening.*'[8]

Clarke had proved himself the Cabinet's outstanding advocate, winning the ultimate political accolade, that he was a safe pair of hands. Both he and Mrs Thatcher now afforded each other a measure of guarded respect, as Lord Parkinson observes: 'She respected his ability to win an argument in the Commons and to drive tough policies through, but she never wholly trusted him.'

In addition, Clarke had another key virtue which his leader could not ignore; he made his mind up. In October 1987 he saw a chance to privatise British Steel, and he handled the subsequent sale with skill. As Lord Young says: 'His chief attribute – and it stands out like a beacon today – is decisiveness. Under Prime Minister Clarke you'd see an entirely different style of government. It won't be politically different, but it will be decisive.'

It was clear to Mrs Thatcher that Clarke was more than ready for his own department. Precious few Thatcherites could match him in the performing arts. Her favourite, John Moore, had been found sadly wanting in the House of Commons, and she was now forced to split his empire and give half of it to Clarke, who considers that 'she had no feel for Health': 'To her it was just a great expense. Norman and I had run a pretty steady ship there – but she though John Moore was going to stop being as soft and wet as Fowler and Clarke and sort it all out. So I was astonished when Margaret moved me there.'

A true believer had been humbled by a quondam Heathman. Clarke was to return to the Health Department where he had once been junior minister – a department, moreover, in the eye of a Thatcherite storm. It was, Norman Fowler believes, a mistake.

CHAPTER 10

A Monumental Row

He's fifteen stone, smokes and drinks and now he's in charge of your health.

Sun

On taking up his new job in Mrs Thatcher's surprise summer reshuffle of 1988, Clarke was greeted in inimitable fashion by the headline writers of the *Sun* newspaper; they gave him just ten more years to live. The *Sun*'s resident medical expert, Dr Vernon Coleman, opined that 'having Mr Clarke as Health Minister is rather like having a convicted burglar as Lord Chief Justice'. The paper had actually exaggerated Clarke's weight by some ten per cent, which led cynics to remark upon the *Sun*'s new standards of accuracy; but it none the less summed up in a few choice words the incongruity of Clarke's appointment. Here, as guardian of the nation's health, was a man who appeared to revel in his vices.

The appointment was politically incongruous, too. Clarke was replacing his antithesis: John Moore, the very model of a modern Thatcher minister. Moore was an American-trained banker whose chiselled good looks had won him the sobriquets 'Action Man' and 'the Thunderbird puppet'. He was also a fitness fanatic. The country had never had a healthier Health Secretary.

At the Department of Health and Social Security, however, they were more concerned with Moore's mental abilities. At first, say insiders, he was seen as 'an extraordinarily good-looking Kennedy-style politician, a right-winger with brains. He looked good and he sounded good.' But this opinion soon changed to the view that he was 'an over-promoted rabbit'. Henceforth the dapper Moore became known at the DHSS as 'the Empty Suit'.

Moore was under pressure. At the start of 1988, somewhat to her Cabinet's surprise, Mrs Thatcher had taken it upon herself to announce, on the BBC Television programme *Panorama*, a review of the National Health Service to be completed within a year. A funding crisis in the winter of 1987 had convinced her of the need for change, a crisis sparked by the decision of Birmingham Children's Hospital to deny patients treatment. Year on year, Mrs Thatcher thought, the government was putting more money into the NHS in real terms, but all it received in return was a constant supply of bad headlines.

Suddenly the arm of government known, fondly or otherwise, as the Department of Stealth and Total Obscurity, emerged from the shadows into the full glare of the Thatcher revolution. For the next six months a small review team, led by the Prime Minister herself, examined every option for the future funding of the health service. John Moore made the mistake of taking Mrs Thatcher's promise of change at her word, going up every radical alley he could find in an effort to produce a truly Thatcherite agenda. But his leader was more pragmatic than he suspected, and as the review team became bogged down in the quicksand of indecision Moore's health collapsed. His debating style, never strong, became the weaker for it, and he lost the confidence of his own side in the Commons.

Confidence was not a commodity of which Clarke was short. Searching for a minister who could reassure the public that the NHS was safe in Conservative hands, yet be tough enough to carry through change, Mrs Thatcher looked no further than her compassionately tough trade and industry minister. He believed in the health service probably more strongly than anyone else in the Cabinet, which would reassure the public; unlike his Prime Minister, he eschewed private health insurance and was fond of calling the right wing's notion of health vouchers 'dotty'; moreover, his daughter worked in the NHS as a student nurse. But at the same time he was no defender of the status quo, of bureaucracy and inefficiency: as junior health minister he had been instrumental in pushing through competitive tendering for catering and laundry services, and had firmly backed Roy Griffiths's report in recommending the introduction of general managers into the service. Clarke was, Mrs Thatcher thought, the ideal man to persuade the doctors and nurses that she wanted a better health service, not a privatised one.

From the outset, Clarke determined that he would be measured by his toughness, or at least by the public face of it. He resolved to tackle the job in a very different way from Moore: 'When wild allegations were made I always went out and replied to them. I didn't allow the public to listen to these "babies are dying" stories without finding out what it was about and saying babies are not dying. John just went in for masterly inactivity.'

Clarke's appointment did not make for an easy relationship across the Cabinet table with his Prime Minister. Like Mrs Thatcher herself, he was fond his own voice, never using one sentence where three would do, and he stood up for himself:

I don't think she appreciated how forceful she could be. I think my relationship with her got warmer as it went on, but it was always rather lively. We had a ferocious row over health when she leaned forward and said, 'Every Cabinet has somebody who talks too much – Robert Carr was like this in Ted Heath's govern-ment.' As a case of the pot calling the kettle black, it really was quite ridiculous![1]

Officials in Clarke's private office, waiting to find out how the latest meeting at No. 10 had gone, used to receive telephone calls from their friends in the Cabinet Office who had marked the day's proceedings on the Richter scale. 'They had some terrible rows over tax breaks for old people's private health insurance,' recalls one political adviser. 'Clarke was dead against it but he had to give in.'

Clarke once discussed Mrs Thatcher's style of leadership with David Mellor, who had moved to Health as a junior minister. Mellor recounted to Clarke that Mrs Thatcher's favourite method of rounding on him in his previous job, at the Foreign Office, was to ask exasperatedly whether he had ever been a Chancery lawyer. Evid-ently, from her time at the Bar, she regarded this as the lowest form of legal life. A few days later Mrs Thatcher and Clarke had another argument over the health service reforms. She leaned across the table towards him and said: 'Ken, were you ever at the Chancery Bar?'

Clarke enjoyed the verbal fisticuffs, however. He was a lawyer and took nothing personally. Despite Mrs Thatcher's being at times 'idiosyncratic, difficult and cajoling,' he also found her fun to work with:

> If after a bit she thought you weren't good enough, she booted you out. And if you had the most frightful rows with her and she thought she quite enjoyed the way you held your corner, you found to your amazement she promoted you. There was always a tension. If you couldn't stand the racket, if you couldn't stand the feeling of permanent crisis and if you started having sleepless nights every time a reshuffle was coming, I'm sure it was hell.

Clarke, of course, liked the feeling of crisis, as he had admitted when he was last at Health.

Clarke's appointment, none the less, summed up the Prime Minister's dilemma. By turning to him, Mrs Thatcher was tacitly admitting that she needed the energy and communication skills that one of her more instinctive supporters could not supply. If Clarke succeeded, she would be handing him the chance to go on to greater things, proving that a capable minister was a greater asset than a true believer who could not cope.

If Clarke failed, it would be the end of his ministerial career. He recognised this straight away: 'I realised I was staking my political career on this. Of all the national organisations I've ever dealt with, the NHS is the most difficult to turn. It's like one of those tankers going down the Channel. You spin the wheel and the damn thing doesn't start moving for a hell of a long time.'[2] If he could turn the ship in the right direction, his leadership chances might get a fair wind. Ahead of him, though, lay rough seas and hidden reefs.

For the next five years, in three different offices of state, Clarke would be the Tories' main destroyer of vested interests. His love of disputation, and his dislike of union obduracy, would combine to earn him a hard-line reputation, although the unions would in turn play upon the fact to their own advantage. The caring side of Clarke, exhibited in his work on the inner cities, would slip from view as he battled to reshape the public services of health, education and the police. It was what the politics of the day demanded. The advantage of having no overreaching political theory is that there are fewer ideals to stand or fall by. For Clarke, there would be some occasions when matters of principle arose, notably when Mrs Thatcher demanded health reforms which he considered called into question the very universality of the service. But on the broad highway along which he allowed himself to travel there were few ideological obstacles for him to surmount.

Kenneth Clarke's first action as Health Secretary was to pack a suitcase for his family holiday in northern Spain. Along with his bird-watching binoculars and sun cream he took a mass of background reading to prepare himself for the battle over the future shape of the NHS. No sooner had he gone than he faced calls from Conservative MPs to return. The new health service team of Clarke, David Mellor and Edwina Currie, picked for their presentational strengths, were all away on holiday at the same time. The nurses' leaders took full advantage, walking out of a meeting with NHS management in an attempt to press home their case for new clinical grading structures. It was August, the time of year when the world is usually quiet and journalists are hungry for news. If the walk-out was prompted by the knowledge that the government could be embarrassed, the nurses were not to be disappointed. The newspapers seized on the story and tried to track down Clarke who was holidaying with his wife, daughter and elderly mother-in-law. They even ran competitions offering prizes to anyone who found him. For a man who keeps his family life private it was more than a little aggravating. He claimed that journalists were offering bribes of up to £10,000 to his staff to obtain the address of his Spanish villa. 'Last summer they were all out in Spain looking for Blackie the donkey; this time they were out there looking for me,' he remarked ruefully.

The journalists scoured the Spanish beaches for a sighting, but they failed to realise that Clarke hates sunbathing and, true to form, was inland, 'monument-bashing' with his wife. He was in such a remote spot that he had no direct communication with his office; to find out what was going on in Britain, he had to pump pesetas into the local phone box and talk to his political adviser, Jonathan Hill. By sheer journalistic fluke the *Daily Mail* tracked him down. Its reporter happened to be driving past the phone box as Clarke was making one of his calls to London. He emerged to concede defeat and gave an interview.

The walk-out in the nurses' dispute had its effect. For the government it was a public relations disaster in which the opposition spokesman Robin Cook, conspicuously not on holiday, revelled. He danced through an interview on Radio 4's *Today* programme, made sure the *London Evening Standard* had the story and then, no doubt still chortling at his own good fortune, dashed off a letter to the Prime Minister questioning the Health Department's holiday arrangements. For twenty-four hours the forces ranged against the government had a free run, until Mrs Currie, the under-secretary, was ordered to break her holiday in North Yorkshire to defend the government's stance. It was an inauspicious start – and proof, if Clarke needed any, that he had the most sensitive job in the Cabinet. These events also showed that there were ministers waiting for him to fail; one remarked anonymously to the newspapers that it was 'most surprising' that the department could not get its holiday rota right. The reorganised Department of Health, it seemed, was not necessarily ready to face the battles ahead.

At the heart of the nurses' row was the regrading of 77,000 ward sisters. They argued that the NHS management was putting too few of them on the higher of two grades, under a review which the government was committed to funding in full. The problem with the regrading exercise was that it had been rushed through at top speed, and no one knew how much it would cost, only that this would be much more than anyone expected. By interpreting the regrading guidelines strictly, Clarke was able to get the overspend down to less than £100 million on top of the £803 million already allocated.

How was Clarke to respond to the nurses? He decided to ignore them. After two months of desultory negotiations, he abruptly refused to meet their leaders. Then, quickly announcing an extra £98 million for their pay award to the Conservative Party conference in Brighton, he pleased the party and divided the forces ranged against him. With some nurses getting back-pay worth up to £2,000 before tax, he calculated that, though their leaders would mutter, their support would evaporate. It summed up Clarke's view of unions; he felt that union leaders usually represented themselves, rather than their members. But it would be a close call. 'If his judgement is right,' wrote Nicholas Timmins in the *Independent*, 'he'll have rescued the Government from what has become close to a billion-pound bungle.

But if the refusal to talk . . . is seen as bullying, or if either the sums or his judgement is wrong, it is another winter of mayhem on the wards.'

The Royal College of Nursing advised disgruntled members to appeal; but both the Confederation of Health Service Employees and the National Union of Public Employees suggested that their members should work to grade. From Manchester to London a rash of hospital disputes broke out. At Birmingham Children's Hospital heart operations had to be cancelled indefinitely. The unions felt the full force of Clarke's rhetoric – they were 'extreme, old-fashioned and bloody minded', he said; 'the NHS still suffers from the style of trade unionism that did so much damage to Britain in the 1970s'.[3] By Christmas the protest had dissipated, though the legacy was once again the bitterness of the dispossessed. Clarke had called the dispute correctly, but the main battle lay ahead.

Once a week for the six months before Clarke's appointment Mrs Thatcher had examined radical options for changing the future funding of the NHS, helped by a small group of ministers: Nigel Lawson, John Moore and his number two Tony Newton, and John Major, the Chief Secretary to the Treasury. Together they had examined paying for the health service through every conceivable method (such as an insurance-based system) and for good measure some inconceivable ones too (a national lottery). Nigel Lawson recalls that 'Margaret . . . having initially been too nervous to do anything at all, once she had accepted the idea, characteristically decided to go the whole hog and reform everything at once.'[4] The evidence they gathered suggested that this was hardly a sensible exercise; but because Mrs Thatcher had talked up the prospect of reform, there were high expectations of success. The government had to deliver to meet those expectations – marginal changes were not enough. There had to be a policy which looked radical, within the tight timetable Mrs Thatcher had imposed.

Clarke returned from his Spanish holiday with some clear ideas about the reforms he would push through. It was just as well, because he had but six months to fulfil Mrs Thatcher's promise to the nation. 'Ken came in without much progress having been made. The pressure was really on him to deliver,' observes David Willetts, the Tory MP who was then advising the review team, as Director of the Centre for Policy Studies. It was already clear that radical funding options were untenable, and that the NHS would have to be improved within the confines of a tax-based service. This suited Clarke. He has always believed in a health care system free at the point of use: 'John Moore was pursuing a line which Margaret was very keen on, which made everything compulsory private medical insurance. I was as bitterly opposed to that as I am now. The American system is a mess. It's the world's worst health service – expensive, inadequate and with a lot of rich doctors.'

As the review team dithered, unable to bring itself to accept its own findings, Clarke was able to give the final push for the service to remain publicly financed, with radical change imposed instead on the supply side. He fully accepted his leader's verdict that the NHS had to be changed; this accorded with his drive for efficiency. That the service was already broadly efficient compared with other countries there could be no doubt, but it had significant problems. Hospitals were caught in an efficiency trap. The more patients they treated, the more their costs went up, but their income remained the same because they were operating on a fixed budget. The budget was unresponsive to their needs because it was handed down from the government under a complex formula based on theoretical need, first to the regions and thence to the districts which set the individual hospital budgets. So when the family doctors, who did not operate within budgetary limits, began to admit more patients to hospital, a funding crisis grew as the chosen hospitals incurred ever greater expenditure. The drive to find a solution to this 'efficiency trap' was a prime motivating force behind the reforms. It still accorded with Clarke's creed: 'Our society must not only be efficient but it must also be humane, just and compassionate. But it you do not strive for efficiency and eliminate waste, all your words about compassion are of no benefit to those at whom they are aimed.'[5] Clarke decided that the reforms would be 'fairly drastic' on the management side, to attack the problems of its 'ramshackle bureaucracy'. He sounded like a minister who had spent three years under Lord Young; the health service needed to be a well-run business. He would impose on the medical world a more efficient way of treating patients within the existing system.

Clarke's main contribution to the NHS review was the suggestion that family doctors should be allowed to manage their own budgets, to become what is known as 'fund-holders'. The genesis of this proposal lay in one of the radical ideas mooted during a review of primary health care in 1985, which led to a Green Paper the following year and suggested changes to the pay and conditions of general practitioners. It had also surfaced at the start of the health review before Clarke joined the team, but was dropped after its members decided that GPs knew little about finance or management. When Clarke came back from his Spanish holiday he urged his civil servants to work on the project. He is still proud to claim that he was its author:

> It was wholly my idea in the teeth of Treasury resistance. I'm a great fan of Nigel Lawson's but when I read his book and see how he organised the reform of the health service I fall about laughing. Nigel had damn all to do with it and in so far as he was at the meetings he was thoroughly unhelpful and just took a straight Treasury line that you mustn't change this except in such a way to give the Treasury tight control over spending in every detail. It was rubbish!

At the end of January 1989 the government's proposed reforms were published in a White Paper, *Working for Patients*, which was followed by eight more detailed working papers for discussion with staff. The proposals aimed to alter the entire financial and administrative structure of the NHS and thus to improve the quality of its care. In a sense, they harked back to the reforms suggested during Clarke's previous stay at Health by Roy Griffiths, the chief executive of Sainsbury's, whose inquiry into the running of the service had proposed pushing responsibility downwards to hospital managers, replacing the old process of continually referring upwards. Clarke, too, wanted to push responsibility downwards, but also to introduce an element of competition. The service was to be broken down into smaller sections while at the same time retaining its monolithic structure.

The main change was the development of the so-called internal market, summed up in the phrase 'the money should follow the patient'. The aim was to end the efficiency trap by scrapping the system whereby the health authorities, because they set the budgets of hospitals they ran, were held to be responsible for both the purchase and the provision of health care. Henceforth the local health authorities would be known as the purchasers, and the hospitals as the providers. The split was made by giving the purchasers the freedom to shop around in the hope that hospital standards would rise and costs come down through competition; they were to be allowed to buy health care on behalf of patients from a range of competing hospitals.

It was here that Clarke's ideas about GP fund-holders came into play. While he accepted the idea of the internal market, he wanted wherever possible to operate it via the GPs. Doctors with at least 11,000 patients were to be given the chance to run their own budgets, enabling them to buy health care for hospital-bound patients wherever they considered they could find the best service and strike the right price. But doctors would have to perform efficiently too; patients were to be given greater freedom to choose or change their GPs. The doctors were given the incentive to work harder and offer a wider range of services by the simple expedient of make more of their pay dependent on the number of patients they treated.

There was one other key reform. Responsibility was to be devolved by allowing hospitals to leave the control of the local health authority and become self-governing 'trusts'. They would be self-financing and rely almost entirely on whatever contracts they could win, although they would be allowed to raise private capital. In this way, the purchaser–provider split would be more than a mere academic distinction. The hospitals were to remain part of the NHS empire, but as self-governing islands. 'Let me make it absolutely clear,' Clarke told the Commons, 'they will still be as much within the NHS as they are now.'

The opposition in Parliament and the country at large needed considerable convincing that this was the case, especially as Labour made much of the charge that the government was in some way privatising the health service. The party's health spokesman, Robin Cook, said that the trust hospitals would be 'indistinguishable from private hospitals'. Clarke had the propaganda battle of his life to win; the good communicator, who had seen the value of the media in his Mansfield days, and who had been schooled by Lord Young in the latest techniques, had to sell his wares again:

To the surprise of the Cabinet I said there is going to be a *monumental* row with the doctors, there is going to be the most fantastic row. It was as if we had picked up every tablet of stone in the British Medical Association's book and smashed it on the pavement in front of Tavistock House. There was nothing in there that the BMA could remotely accept. I don't think any of the Cabinet believed me. They probably still blame me for making the row.

The question that goes to the heart of Clarke's political style is whether or not he exacerbated it.

To begin with, Clarke organised a closed-circuit television link-up so that he could answer questions from NHS staff around the country; a video was also screened to show a Pathe newsreel from 1948, when the health service was founded. In it, mothers were handed free orange juice for their babies. The message was that the service had to adopt to meet more modern needs. It was a message which also summed up Clarke's political beliefs; while he held the NHS dear, it had to adapt to survive.

The inevitable roadshow started in Birmingham, the city which was arguably the catalyst for Mrs Thatcher's determination to reform the health service. For more than an hour and a half Clarke answered questions from managers, consultants and GPs about the detail of the changes. Some of the questions were hostile, a sign of the opposition to come, and although Clarke felt he won more friends than enemies in his first sortie out of London, the doctors were the group to express the greatest fears. Clarke recognised the danger. He declared that the BMA 'in my unbiased opinion' had never been in favour of change of any kind 'on any subject whatsoever' for as long as he could remember. The newspapers ignored the portents and were impressed by Clarke's handling of the reforms; the changes 'needed stage managing', gushed the *Daily Mail*, 'and Clarke has done just that, brilliantly . . . [he] has set a scorching pace in putting across the case for change . . . Thatcher has probably got the best minister she could deploy in the whole Cabinet.' John Moore, left to contemplate the remains of his divided empire, must have wondered where he had gone wrong.

The selling of the NHS reforms revealed both Clarke's strengths and his weaknesses. Here was an energetic, enthusiastic, affable minister who could promote his message so well that even people who took issue with him warmed to his style and approach. He was as tough as the Iron Lady herself, although that, as she herself would demonstrate, was a political virtue which was none the less liable to metal fatigue. The doctors' angry protests – partly against the health reforms, but mainly against the narrower issue of the new contracts which were being imposed on them – provoked a furious and protracted clash with Clarke which dented his caring image and saw him outmanoeuvred for long periods in the propaganda ware. The biggest mistake had already been made, in publishing the doctors' new contracts a week after the White Paper, allowing the doctors to conflate the two issues. 'It just messed up the whole damn thing,' according to one of Clarke's advisers. 'I just don't believe it was necessary to upset those doctors in the way they were upset.'

Clarke and the doctors had never seen eye to eye. He referred to the BMA, witheringly, as the doctors' trade union. As the junior health minister back in the mid-1980s he had been heavily involved in the primary care review under Norman Fowler and had toured the country on a big consultation exercise for the Green Paper which the government produced. David Willets considers that 'At that time he'd tried to handle the profession gently. But they didn't take it seriously. They just tried to veto everything and that led to some sort of determination by ministers that next time they'd handle it differently.' Clarke had also produced new rules governing the doctors' use of deputising services at night and at weekends, which were bitterly resisted; and he had won his battle against the BMA over the government's insistence on the use of cheaper, generic drugs, when the doctors' association made the mistake of sending a standard appeal to MPs on drug company notepaper.

The two sides, then, knew each other of old, and both were wary. Both had learned lessons. Clarke had discovered the BMA's resistance to changes he wanted to push through; and the BMA realised it had to smarten up its publicity act if it was to make an impression on the government. In a sense, therefore, the war which broke out between them in 1989 was but the battle delayed from their previous encounter.

Clarke regarded the doctors' representatives as he regarded many union leaders: with a large dose of scepticism. They were, he considered, representative only of their own self-interest, and not of their members' views. In the last few years, however, the BMA had been taking steps to improve its image. No longer was it dubbed by the public the 'British Money Association'. A series of high-profile campaigns on smoking, drinking and seat belts in cars had seen to that. The medical profession had, remarked Nicholas Ridley sardonically, largely taken the place of vicars in the community.[6] Clarke appeared not to have noticed the difference in the public's perception since his last spell at Health: 'It was always going to be combustible. I told my junior ministers and officials that all hell was going to break loose. So I commended the rules of a certain rugby football club – get your retaliation in first.'

The BMA started with one significant tactical advantage; it had discovered the enemy's plan. Long before the date of the White Paper became known, the doctors' top brass had arranged a meeting in Stratford-upon-Avon on a completely different issue – the running of the BMA itself. By chance, this took place a week before the White Paper was officially published. But Robin Cook obtained some leaked copies in time for the meeting and, in the words of one doctor, 'threw them around like confetti'.

At first the doctors' leaders thought the White Paper was a hoax. Then, as the truth dawned, their mood changed to anger. The proposals would lead to the fragmentation of the health service, they thought, and the closing of hospitals. The government's claim that there would be increased choice for patients was, they believed, a fiction; patients would have no choice at all. As they considered their option, they remembered the battles of the past, and how they had shot themselves in the foot over the drugs list. This time, they decided, the battle-plan was going to be carefully controlled and co-ordinated. The Health Secretary would be taken on at his own game: playing the media. All nine of the Royal Colleges added their weight to the campaign against Clarke. Whereas Aneurin Bevan had won his battle against the doctors by dividing the medical profession, Clarke had, within seven weeks, succeeded in uniting it. The GPs were, essentially, involved in a dispute over pay and conditions; but they were not averse to supporting Labour's claim that the NHS was being privatised. Clarke, who knew he had a complicated set of reforms which had to be presented clearly to a confused nation, was forced on the defensive as the concept of what the government was trying to do to the health service became more and more obscure. Opinion polls showed that only 12 per cent of the public believed the changes would benefit the NHS, while 50 per cent thought they would make it worse. Unfortunately, no polling organisation asked voters whether they understood what was going on.

The government had an even deeper problem, which Clarke could do nothing to solve. Few voters seemed to trust Mrs Thatcher when she pledged herself undyingly to the continuation of the NHS as a truly national service, free at the point of use. The irony was that Clarke was a stout defender of the service; he wanted it to be as efficiently run as a private-sector organisation, with an adequate management structure no longer dominated by over-strong unions. His difficulty was that, in trying to inject the market-place into a public service, he was stoking fears about the Tories' true intent, or at least leaving himself vulnerable to opposition attacks. It sounded like an ideological exercise, not a pragmatic attempt to bring efficiency into the service.

The doctors had a problem, too. They had to present themselves as concerned only for their patients, and not act too obviously as a trade union. But they had only one ultimate deterrent: mass resignation, and that would undermine their credentials as a caring profession. They could hope only to amend the reforms, not stop them altogether. It made Clarke's task harder; the doctors' leaders determined to fight a propaganda war to match the government, the like of which they had not fought before.

The BMA dug deep in its pocket, spending more than £2.5 million. First, it printed eleven million leaflets attacking the government's proposals, sending two hundred of them to every one of the 32,000 family doctors. Then it went to a leading advertising agency, Abbot Mead Vickers. The first poster the agency produced was too powerful even for the doctors. It pictured a railway line leading into a hospital. 'It looked just like Belsen,' the BMA's then leader, Dr John Marks, remembers. 'I just took one look at it and said there's no way we're having that.' But the copywriters soon hit their stride and their aggressive advertisements appeared in ten national newspapers, appealing to the public to complain to MPs. Patients were being treated 'like Clarke's processed peas'; 'making medicine pay could become more important than making people well'; and 'Mr Clarke wants to introduce a new spirit of competition within the NHS – the health of the patient versus the cost of the treatment.' All carried the same theme, that the NHS was 'underfunded, undermined and under threat'.

Clarke himself showed no signs of the pressure and resolved to stand firm in the face of this unparalleled advertising campaign. 'He can be persuaded off a course, and he can be convinced to go in another direction, but he will not be pushed off it by bloody-mindedness or by straightforward destructive opposition,' thinks John Major. Unfortunately, this time Clarke did more than stand firm, and the GPs' resentment was stoked accordingly. One night, shortly after the White Paper was launched, the retired consultant surgeon Sir Arnold Elton, a former President of the Consultants' Medical Association, invited Clarke to dinner at the Carlton Club – to try to take the heat out of the dispute. John Marks and the secretary of the BMA, John Harvard, were also there. In a private room, the men tried to hammer out their differences. The doctors were desperate for the reforms to be tried in a pilot area. It was an idea which had some powerful advocates; apart from politicians, an American academic named Professor Alain Enthoven who had been consulted by Clarke about the health reforms was also calling publicly for a demonstration project. The doctors asked Clarke to allow them to give the reforms a trial run in one region. Angrily, he refused point-blank: 'No, because you buggers will sabotage it.'

Clarke found it intolerable that the doctors' lobby was prepared to defend even the elderly GP in a lock-up surgery who offered no preventive medicine at all. He believed they were circling the wagons, trying to protect the strength of their profession by defending even their weakest members. Clarke's abrasiveness in the face of opposition was both his greatest asset and his greatest weakness. It gave him the strength to face down the doctors – accusing them, for example, of irresponsible shroud-waving – but it also exacerbated the dispute.

There was one incident, above all, that Clarke lived to regret. Three months after the launch of the White Paper, on 9 March 1989, he attended the annual dinner of the Royal College of General Practitioners, as was the custom for a Health Secretary. The evening passed off amicably until Clarke rose to make his after-dinner speech. Facing the serried rows of the medical great and the good in the Prince's Room of BMA House, and standing next to the President of the Royal College, Clarke uttered a phrase which would come back to haunt him. The medical professions had always resisted change, he stated, and 'I do wish the more suspicious of our GPs would stop feeling nervously for their wallets every time I mention the word reform.' He also had a go at the hospital consultants; the changes to GPs' budgets would 'make some consultants pay more attention to GPs than they do now'.

The fall-out was immediate. The President of the Royal Medical Colleges, Professor Sir Dillwyn Williams, who was at the dinner, went white with anger. Tory MPs were flooded were complaints from their constituents (many of whom were prompted to write by their doctors). Clarke had given voice to what many Tories were thinking, but the problem was that he had dared to say it. Clarke's friends still stand by his remark. Former health minister David Mellor observes: 'After the low, underhand way in which the BMA had conducted its campaign, for the doctors to resent him coming along and having a jibe at their expense is a sign of how far they traded upon the fact that 90 per cent of the public trust doctors and 10 per cent trust politicians.' Clarke's speech none the less represented political misjudgement, not an ad-libbed aside. He had arrived for work earlier that morning with the offending words written on a piece of paper in his pocket, and had proudly showed them to his staff.

The Conservative Party is the party of cricketing metaphors; the closing of Mrs Thatcher's final innings was dominated by them. Some years after his injudicious remarks, Clarke likened his attack on the doctors to when a batsman makes 'a silly stroke that he regrets the instant he puts his bat there'. It was, he said, an after-dinner joke – 'I was merely trying to point out to them that health service reforms didn't threaten their wallets. But it took me years to live down.'[7] It also set back his cause in the propaganda war. So why did such a skilled political batsman do it? One serving minister, a political ally, picks up the cricketing theme:

Just occasionally, it may be exuberance or plain over-confidence, but when he feels he's totally in command of the bowling he comes close to being flippant. The wallet remark hurt, it gave offence, because it just may have been close to the truth. The real question is one of judgement – should he have made that remark? They're the faults of a very confident player. It's a bit like Vivian Richards having such a good eye that ball after ball coming down on the off-stump he could pull through midwicket no matter how fast the bowling, because his timing is so superb; but once in a while he'll get it wrong. That's the greatest fault you could level against Ken.

Some of Clarke's Cabinet colleagues were taken aback by his sandpaper approach to the dispute. One night his old mentor Sir Geoffrey Howe organised a meeting in Reigate to give voters from the three local constituencies a chance to debate with the Health Secretary. Howe invited key figures from the caring professions to attend – doctors, administrators and nurses. Some three hundred people came to the large school hall to question Clarke. It was not an entirely successful occasion. 'I think he just harangued them a touch too much,' remembers Lord Howe. 'He was clearly involved, engaged, committed, concerned and knowledgeable but he somehow seemed to look more often than was necessary for the half-volley.' After Howe had proposed the vote of thanks at the end of the meeting, trying to lighten the atmosphere with a joke or two, he tackled Clarke about his aggressive attitude. He found Clarke unapologetic, insistent that it was the only way to get his message across.

The BMA took full advantage of the way Clarke was perceived, stepping up its attacks on the reforms. Posters appeared at strategic sites around the country – the first depicting a driverless steamroller, underneath which was printed : 'Mrs Thatcher's plans for the NHS'. There was no doubt that the doctors were winning the argument. Clarke himself admitted he was losing the presentation battle. He was impaled on the reputation of the right-wing radicals in his party. Time and time again he tried to hammer home the message that he was not one of the Conservatives who wanted to privatise the NHS, and that he was merely trying to introduce market efficiency into the system. He was, he said, opposed by the forces of pure reaction, the middle-class and professional trade unions in particular.

As a sign that the changes would go ahead, come what may, Clarke announced a list of more than 150 hospitals which had expressed interest in running their own affairs, together with a £750,000 publicity drive to sell the reforms and fight the BMA. Half a million leaflets were sent out to public-sector workers and health service staff. But within a month he was being undermined by some of his own MPs; the Commons Select Committee on Social Services demanded local ballots before hospitals were allowed to go their own way, with two senior Conservatives, the Eastleigh MP Sir David Price and the maverick Macclesfield MP Nicholas Winterton supporting the idea. There was, however, a split on the committee and Clarke was able to shrug off its findings. It was a great myth, he said, that 'if only I spoke nicely to the doctors all the time it would all go so much better. I'd just be frozen in the job. You have to defend yourself against what in the last resort is a pretty ruthless lobby.'

The Cabinet began to get the jitters. The government had fared badly in the European elections and it was searching for a scapegoat. At one Cabinet meeting the Energy Secretary, Cecil Parkinson, reportedly broke rank and warned that the doctors were becoming more, rather than less, entrenched. Today he says that 'What made a number of Ken Clarke's colleagues uneasy was that you had the feeling he actually liked attacking people.' The Cabinet's stand forced Clarke to soften his line, and he postponed his threat to try to impose the contracts on the reluctant doctors rather than imperil his wider reforms. A Conservative Party document presenting a firm defence of the reforms was also launched. Such moves were seen as attempts to bail the government out of trouble.

Ironically, the doctors' own belief in their case, and their willingness to pursue it so aggressively, was to be their undoing. Abbot Mead Vickers came up with a new poster, which the BMA held to be quite brilliant; it had by far the most memorable slogan of the campaign, and went on display at a thousand poster sites throughout Britain. It seemed only a matter of time before it won the advertising agency an award and the BMA its battle against the government. The poster had no picture. It was simply bright yellow with a large black caption in block capitals which read: 'WHAT DO YOU CALL A MAN WHO IGNORES MEDICAL ADVICE? MR CLARKE.'

The BMA was right; it was the most memorable poster of the campaign, but for all the wrong reasons. The doctors' leaders had committed the unforgivable error in the eyes of their members of personalising their attacks. Hundreds of doctors objected, and many wrote to their house magazine, the *British Medical Journal*, to say so. The BMA's 'half-truths', wrote some, have 'poisoned' the minds of patients. 'It was a brilliant poster – they were thinking of putting it in for a competition,' John Marks laments. 'But it was too good. It upset a lot of our members because it personalised the issues too much.'

The turn of events dug Clarke out of a hole. Within six weeks he was buoyantly addressing the Conservative Party conference in Blackpool, an event which in other circumstances would have been an endurance test. He was able to turn the tables neatly on his opponents, telling the faithful: 'I rather enjoy controversy. I have acquired a politician's thick skin, fortified by common sense. Common sense tells me one thing. I know when my critics are reduced to personal abuse they must be getting desperately short of better arguments. So what *do* you call a man who will not take medical advice? I call him healthy.'[9]

Clarke had always doubted whether the BMA fully represented the feelings of its rank and file, though Dr Marks had been careful not to make any move which had not been approved democratically. Now the Health Secretary had received confirmation of his views. He spotted the opening which the campaign against him presented and seized it with grateful hands. He simply imposed the new contracts on the doctors.

After an eight-hour meeting of its family doctors' committee, the BMA bowed to the inevitable, going out in flurry of invective. 'Unethical', 'misguided', 'ill-conceived' and 'wasteful' were some of the more polite words used about Clarke's decision and the new contracts. But the alternative to acceptance was mass resignation, the very weapon the doctors had ruled out from the start. Clarke was more than pleased with his handiwork. Asked on television whether he had beaten the BMA, he took the bait: 'Well, I think I won. But you use those words, I don't.'

The battle over the doctors' contracts, and the wider issue of the health service reforms, left scars in the medical profession which have still to heal properly. Part of that, undoubtedly, was the result of

Clarke's style, his aggressive promotion of radical change, although he felt this was the only way to shift the die-hard forces of medical resistance. Part of it, too, resulted from the BMA's focusing its campaign on Clarke's character. 'I always say', he declares, 'that my hard-line reputation is the result of a multi-million-pound advertising campaign.' As one former minister who was in the Cabinet during Clarke's time at Health sums it up: 'He just adores having a go at people. He's been landed with some tough jobs and he did have to take on a lot of vested interests, but you get the feeling that just roughing people up was a desirable end in itself. Crippled nurses would be right up Ken's street.'

Did Clarke win the battle only to find, as the years unfolded, that he had lost on the wider front, failing to make the NHS more efficient? His legacy is still in dispute. In 1993 health service professionals and politicians were still arguing over the reason for the explosion in the number of NHS managers, or 'grey suits', as the Welsh Secretary John Redwood described them, required to run the new model service – a picture confused by the inclusion of nurses among the tiers of management. 'The health service is a hell of a lot better,' Clarke insists. 'It was a hopeless bureaucracy, a muddle with no one in charge. Every winter you had a funding crisis. There was no way in which the universal system could have gone on much longer. It was the last-chance saloon, to coin a phrase.'

It is undoubtedly true that when the reforms were introduced neither their proponents nor their opponents knew how they would work in practice. Poised between the White Paper and the National Health Service Reform Bill itself, Clarke could cheerfully admit: 'Yes, there is a lot of detail to be filled in. The more you go into it, the more you unfold questions to which you have to have an answer.'[10] Because he had rejected pilot schemes, for the reason that he did not trust those selfsame forces of medical resistance, no one knew how the NHS would react. Would it, like most forty-year-old patients, be incapable of learning new ways? Or would it respond eagerly to a new challenge in middle age, losing weight, gaining enthusiasm and deciding that life did, after all, begin at forty? Even Mrs Thatcher seemed unsure; she praises Clarke's advocacy of the changes but, ignoring her own role in promoting sweeping reform, recalls that she was 'less convinced . . . about whether Ken Clarke and the Department of

Health had really thought through the detailed implementation of what we are doing'.[11] At one point, she became so worried about the pace of change, particularly in London, that she sent one of her political advisers to the Health Department to run the rule over Clarke. The Health Secretary was so clear about what he wanted to do that she accepted his views.

The impact of Clarke's reforms suggests that there were some benefits, but not necessarily the ones the government anticipated. The efficiency trap is still with the NHS; hospitals still run out of money because they treat too many patients without being rewarded for their productivity. On the other hand, the reforms have succeeded in shifting the balance of power within the health service. The very doctors who fought so long and hard against Clarke now have more influence over how the service is financed and run than they did before the reforms. Clarke himself is still an aggressive supporter of the changes he introduced:

> Before the reforms nobody could make the doctors do anything. We took away from doctors the total licence to decide what they did. The job was what they made it. No one could require a consultant to do anything either. Many consultants at London hospitals never turned up to do their own casework at all. They did the cases they chose; they organised their own waiting lists; and if they had heavy demands on their time with their private waiting lists and their overseas lecture tours, that was a matter for them.

Structural problems remain, however. Fund-holding GPs have better access to hospital care than their non-fund-holding colleagues. Some hospitals have had to close altogether because of the new 'market'. That much was predictable. But some *trust* hospitals have also found it hard to survive in the stiff world of competition. Many were given the go-ahead to run their own affairs too quickly, with insufficient attention paid to their financial stability. Clarke rushed through reforms which effectively used the NHS as a guinea pig, and although he was under political pressure from his leader for fast results, that was what he wanted too. Either he moved quickly against the 'vested interests' which opposed him, or, he felt, little would be altered a decade hence. As a policy it brought the desired change, without a full appreciation of what might result. As one of Britain's leading health experts, Professor Chris Ham of Birmingham University, puts it: 'We've been making it up as we go along.' Clarke seems almost to accept the point. When Mrs Thatcher moved him from the Health Department in November 1990 he argued that he should stay because he wanted to see how the reforms worked in practice. He was convinced they would succeed but could not be sure: 'I remember saying to her, I think it's going to work, it's like a rocket – it's going to take off, and if it fizzes round into the sea, you won't have to fire me, I'll resign.'

Clarke had survived intact this first major test of his political career. Moreover, the opponents with whom he fought hand-to-hand for more than year, the same opponents who launched a vitriolic campaign against him and who even now are still deeply angered by his reforms, have no personal dislike for him. 'He is a thug and a bully who will be loathed by GPs till time immemorial because he produced a completely cock-eyed scheme moved by pure political dogma,' says Dr Marks. 'But I have a certain admiration for the man because he knows exactly what he's doing and he's prepared to fight his corner.'

The fact that Clarke always seemed to win his battles appealed to his Prime Minister. He was never one of the inner circle, but Mrs Thatcher came to appreciate his strengths. Was he a soldier in search of war, preferring the heat of battle to peace, as he had himself once suggested? Kenneth Baker, his Cabinet colleague at the time, believes so:

> Ken is a naturally belligerent soul who basically likes action and he's not a painstaking administrator. He likes the sheer flow of events and being at the centre of them. He's the minister who likes to have a go. He's not a great conceptual thinker – he has a series of instincts and attitudes, but he's basically a goer and a battler.

This approach had many advantages. Unlike Moore he did not crumple; unlike William Waldegrave, who was to inherit the Department of Health, he never looked discomfited. But there was also a major disadvantage. For all his compassionate credentials, Clarke looked and sounded like a bar-room bully. Kenneth Baker, as party chairman, thought he had the answer to help his embattled colleague, as well as two other ministers with 'image problems', Home Secretary David Waddington and Education Secretary John Mac-Gregor. It lay, as ever, in the power of the advertising men.

Kenneth Clarke, like David Waddington, had a hard-line image. John MacGregor had the opposite problem and more; he had no image at all. So Baker suggested that the chairman of the Young & Rubicam agency, John Banks, should act as a personal valet to Clarke, with Tim Bell, deputy chairman of Lowe Bell, acting in a similar capacity for Waddington, and Robin Wight, chairman of Wight Collins Rutherford & Scott, advising MacGregor. The idea originated at a dinner hosted by Baker for the image consultants where they analysed the government's travails. As ever, presentation rather than policy was blamed. The group felt that many of the government's policies were so radical that they were vulnerable to misinterpretation. Hence Mrs Thatcher's favourite image-maker, Gordon Reece, suggested allocating a communicator to each minister in trouble.

John Banks, who had masterminded the 'Sid' advertising campaign for the privatisation of British Gas in 1987, now found himself having to sell shares in 'Ken'. Since 1984 he had been undertaking 'lifestyle research' for Mrs Thatcher and a small number of ministers, including Willie Whitelaw, to try to ensure they kept in touch with public opinion. He had been particularly helpful during the Westland affair.

That Clarke would accept advice from an image consultant was as likely as Dracula not just renouncing his nocturnal habits but offering to become an NHS blood donor into the bargain. While the prospect of the 'before' and 'after' shots held out the tantalising hope of professional immortality to the adviser who could transform him, by much the same token Clarke was cheerfully impervious to any such entreaties from the advertising world. He had been willing to take lessons from Lord Young on the presentation of policies, but he was equally concerned to preserve his own image unchanged. In the age of the blow-waved politician, it took little time for Banks to decide that Clarke was beyond redemption: 'Pointless! I mean, you can say, look, you shouldn't wear suede with grey, and really the beer belly isn't on, and you'll have to put the cigars out because it's the NHS – and his view would be, I'm sorry, take me for what I am.'

Clarke seemed positively to rejoice in his smoking, drinking image. At a late-night fringe meeting at the Conservative conference in Brighton in 1988 he posed unashamedly for the *Sun* photographer, glass of wine in hand, cigar in mouth. The headline was predictable: 'Cigar in mouth, tummy hanging over belt . . . we give you the Health Minister'. Clarke has in fact twice given up smoking his 'small, cheap cigars', as he calls them, for nearly two years on each occasion, but he considers the habit 'relaxing in a childish way in the course of a busy day'.[12] But why, even as Health Secretary, did he choose to flaunt the fact of his smoking and drinking, just as later, as Home Secretary, he would ban the imposition of No Smoking Day in his department? He cannot stand hypocrisy, explain his friends, so he made no attempt to hide his vices. Lord Parkinson has a different view: 'It was absolutely inevitable that he would smoke, drink beer and give two fingers to basic fitness when he was minister for health. It was entirely in character. He just likes that; he just likes the contrast.'

Banks's relationship with Clarke was destined to end quickly, but he saw enough to be convinced that Clarke was 'a great politician. He's so well in control. I think he's extremely confident. Thatcher was extremely confident. With Clarke you get a feeling that you'll go up that hill with him as he leads the troops.'

Successful commanders, however, lead a united force; they win not just through a superior battle plan and weaponry, but through discipline. And Clarke's Health Department was not a united unit. In David Mellor he had a comparable political force: a fast-talking barrister, well versed in the rough-and-tumble of the macho end of politics, and a fellow smoker too. Edwina Currie, on the other hand, was only some of these things; there were none faster at talking, none better at winning personal publicity, but she was self-evidently neither a man nor a smoker. She felt isolated and desperately unhappy with Clarke's leadership. 'A great big chunk of Ken doesn't care,' according to one of her friends. 'He has a tremendous subconscious arrogance. He gets his teeth into an argument and he's convinced he's right. He treats people like a punchbag. He's a strong-minded man determined to be in the thick of things and he loves to row. If there isn't a real row, he'll invent one.'

182

There would be no need to invent any rows with Mrs Currie in the department. Plenty of tensions arose before the final dispute, over salmonella in eggs, wrecked her political career. And if the fate of Mrs Currie and a few million eggs seems unimportant in the great political scheme of things, then Kenneth Baker looks back on the episode as a turning-point for the government, after which everything that happened seemed to go wrong.

CHAPTER 11

A Postcard and a Letter

Errors look so very ugly in persons of small means – one feels they are taking quite a liberty in going astray; whereas people of fortune may naturally indulge in a few delinquencies.

George Eliot, *Scenes of Clerical Life*

Political leaders may fear events, but they have to manage them. It is as much a part of their job as the laying down of policy, even though some ministers may prefer to retreat to the sanctuary of their own departments, to do little in the hope that they will be seen as a safe pair of hands. Clarke had never shown much anxiety about tackling the real world outside. No Tory enjoys standing twice in Mansfield without relishing the fray. But between 1988 and 1990 two events were to overtake him alarmingly, leaving him gasping for political breath. The first of these appeared trivial but lost him and the government the services of a minister. The second was more serious – an ambulance crews' strike which, like the dispute with the doctors, forced Clarke on to the defensive. Both events brought Clarke's instinctive political judgement into question.

Edwina Currie was a phenomenon, a junior minister whose fame outstripped her rank, making her a far more recognisable politician than Kenneth Clarke – five times more so, according to a national opinion poll. This did not mean, however, that she was an easy politician to work with. The former Cabinet minister John Biffen once observed: 'Right from her arrival in this House, she should have borne a label saying she was a political health hazard, with her quite extraordinary genius in every quality except being a subordinate.'[1] When Mrs Currie's genius for publicity, combined with an outbreak of *Salmonella enteritidis* phage type 4, killed her off politically,

Kenneth Clarke was condemned for not acting more decisely to contain the crisis she precipitated.

The affair revealed at close quarters how Clarke is perceived by a junior minister who does not appreciate his style of management. Many ministers welcome Clarke's decisiveness and political skill; he does not court supporters but nevertheless inspires great loyalty from his friends – who are generally of the 'matey' variety. Mrs Currie, however, was hardly of that ilk; she was unhappy working for Clarke, and long before the eggs affair she was discontented. She reportedly felt that he wasn't a good team leader, failed to appraise her work and took little notice her holiday plans or personal circumstances when it came to sharing out the work.

The next cause of friction for Mrs Currie was the issue of smoking, which she vehemently opposes. The previous team at the DHSS, before it was split, had all been non-smokers apart from Tony Newton, who had been apologetic about his addiction. Clarke had chosen as his office not John Moore's old room, which he did not like, but a new room with a low ceiling, which trapped his cigar smoke. 'Every meeting was held in a smoke-filled room,' says one insider. 'He was saying I'm the boss. He never noticed people were going green.' Shortly before her resignation, Mrs Currie agreed to a European Community request to put tougher health warnings on cigarette packets, a concession which infuriated Clarke.

The main catalyst to Edwina Currie's falling out with Kenneth Clarke, as far as she was concerned, immediately preceded the salmonella affair which led to her resignation. She had spent seven years on Birmingham City Council's social services committee, which she chaired, developing a special interest in the problems of caring for the mentally ill. It was an interest shared by the Chief Whip at the time, David Waddington, and one night he hosted a meeting at 12 Downing Street for the organisation SANE, which helps mentally ill people. SANE claimed that the government was closing psychiatric hospitals too quickly, and Mrs Currie agreed. She wanted a review of the policy. Clarke resisted this. As luck would have it, while the Downing Street reception was still in full swing, he appeared on a television programme to declare his opposition to change.

Mrs Currie had now become so disenchanted with her life as junior health minister that she had been to see the whips about her future.

'She was fed up,' one friend remembers. 'The relationship was always going to be destructive, because he didn't understand her.' As if to prove the point, one summer the fastidious Mrs Currie was appalled to receive a postcard from the holidaying Clarke which depicted a bedridden hospital patient attached to several intravenous drips that were connected to bottles of red wine.

In the autumn of 1988 health officials told Mrs Currie that the number of cases of salmonella food poisoning in the first ten months of the year had already reached double the total for the same period of the previous year. Not even the House of Lords had proved immune, with a number of peers laid low by a dessert at a reception for the London Magistrates' Association. Health warnings about the use of raw eggs had gone out to NHS catering managers in the summer, when they were advised to use pasteurised eggs instead, and in November the public was warned to cook any food thoroughly to kill the bug.

One weekend, when news is generally more scarce, an ITV regional reporter approached Mrs Currie to gain her reaction to the decision by Plymouth Health Authority to switch from shell eggs to pasteurised eggs. As the change had been suggested five months earlier, it was hardly a big news story. Even so, the Department of Health was also trying to find her, to warn her to say nothing because the Chief Medical Officer was handling the case. The television reporter reached Mrs Currie first. On the outskirts of Derby, in a small council estate which she had been visiting as part of the 'Keep Warm, Keep Well' campaign, Mrs Currie sealed her own political fate. At the end of a short interview she declared: 'We do warn people now that most of the egg production in this country, sadly, is now infected with salmonella' – words which were broadcast on the evening television news.

The political uproar was immediate – the poultry farmers made sure of that. For more than a week the newspapers and television analysed the disease, its causes, alternative recipes, modern farming methods and the financial damage done to the industry by a chance remark. A major egg producer began legal proceedings to sue Mrs Currie. Arriving for work on Monday 5 December, Mrs Currie was told by Clarke to keep her head down and say nothing which could inflame the situation – a message he had to repeat the following day, because she assumed it was only a 24-hour interdict. 'I rather misunderstood his instruction,' says Mrs Currie mildly, 'but he made himself clearer on the Tuesday in a kindly way.'[2] To this day she thinks she should have been allowed to defend herself; she apparently believes Clarke refused to let her do so because he thought she was entirely to blame.

Mrs Currie's friends say in her defence that health officials had been 'twitching like mad' about salmonella poisoning all summer, and that Clarke had taken no notice. 'The red boxes were full of stuff about it,' remarks one: 'his problem is that he's very bright and very quick but he likes to be briefed in two- to three-hour meetings, without notes, so he gets the case in his head. He doesn't do any unnecessary reading at all. So when things happen, he doesn't understand them – especially if he has a minister who's a bit of a pain.' Clarke denies this:

> There was a serious problem with salmonella, but she'd overstated it. So I advised her to get off the air, because she hadn't used the right words. I was driving my car somewhere and the next thing I knew she was on the radio again, laying into the egg farmers and repeating what she'd said. The whole thing was in flames again. What she should have done, at an early stage, was modify the slip.

He thinks that if she had kept her head down the storm might have blown over.

However, Kenneth Baker is also critical of Clarke's handling of the ·affair: 'For whatever reason, the smack of firm government failed to descend.'[3] Clarke felt that if Mrs Currie kept silent the media would concentrate on the assurances being put out by the Chief Medical Officer, Sir Donald Acheson, who had issued the original warning about eggs in the summer. 'What she should have said is that "We have a serious problem with salmonella. I may have overstated the case when I said most egg production is infected, but it's no good the egg farmers carrying on, it really is getting worse." But instead she just told me "Never apologise, never explain." So she was getting herself into more trouble.'

Clarke made a staunch defence of Mrs Currie's position in the Commons on the Tuesday following her comments, dismissing the clamour from the Tory back benches for her head. 'It is right we draw the public's attention to the need to be careful in the way they handle and cook food,' he told MPs. 'Edwina Currie is in my opinion an extremely valuable member of the health team and of the Government. It may be that many members of this House are envious of her natural gift of obtaining publicity.'[4] But ten days later Mrs Currie was forced to resign. Clarke, who says he argued with Mrs Thatcher that his minister should stay, was sent to break the bad news. After it was all over, he sent her what one of Mrs Currie's supporters calls 'a kind, sad note'.

No one emerges from this very British saga with credit. Mrs Currie had allowed her natural delight in publicity to run away with her. The poultry farmers' method of feeding hens on the recycled remains of their feathered friends had been revealed to the public gaze. The Ministry of Agriculture, Fisheries and Food had showed a consummate lack of urgency. And Clarke stood condemned for his crisis management. A report by the Conservative-controlled Commons agriculture committee concluded that, given Mrs Currie's high profile, it was hopelessly inadequate to think that the affair would go away by ordering her to keep quiet. The decision to let Sir Donald Acheson do the talking 'may have been right in principle' but was 'naïve'. 'Mr Clarke, and any other ministers he consulted, badly misjudged the situation.' The Ministry of Agriculture was also told it was to blame. But Clarke, typically, tried to shrug off the condemnation, calling it 'ridiculous' and just part of the 'political froth' of the affair. But others questioned his judgement. John Biffen told the Commons that Clarke had relied too much on Acheson for enduring the 'political hazards of the affair . . . [he] was wrong to have held back in the way he did . . . it was a mistaken judgement of what was required'. Kenneth Baker says this is a fair assessment of some of Clarke's overall decision-making: 'Ken's judgement I found to be very varied. At times I thought he was spot on. At other times he was wildly out. There were times I thought he was naïvely wrong.'

More than four years later John Major offered Edwina Currie the chance to return to government as a Home Office minister, working under Kenneth Clarke again. Partly because she had developed a political interest in Europe, but also because she didn't want to repeat the experience, she refused. Apart from John Major, only the Prime Minister's private secretary was at the meeting, and Mrs Currie wanted the conversation to remain confidential. She was upset, therefore, to read reports of the job offer, and of Clarke's reaction to her refusal, in the next day's papers. Clarke, who never fully appreciated the gulf between them, duly sent her another pleasant note in his usual felt-tip, expressing his sadness at her decision not to join his team, but welcoming her enthusiasm for Europe.

At Health, Clarke had played it tough over the nurses' regrading claims, the health service reforms and the salmonella affair. If he felt the pressure, it didn't show. David Mellor believes 'It never got to him. I never found him with his head in his hands. When I left he wrote me a charming letter saying thank you for helping me appreciate that one can enjoy life even in the worst times – and that was the way we approached it.'

Clarke needed to be pressure-resistant, because what lay ahead of him was dispute with yet another group of workers with whom the public would instinctively side: the ambulance crews. It was, he says, his lowest point in politics:

> Given that it all ends in tears, and that sooner or later you get the boot, that was the time I was clinging on by my fingernails. If we'd lost it, I thought there would have to be a scapegoat and that Margaret would fire me. One of the reasons I supported her in the first round of her leadership election against Michael Heseltine was that I was heavily in her debt; a lot of Prime Ministers would have cut their losses and got rid of me, and I'm sure some people wanted her to.

The ambulance crews wanted more money – nearly double the 6.5 per cent the government was offering. But they also wanted a pay formula to match the fire crews. Clarke had already predicted there would be trouble in the NHS, warning the Cabinet of the dangers of the 8.8 per cent deal awarded to striking rail workers the previous summer. He felt that if he agreed to the ambulance crews' demands there would be a wage explosion within the NHS, and half the service would go on strike in another winter of discontent. 'Of all the things you can spend money on in the health service, buying off strikes is the worst,' he insisted.[5] In August 1989 the ambulance crews began an indefinite ban on overtime and rest-day working, and their leaders in the

National Union of Public Employees put into operation a plan of action to defeat Clarke.

The health unions had learned much from previous disputes. They set out to capitalise on the public support which was their due for the jobs they did, rather than alienate the country at large by any show of extremism. To do this, NUPE, in particular, had to appear as the acceptable face of trade unionism – to show the merits of the ambulance crews' claim and the iniquity of the government's stand, without making the dispute overtly political. It selected the young, dapper secretary of the union's ambulance council, Roger Poole, to present its case. The choice could not have been better. He fitted no known Tory identikit picture of a militant trade union leader, possessing neither triple chins nor an aggressive, embittered manner. Instead he appeared to be the very image of the moderate unionist which the Tories had espoused; no one could take offence at his clean-cut manner and his friendly but determined West Country burr. But he was far from moderate in his tenacity. He proved to be a fearsome adversary, as quick witted as Clarke and just as proficient a television performer. Poole and his union colleagues 'decided from day one that we were going to try to present the whole issue in such a way that we'd try to get a majority of the population on our side and not allow the government to portray us as just another bunch of trade unionists trying to bring the government down'.

The union's plan was to appear reasonable and moderate. Under no circumstances must the public think that right was not on its side. So there would be no all-out strike, whatever the members demanded. Public sympathy was all, Poole explains: 'Disputes in the services are won or lost because the world out there decides that you should win or lose.' It made Clarke's dilemma all the greater. He was in the Cabinet because of his capacity to tough it out, but while his style had proved politically advantageous to his career, it did not instinctively appeal to the public in the disputes which came his way.

The trick for the union was to try to capture the media's attention, even though it had not called an all-out strike. Each day, immediately after breakfast television had finished broadcasting, its strategy team met in an operations room at the TUC's Transport House to plot the course of the campaign for the next twenty-four hours. Poole, the national officers and the union's press officers all attended the briefing. Their plan was to keep the story moving, hour by hour, and to respond to any government initiative with one of their own. Moderation was the watchword. They were determined to ask for nothing that seemed extortionate, nothing that they would have difficulty defending, nothing that would lose them sympathy.

Clarke, supported by Mrs Thatcher, was not interested in the sympathy vote, though he was conscious of being on the wrong side of it. ' "Support the mercy men" may be an easy slogan,' he wrote. 'But what are the facts?'[6] He valued the work of the highly skilled paramedical teams, but saw the union leaders were trying to win a bigger pay award for every ambulance crew, even though he considered, in David Mellor's words, 'that a lot of the work they were doing was basically just drivers' work – it didn't require specialist skills at all'. In his eyes they were trading on a small percentage of their work to justify the rest of it. 'He wanted efficiency,' says Mellor. 'He wanted value for money.'

Clarke's presentational problem was similar to the one he had in the dispute with the doctors. The only way he could possibly gain public support was by depicting the union ranged against him as the menace he had fought against for most of his political life. Yet that was not how the public saw it. Clarke vainly tried to raise the spectre of the Winter of Discontent: 'Remember 1979? Why are we seeing a glimpse of history?'[7] More personally, he remembered his days as health minister in 1982, when NUPE was the most militant of the five unions opposing him.

The problem now was that NUPE, under Roger Poole's leadership, resolutely refused to live up to Clarke's description. Poole's moderate approach enabled him to ensure that the government and not the union was the target of public wrath. As one Clarke adviser puts it: 'Roger Poole looked so great on the television set, and the government looked horrible.' By November 1989 the situation in London was reaching crisis point, with ambulance services at a virtual standstill. When more than three-quarters of the capital's crews staged sit-ins at their stations, the police had to act as a makeshift ambulance service. Clarke was forced to go before the Commons twice in twenty-four hours to explain that the Army was being brought in to provide emergency cover. The unions had succeeded in their aim; the Army was on the streets, attracting the attention of every newspaper and television station, yet they had not actually gone on strike, and they had managed to retain public support. Clarke knew exactly what had happened to him: 'I admire NUPE officials for their skill in their chosen trade . . . they have caused a strike without making it look like a strike.'[8]

For much of the dispute, Clarke hid behind the fiction that it was the responsibility of the new NHS chief executive, Duncan Nichol, to decide what action to take. The tactic had been proposed by Don Wilson, chairman of the Merseyside Regional Health Authority. Clarke recalls having

a lot of difficulty persuading Margaret. But it worked because Duncan had the loyalty of the regional managers to a tremendous extent. They wanted to deliver for Duncan, but they were far more distant from me. What didn't work was that Duncan was not allowed to become this large public figure helping to lead the service, largely because that's not the way politics works in the health service.

The unions preyed upon the point; their strategy was to drag Clarke into the dispute. It soon became clear that he could not stay out for much longer. Even the *Sun* appeared to be siding with the crews, running a large headline which read: 'HEAL THIS WOUND NOW, MR CLARKE'. But Clarke felt that if he ordered Nichol to settle he would undermine the authority of his own management team and establish Roger Poole as a leader who had shown the other unions the way to get more money.

Painted into a corner, Clarke found himself the victim of his own abrasive past and NUPE's new-found moderation. 'Whatever happened to caring Ken?' asked the *Daily Express*. 'Instead of the matey, jolly fellow once known to colleagues and public we now have a truculent, bad-tempered bully.' The newspaper argued that Clarke had been given a personality transplant on the NHS, 'and it is beginning to look more and more probable that the donor was his colleague Nicholas Ridley'.[9] It wasn't true. The toughness, though stepped up under Mrs Thatcher, was always part of Clarke's mixed political personality, and when it needed to emerge it simply overshadowed the liberal side of his politics which he had been able to express when the circumstances favoured him, as inner-cities minister.

As the dispute dragged on, Clarke's views about the 'two-tier' nature of ambulance work became more pronounced, and his language grew more vehement. While he felt he had to stand up to the union's pay claim for the greater good of the NHS, and while the union undoubtedly exploited the ambulance crews' caring image, Clarke nevertheless fell headlong, once more, into a public relations disaster of his own making.

It was the season of good cheer, Christmas 1989, when the fifteen-year-old daughter of a Nottingham ambulance man wrote to Clarke to express her feelings about the dispute. Lisa Mitchell felt her father was getting a raw deal: 'My father is a fully trained ambulanceman whose basic skills include life-saving, resuscitation plus the ability to diagnose any medical situations that may lead to loss of life.' There then followed a surprisingly accurate and detailed comparison of the salaries of a police officer with five years' service (£15,000 a year), a fire-fighter (£13,850) and an ambulance crew member (£10,093). She concluded: 'I would like you to think about this very carefully before they are all on strike and people start dying because of this.'

It would have been easy for Clarke to respond with a polite but firm letter detailing his resistance to the pay claim and his overall concern for the NHS budget, not just for one group of workers. Whatever his suspicions about the guiding force behind the letter, that is what he should have done. Instead of pitching the letter directly at the teenager, however, Clarke effectively addressed his reply to the girl's father, and to the world at large, sounding like Scrooge into the bargain:

> You describe the accident and emergency work that your father sometimes carries out. Such cases represent one in ten of all patients carried . . . You describe your father's life-saving skills. The vast majority of ambulance staff have had no extended paramedical training at all. They are professional drivers, a worthwhile job – but not an exceptional one at all.

The strategists closeted at Transport House were quick to spot their opening. They believed the insult was deliberate, to provoke an all-out strike which might undermine their support. If they could just keep the protest running at the same level of intensity, without a full-scale walk-out, they might exploit Clarke's ill-chosen words to win another public relations victory. Support came at once from the Chief Ambulance Officers' Association, which had hitherto remained silent. The group declared that the government had set out to destroy the worth of any group involved in a pay dispute and 'would reap the rewards of a disillusioned and disgruntled workforce'.

Clarke's injudicious reply also had repercussions at Westminster, among supporters in his own party. The former health minister Sir Gerard Vaughan warned that the dispute was doing much damage politically, while the Leominster MP Peter Temple-Morris declared that he did not like the efforts being made to diminish the ambulance crews' work: 'The public does not see ambulancemen as an irresponsible bunch of Arthur Scargills.'[10] Deep in the Ministry of Defence, Alan Clark was playing three-dimensional political chess with the careers of his boss, Tom King, and Clarke: 'My present solution is to move TK to Health, where he could be pinkly affable and repair some of the damage caused by my "abrasive" namesake. But that could only happen if Clarke has a nervous breakdown – unlikely in one so fat – or – perfectly possible at any time, he must make the Norwich Union wince – something "happens to" him.'[11]

The weekend after the publication of Clarke's letter, the *Sunday Times* reported that 'a furious Clarke' had accused Cabinet colleagues of deserting him over the handling of the dispute. That the accompanying photograph pictured him looking not at all furious, but cheerfully enjoying a Notts County football match, made no difference to the import of the story. The paper said he was 'believed to be especially critical of the lack of support from Kenneth Baker, the Tory party chairman'. Baker himself will comment only that Clarke is

naturally provocative and he certainly provoked. I felt that the presentation of the government's case was not all that good. We should have taken it in a different way. I think there was no sense of trying to appeal to the patients or to the general public over the heads of the ambulance men. Presentationally it could have been handled in a more persuasive way.

Clarke's opinion about this turn of events is that 'You don't half discover who your friends are when you're in trouble. Nameless colleagues, who I've never had any time for since, distanced themselves rapidly from this difficulty.'[12] Baker's silence was apparently hurtful and remains so to this day. Publicly the two are friends, and Clarke appeared on Baker's BBC Television series based on his book, *The Turbulent Years*. But one of their mutual friends, a former minister, says Clarke will never forgive Baker for his lack of support during the ambulance dispute: 'He feels that Baker undermined him. Nothing would surprise me less. I think Baker has quite a lot to do to establish that he didn't. Ken has no illusions about him. He'll never forget that.' By contrast, John Major, who was by this time Chancellor of the Exchequer, offered his full support – and Clarke never forgot that, either. 'I thought his arguments were good,' Major remarks. 'What he was trying to do was right. He had advanced a policy; it was a collective policy; I think he deserved support, so I gave him support whenever I could.'

Clarke felt the dispute had pitched him into serious political trouble. One of his former political advisers says that Clarke was called into No. 10 and given 'a carpeting' for his handling of the affair. Some reports even suggested he was fighting for his political life, although according to his colleagues that was not the case because Mrs Thatcher always backed a minister who was fighting a public spending battle, however unpopular the cause. 'Actually, although I hadn't consulted her before the dispute started, and some of my colleagues complained that this had happened without me telling them, she quite obviously agreed with me, so she stuck with me through thick and thin,' Clarke reflects. 'But my popularity in the party plunged to depths that I have never plunged to before or since.' The political columnist Hugo Young wrote that Clarke's handling of the dispute 'causes him now to be regarded with extreme wariness by his colleagues . . . another golden boy is showing himself to be not very good at his trade, which is, at bottom, not health but politics'.[13]

Clarke may have tripped up presentationally, but there was no deep-seated animosity between him and Roger Poole. In the middle of the dispute, they bumped into each other in the small BBC Television studio in the basement of Broadcasting House. Neither of them knew that the other had been invited on to breakfast television, because they were being interviewed separately. As Clarke emerged from the studio, Poole asked him if they could have a meeting. The worst place to have a private talk about the way to solve an industrial dispute is probably the BBC; within minutes, journalists were buzzing around the pair, who had to ask for a quiet room in which to continue their discussions. They spent nearly three-quarters of an hour together, trying to find a way to end the ambulance crews' action. But there was a major sticking point to overcome in any settlement: Mrs Thatcher. So bad were relations between No. 10 and the unions that the latter had to employ a public relations firm with contacts in Downing Street to see if there was any hope of compromise. The answer they got back was short and to the point: no.

As the dispute hardened, Clarke's handling of it became increasingly less certain. Within a few days of his unfortunate letter the *Observer* reported that he was prepared to offer more money to the ambulance crews if they dropped their demand for a pay formula. The story had emerged from a briefing which Clarke had given to journalists at the Department of Health on lobby, or off-the-record, terms. But at the same time that Clarke was meeting the representatives of seven Sunday papers, NHS chief executive Duncan Nichol was telling other reporters there would be no concessions to the unions. Confusion reigned. The Department of Health first told the Press Association that the *Observer* report was correct, only to retract its statement half an hour later. The unions, with their smaller, tighter campaign team, appeared to be a much more disciplined force. The feeling deepened that the strike was being mishandled. Twice at Prime Minister's Questions, Mrs Thatcher declined to endorse Clarke's description of the crews as 'professional drivers'.

Clarke desperately needed to start winning the media battle. A telephone poll suggested that 80 per cent of those questioned were sympathetic to the ambulance crews and only 10 per cent to the government. Even among Conservative voters, 65 per cent backed the workers and only 19 per cent their own party. Just then a chance arose to repair some of the damage, in the unlikely form of an invitation to become a television reporter. *Channel 4 News* had covered the dispute from the beginning, but its senior journalists considered that the issues which both sides were raising were becoming lost in the day-to-day coverage of the industrial action itself. So it asked Kenneth Clarke and Roger Poole to make their own films about the ambulance strike. Each would be given their own producer and camera crew, who would advise solely on the most effective way of imparting their message televisually, and each would be given full access to ITN's facilities.

The Health Secretary decided to visit the Northumbria ambulance service, to hammer home his point about the two-tier nature of the crews' work. Northumbria had separate staff handling emergency and non-emergency work, with much routine transport handled by private operators. Clarke hit upon a stunning way to start his report. Wearing a set of headphones with a microphone attached, he swung round in the passenger seat of the service's helicopter to the camera behind him, so that viewers could see the River Tyne far below him as he spoke:

> I'm in a new helicopter that's just about to come into service with Northumbria's ambulance service. They serve a big rural area and this helicopter's going to save lives as they bring patients down from the hills. Now the reason they've been able to invest half a million pounds in this helicopter is because of the very effective way they've improved their service.[14]

For a man widely perceived to be losing the public relations offensive, Clarke seemed unusually assured. As the film progressed, there was Clarke in an ambulance on his way to an emergency; Clarke in a hard hat interviewing Duncan Nichol; and Clarke arguing to camera that local change and flexibility were the only way forward – that paramedics should earn more than the 'drivers' who picked up pensioners.

To make his point, Clarke went out with a paramedic team as it sped to an emergency. He was pictured bouncing along in the back of an ambulance as it sped to Newcastle University, where a man had collapsed on the pavement. When they arrived, he could only watch impotently, clasping and unclasping his hands inside his black gloves, as the paramedics fought vainly for the man's life. The tragedy, reported as headline news in *The Times*, made grim breakfast-time reading for the Prime Minister the next day.

Roger Poole's film was as elegantly made as Clarke's and he was as natural a television performer. But he concentrated heavily on statistics to try to justify his members' pay claim, and he stressed Clarke's intransigence: 'He's said no to arbitration; he's said no to a pay formula; he's said no to a live debate with the unions. Mr Clarke says nothing but no.' Ultimately, however, he could not match the opening shot of the helicopter high above the Newcastle skyline. Afterwards ITN's editor, David Nicholas, sent a congratulatory note to the production staff who had helped to shape the two films. Both films had been very good, he opined, but in his view Clarke had won.

It was to be a turning-point. The dispute dragged on for another month, with both sides standing firm. But it was obvious that it was going nowhere, and that for the action to end there had to be a compromise which would allow both sides to claim victory. And so it proved. On 23 February 1990 the government and the ambulance crews' leaders finally hammered out a deal after twenty-four weeks of hard pounding.

The new two-year pay deal of 17.6 per cent offered little more than an eighteen-month deal which had already been rejected by the crews, so the government could now claim that its strategy of holding out had been rewarded. Downing Street called the peace terms 'fair and reasonable', affording Clarke the chance to rebuild his reputation. He had held the line against an automatic pay formula, and he had been vindicated.

But the unions could claim victory, too. So complicated was the offer that Roger Poole was able to claim that he had 'driven a coach and horses' through the government's pay policy, with little fear of contradiction from his members. More importantly, perhaps, he had driven a coach and horses through the government's public relations machine. 'Roger Poole stuffed us on the PR front,' says a Clarke adviser succinctly. The Health Secretary's rehabilitation would take time.

Clarke had made some gains, however. *The Times* in an editorial said that he deserved the gratitude of this Cabinet colleagues for holding the line on two sectors of the front simultaneously – health reforms and the ambulance dispute. Weaker personalities would probably have buckled under the strain. Yet Clarke's abrasive style, while perhaps not actually lengthening the dispute with the doctors and the ambulance crews, had none the less played into the hands of two sets of workers who were eager to exploit their public popularity at the expense of their political masters. 'What I said throughout and what I believed was that the only thing people remember about industrial disputes is who won, and whether it was worth it,' Clarke thinks. 'I was convinced that to concede to the ambulance crews would leave the health service in a totally unmanageable situation, with the ancillary workers demanding the same deal. I hadn't got the money for it, and it would have had a chaotic effect on public service pay settlements generally.'

Overall, Clarke's time as Health Secretary set back his career and ultimately cost him a place in the leadership race when Mrs Thatcher resigned. He told David Mellor it would take him at least three years to recover politically: 'He knew the price he'd paid, but that wouldn't stop him paying it. He was not prepared to be an emollient soft touch in order to be the smiling face that meant people would say, "That Ken Clarke, let's have him as our leader."'

There was more to the story than this, however. For a man versed in the Lord Young school of advertising, and possessed of finely tuned political instincts, it was extraordinary that Clarke should have scored two public relations own goals with stray remarks regarding the doctors and the ambulance crews. Sir Norman Fowler believes that part of the explanation lies in the fact that Clarke had already served one term at the Health Department as a junior minister, so he felt he knew the ropes: 'I think it was a mistake actually to send him back to do the same job again. That was the one time his career really faltered. I think the trouble was that he came back as a secretary of state thinking that he slightly knew it all and he slightly overdid it.'

A deeper explanation lies in Clarke's personality. The very toughness that ensured his survival as Health Secretary, and his delight in its display, prompted the verbal infelicities which added to the already severe pressure he was under. Politics for Clarke was a verbal contest, both in and out of the chamber; he could express his lifetime's detestation of vested interests and condemn the organisations represented by John Marks and Roger Poole but do so without personal animosity. It was like the sport which he sometimes watches: a boxing match, where the protagonists traded blow after blow for fifteen rounds as if their lives depended on it, only for them to embrace each other when the final bell had sounded. One of Clarke's former advisers agrees: 'He takes nothing personally, because he's so self-contained. There's never any personal rancour between him and his opponents. People can say whatever they like about him, but it just bounces off.'

To an extent, then, Mrs Thatcher's suspicions had proved to be correct; Clarke was a hard minister to control. But on policy they had a pragmatic accord. On specific problems, such as the reform of the NHS, they agreed on the broad sweep of the changes required. Clarke readily accepts this: 'I was never one of her close entourage. But when it came to practical problems . . . then the two of us enjoyed working together.'[15] If he did occasionally overstep the mark, his speaking style showed that there was a Thatcherite toughness about him; if she knew him to be a wet, she need not fear he was a wimp. 'Whatever the philosophical differences between us,' she writes, 'he was . . . extremely effective . . . tough in dealing with vested interests and trade unions, direct and persuasive in his exposition of government policy.'[16]

As the political strength of Mrs Thatcher's government waned, so, in inverse proportion, Clarke's presentational abilities grew in importance to the Tories until they became the very rock on which the government itself was founded. He was more like Mrs Thatcher than anyone else in government in the certitude with which he expressed himself. He might do so with more humour than she ever attempted, and he might genuinely be a man of the people rather than just on their wavelength. But he was nevertheless Thatcherite in his approach to politics: he liked to speak; he expressed himself forcefully; and he was, in his own mind, always right. In time, these Thatcher-like qualities would become the sheet-anchor of John Major's enfeebled administration. Major acknowledges Clarke's toughness and experience:

Having fixed upon a course, he will not be pushed off it by silly or short-term arguments. I think that is a considerable strength of his. He is very experienced. People forget how long he has been around in politics; he's seen many of the things that happen before. You learn from that. The second time a problem comes around, you are aware of the drawbacks that are not immediately apparent first time round.

Clarke had survived the ten thousand hells of Health. His reputation had taken a battering only because he had appeared to be too tough. And strong, decisive ministers, it seemed, were what Mrs Thatcher wanted. In the reshuffle sparked by Sir Geoffrey Howe's resignation, she asked Clarke to replace John MacGregor and sort out Education. It was his sixth move in eleven years and the only one he has argued against.

The night before the reshuffle Clarke had confidently told his staff that he and Education Secretary John MacGregor were the two Cabinet ministers who would not be moved, because they were both in the middle of putting through controversial reforms. He was wrong. On Friday 2 November 1990 the call came from No. 10. Clarke was in his office at the Health Department with his political adviser and his private secretary: 'Margaret told me, "It's all over now, you've done the job", and I said, don't you believe it, there'll be an awful lot happening between now and next April.' He felt he was being demoted, so he tried a different tack, saying that she could not possibly move John MacGregor. 'She told me, I'm not sure altogether truthfully, that John had already agreed.' Clarke told Mrs Thatcher that he would think about it and ring her back in ten minutes.

Clarke then tried a last line of defence. He asked the Prime Minister who she wanted to appoint in his place at Health. 'When she told me it was William Waldegrave, I said, "Marvellous! Ideal! Fellow of All Souls! Born to be Secretary of State for *Education*!"' And she said, "Kenneth, you can't have an old Etonian as Secretary of State for Education." On the strength of that I conceded.' But he also wanted Mrs Thatcher to promise that he would not have to introduce education vouchers for school places, as she desired. She readily agreed.

It was the last time Mrs Thatcher would reshuffle Kenneth Clarke. Their turbulent relationship was nearly at an end. Within a month she was out of office.

CHAPTER 12

The End of History

*Better passion and death than any more of these 'isms'. No more of the old
purpose done up in aspic. Better passion and death.*
D. H. Lawrence, *Fantasia of the Unconscious*

On taking office in 1979 Mrs Thatcher had famously invoked St
Francis of Assisi by promising to replace discord with harmony, error
with truth, doubt with faith and despair with hope. The only trouble
with her invocation was that it was never very clear that St Francis was
a Tory, or indeed that Mrs Thatcher seriously wanted the Tories to be
good Franciscans. It was fitting, therefore, that she should leave office
amid much discord and not little political error and despair. The
doubt came later, under John Major's leadership.

The causes of Mrs Thatcher's downfall were many and varied but,
with hindsight, the sources of discontent which hitherto had seemed
unconnected became conterminous. John Biffen compares this to one
of the maps on the Paris Métro which light up when you press a button
to go from A to B: 'Someone pressed a button, and all the connections
lit up.'[1] There were plenty of indicators along the way: initially,
Michael Heseltine's self-imposed exile after the Westland affair,
which left a dangerous rival lurking on the back benches; increasingly, Mrs Thatcher's style of leadership, in which she seemed to see
herself as the embodiment of party, government and country; and
specifically, her unpopularity with the voters which sprang from her
adherence to the poll tax. Finally, Sir Geoffrey Howe, removed from
the Foreign Office and no longer wrestling with his own response to
what he called 'the tragic conflict of loyalties' which Mrs Thatcher had
provoked, pressed the button on the route map to find the way to
Europe.

The downfall of the Prime Minister was replete with irony. Like Ted Heath, she was brought down by backbench unpopularity, the very reason for her success when she had seized the moment to topple him in 1975. Fifteen years on, Mrs Thatcher had forgotten the lessons of history and had neglected her supporters. Indeed, Clarke sees a similarity in the leadership style of Heath and Thatcher which contributed to their eventual shared perdition:

> They were both fairly authoritarian and both extremely decisive. They had very strong opinions which they stamped on their governments. Neither was always terribly open to fresh advice. Collective discussion was not a search for the truth taking a variety of views round the table. They were both people of ferociously strong opinions.

But there the similarities ended. Mrs Thatcher was thrice undefeated at the polls, whereas Heath had thrice been vanquished.

However, if Mrs Thatcher was the mistress of the revolution which had rejected Heath's brand of consensus Toryism, her hijacking of the party was none the less incomplete. She led a Cabinet which did not fully reflect her image and a party which had never fully decided whether or not she was an aberration in the broad sweep of its history. Accordingly, her supporters still distrust the faint-hearts who, they suspect, wanted her to fail so that they could return the party to the smooth surface of the main highway after all its years away. Kenneth Clarke is a main target for their ire.

The beginning of the end for Margaret Thatcher came on Tuesday 20 November 1990, when she beat Michael Heseltine by fifty-two votes in the contest he had precipitated for the leadership of the Tory Party. Although she had an absolute majority she was a tantalising four votes short of the 15 per cent margin the rules demanded. It was a result decisive only in its indecisiveness. She was at one and the same time the clear winner and the clear loser. She was so near to overall victory that her supporters still held out the hope of eventual success; but she was so far away that her less enthusiastic, and ultimately more realistic, colleagues could see nothing but disaster for the party if she stood again. Yet that, it appeared, was fully her intention as the judgement was delivered to her in Paris – her presence there a reflection of her ill-organised campaign. Bustling down the steps of the British Embassy, Mrs Thatcher pronounced herself a candidate for round two.

To say that Clarke was unhappy at her decision underestimates both his feelings and the powers of his advocacy. He had grown alarmed over the previous weekend that her support was ebbing and that, although she might win, it would not be by a big enough margin. So a few hours before the ballot result he had gathered with John Gummer in the Commons room of the Energy Secretary, John Wakeham. The political columnist Alan Watkins argues that Clarke and Gummer wanted to impress on Wakeham, a man who had the Prime Minister's ear, that Mrs Thatcher could not expect to stand twice without damaging the government and her own authority.[2] But Gummer angrily denies it was a plot:

> That is rubbish. The truth is that we gathered to plan what we could do to help her. We assumed she was going to win, because that was the advice. But we said what happens if the unthinkable happens. We were three old whips, and we just felt all these figures were too good to be true, because in a private vote there would be quite a few people who would promise to vote both ways. The discussion then was, if she didn't do very well, what should we do, as her supporters, to make sure she was seen at her best?

That night Clarke dutifully trooped around the television studios on his leader's behalf to back her decision to the hilt: the professional lawyer at work, defending his leader in the hope that she would do the honourable thing, or that the party would point out to her the room in which the pearl-handled revolver lay. 'It's just not going to work, it can't, it's impossible!' he told his advisers as Mrs Thatcher hung on. 'He was completely adamant from the moment it happened,' recalls his special adviser Tessa Keswick. 'He thought it was unfair that she should even think of staying. He was convinced that the pay vote would collapse.'

The next day, Wednesday 21st, Clarke told the Leader of the House, John MacGregor, who was canvassing Cabinet opinion, that he would not support Mrs Thatcher any more because he believed that a further contest with Heseltine would split the party disastrously. But as time went on, there was no sign of an arranged suicide. In the afternoon Clarke watched with growing anger as Mrs Thatcher reported back to the Commons on her Paris trip. To Clarke, she seemed to speak with the insouciance of a leader who had chosen to ignore the show of force against her and was determined to go on and on in office. Time was running out for her to stand down; nominations had to close by midday on Thursday. So Clarke demanded that a full Cabinet meeting be held that night. 'He was coming to the conclusion that if Mrs Thatcher wouldn't free her supporters, then he ought to free his own hands to run, or get Chris Patten to run,' Clarke's friend John Barnes remembers.

Instead of a full Cabinet meeting, the ministers went in one by one. They were summoned individually to sit on the sofa in front of the Prime Minister and deliver themselves of their views. Clarke, famously, was the first Cabinet minister to go in, by virtue of both alphabetical order and the fact that he was free at 6 p.m. He set the pattern for the night, declaring bluntly that if she stood she would lose, and that by doing so she would deprive both John Major and Douglas Hurd of the chance to run. It was, he said, like the charge of the Light Brigade: 'C'est magnifique, mais ce n'est pas la guerre.' When asked, he said he could not support her and he did not believe she could win. It was all delivered in a typically robust manner, in what Mrs Thatcher calls 'the brutalist style he has cultivated: the candid friend'.[3] The man who had seen off the doctors and the ambulance crews spared no sympathy on his leader. She remembers: 'In his rather bruising style, he said the whole process was farcical, that he personally could support me for another five or ten years but most of the Cabinet thought I would lose.'[4] Lord Parkinson thinks Clarke even told Mrs Thatcher: '"I'm sick of all this, I'm going to the cinema." It was typical Clarke way of breaking bad news about as badly as you can.' It was certainly a difficult meeting, in Clarke's view: 'Anybody who loses any job gets emotional. It causes a lump in the throat, and the fact is, as we know, women are inclined to cry on such occasions.'[5]

Although Clarke did not actually tell Mrs Thatcher he would resign if she stayed on, that was his clear intent, because he would have voted for Michael Heseltine in the second round against her:

I thought she was destroying the whole credibility of the government by going on. I told her I wouldn't campaign for her – I wasn't going to vote for her on the second ballot. I thought it would be wrong to sit there in the Cabinet probably speaking for and certainly voting for her opponent. I would have voted for Heseltine. But the main thing I was desperate to ensure was that we had more candidates.

He likens the efforts to make Mrs Thatcher aware of the mood of the party to those of 'the generals trying to persuade Napoleon to leave the field at the Battle of Waterloo'. He felt that if she remained in office her authority, and the authority of the party and the government, would be inexorably weakened. Neither she nor Heseltine, he thought, could hope to lead a united party: 'I acted on the principle that if you're serving a friend as your boss, what you owe that boss is your candid, truthful, non-self-interested advice. And I advised her that she could not go on, and in my opinion she ought to step down.'[6] He spent the evening contacting other Tory MPs and telling them he would resign if she stayed, 'as we are crashing to a great folly'.[7]

One former Cabinet minister believes that Clarke was fed up with the Prime Minister and saw an opportunity to get rid of her after the inconclusive first ballot. But Clarke did what he had been doing throughout his career; he faced a specific political problem and came up with a specific answer. Love is blind, but even Mrs Thatcher's greatest admirer, Alan Clark, told her she would lose, although he insisted it was her duty to go down fighting. Kenneth Clarke was less romantically inclined. Typically, when Mrs Thatcher decided to leave the Commons at the next general election, his reaction stood out for its dry pragmatism amid a sea of tears. While John Major paid tribute to her greatness, and Chris Patten to her unrivalled experience, Clarke merely observed that the move 'seems to make inevitable sense'.

From Mrs Thatcher downwards the Thatcherites suspected, if not a plot to unseat her, then a prior agreement that she must go. As she interviewed her Cabinet individually, she came to the conclusion that the dozen ministers who opposed her had agreed on a set formula – that they would support her if she stood, but that she couldn't possibly win. She calls this 'treachery with smile on its face, perhaps that was the worst thing of all'.[8] Clarke denies the charge:

There was no treachery against her. There was a pattern of events which was what it appeared to be, and a Cabinet that was prepared to support her gave her wholly sensible advice that she had been defeated, that she must now withdraw. That was good advice; she had been defeated, she had no chance of winning in the second ballot. But that was nothing to do with the Cabinet. It was the parliamentary party where she'd suffered the defeat.

Mrs Thatcher hadn't actually been defeated; indeed, she was ousted despite mustering more votes than John Major managed when he won. It gave her dyed-in-the-wool supporters such as Alan Clark the chance to allege that even before the result ministers like Clarke wanted Mrs Thatcher to go so badly 'that they don't need even to blink'.[9] This was certainly not true. Clarke backed Mrs Thatcher in the first round, and John Wakeham had even proposed him as her campaign manager for the second vote, a sign that Clarke's views were not as suspect as Alan Clark maintains, but also perhaps a sign of how out of touch the Thatcher team was with the mood of the party.

None the less, Clarke seemed disturbingly cheerful about the whole business. One former minister describes how Clarke strode along to his meeting with Mrs Thatcher: 'He said, "I'm just going to see her now. I think I'm going to tell her it's got to come to an end." He was quite jaunty. He wasn't actually whistling, but he was close to it.' Sir Leon Brittan says that Clarke 'neither felt nor pretended to be deeply distressed'. In fact, he did not enjoy his meeting with Mrs Thatcher; if he was close to whistling, it was to keep his spirits up, and if he was brutal, he says it was because he feared she would not get the message that John Major and Douglas Hurd must be allowed to run, to heal the party. Even then, he was unsure the job was done. He phoned John Major, who was at his Huntingdon home recovering from a wisdom tooth operation, to try to stop him signing Mrs Thatcher's nomination papers. And he once again asked John Wakeham for an immediate Cabinet meeting.

On Thursday 22 November, Mrs Thatcher finally told her Cabinet she would step down. As she walked through the small antechamber to the Cabinet room where she was to read out her tearful resignation statement, she found her ministers huddled together, averting their eyes. One of those present says Clarke informed them, 'If she isn't gone by midday, I'm leaving', but that when Mrs Thatcher told the Cabinet of her decision he told her, 'Don't worry, we'll pin regicide on Heseltine.'

Clarke gave some thought, briefly, to standing for the leadership against Major and Hurd, but just as quickly discounted it. 'It crossed my mind, but I wouldn't have had a prayer. I realised I didn't have the slightest chance of winning. The timing was wrong. It was too near the ambulance strike. Another twelve months and I could have been a contender. Another twelve months in education and I could have given them a good run for their money.'

Before Mrs Thatcher's fall, Clarke had told the *Financial Times* political editor Philip Stephens that the two colleagues he would be willing to serve under were Chris Patten and John Major. Instead, like Chris Patten, he supported Hurd. The combination, although understandable politically given Hurd's Heathite roots, was still a strange one: the toff and the serf. Hurd was the nearest the Cabinet had to a Tory grandee, an Eton man whose background was exploited by John Major in his campaign appeal for a classless society. Hurd might claim to be the son of a tenant farmer; he looked and sounded like a representative of the era Mrs Thatcher had overthrown, whereas Clarke was the minister who had perfected the art of blokeishness. One night during the campaign David Mellor met him at the studios of the BBC Television programme *Newsnight*. Mellor was there to press the case for Major, Clarke to do the same for Hurd. Afterwards Mellor asked him: 'What's a grammar-school boy like you doing on Douglas Hurd's team?' 'Oh, I'm the token peasant,' Clarke replied. 'They need me to pour the drinks.'

Part of the reason for Clarke's decision to back Hurd lay in his long-standing respect for the Foreign Secretary and in his view that Hurd's patriarchal figure would be able to unite the party. For similar reasons he now rejected Heseltine:

I think he's got great style but the reason I was vehemently against him on this occasion was that I thought it would have split and destroyed the party. I couldn't see how he could be leader. For the regicide to take over the leadership, not only would it not have won the election but it would have taken years to put the pieces back together again.

Undoubtedly, Clarke's own desire to be Prime Minister also entered the calculation. 'In terms of age, it would have been crazy for him not to back Hurd,' admits an adviser. If Hurd became Prime Minister, Clarke would still have a clear chance of fulfilling the ambition he first expressed as a schoolboy. Hurd is Clarke's senior by a decade and held out the prospect of a short reign, whereas Major is nearly three years younger than Clarke. Norman Lamont tried to get Clarke to support Major: 'I think he wanted me to nominate him. I explained that my reason was Europe. I thought that Margaret had destroyed herself on Europe and it was time we needed a clear pro-European policy. I also thought Douglas would be a more unifying influence. That was my reason for not supporting John.' But Clarke helped persuade Hurd and Major to run against each other, which they were reluctant to do:

> We all agreed that there would be no personal attacks – because Margaret's team were preparing the most appalling attacks on Michael Heseltine when they thought she was going to fight a second round. I had a conversation halfway through with John Major when he checked with me that there were no hard feelings creeping into any of this.

Clarke was calculating the impact on his career of a new leader but refused to show his hand, even to his friends. David Trippier stayed at Clarke's house in Nottingham the weekend before the second leadership vote. The two men sat up into the small hours, chewing the political fat, with Trippier anxious to convert Clarke to the Heseltine camp. At two o'clock in the morning, after several drinks, Trippier decided to appeal to Clarke's ambition:

> I said to him the pity of it is that if John gets it, it knocks you back quite a bit, but if Michael gets it there's probably time . . . and he said yeah. But it was very frustrating because instead of saying, 'Yeah, I've thought of that', all he'd say was, 'Yeah, if you say so.' Really, I could have thumped him on the chin. He knew exactly what I was saying and he'd sort of nod but he wouldn't even say to me, yes it's a pity, I've blown my chances.

However, Clarke was still a lucky politician. When John Major won the leadership race, he had one key decision to make about his new

Cabinet: how to replace himself as Chancellor. According to Sir Norman Fowler, this was a much more difficult decision than is commonly supposed. The Chief Secretary to the Treasury, Norman Lamont, had been a key member of his campaign team and hoped thereby to become Chancellor. Indeed, when asked on *Newsnight* whether he hoped to gain his reward if John Major won the leadership battle, he parried the question but failed to suppress a self-conscious smile of expectation when it was put again. The trouble was that Lamont, although a junior minister since 1979, had never run a department, and Major was unsure whether to pitch his friend straight into the Chancellor's job. His alternative was Clarke. Fowler says the decision was close, Clarke's toughness against Lamont's role in the campaign, and the fact that Major had worked with Lamont before at the Treasury: 'It was a complete toss-up who was going to become Chancellor of the Exchequer. I don't think anyone did actually toss a coin but they jolly nearly did. It would have done everyone a favour had the decision gone the other way.'

John Major says, however, that his main priority was to keep Clarke at Education:

He was in the middle of some extremely important educational reforms. One of the difficulties I have seen over the past ten years, partly from outside, is that ministers move around too soon, too speedily. I think ministers often should stay longer in the same department. I want to know that the advice I get around this Cabinet table comes from the minister who knows what he is talking about, who has seen political events in that department for a while, who has thoroughly learned his brief, who is actually able to operate from the basis of experience in this department and not information from a brief provided from a civil servant who may have been transferred from a different department the week before. So I do not favour moving people around too much.

Some academics subscribe to the Cleopatra's nose theory of history. This theory, derived from Pascal, holds that if Cleopatra's nose had been shorter, and her face accordingly less beautiful, then Mark Antony would not have fallen in love with her, and the entire history of the classical world would have been different. The ERM theory about

211

Clarke is somewhat similar. If John Major had backed him rather than Lamont, Clarke would have been Chancellor when the Exchange Rate Mechanism crisis broke – the single event which, fairly or not, did most to undermine Lamont's credibility. As James Callaghan had realised when he resigned as Chancellor over the Labour devaluation of sterling in November 1967, the fate of the pound and that of the tenant of 11 Downing Street are inextricably linked. The ERM crisis would have dealt Clarke's career a blow from which it would have struggled to recover. He would doubtless have been as powerless as Lamont on Black Wednesday, swept away by the flood tide of financial speculation, though he might have handled the clean-up operation with more assurance. But he would have been severely damaged, the more so after his Health battles of recent memory.

Instead, the luck which had guided Clarke into a safe seat in Rushcliffe more than two decades before still held. He remained at Education in the run-up to the general election – and the new Prime Minister declared that education was top of his personal agenda, crucial for the classless society he envisaged, and he called it the passport of opportunity for individuals and the nation. It became a key issue in the long pre-election war against Labour. Clarke knew the score. He was fighting on what he called 'the principal battleground' between Right and Left. 'Nowhere', he said, 'is the battlefield more fierce than in the two services which impinge directly on the personal experience of the general public.'[10] Labour had been making the running. His task was to win back lost ground.

Trouble was brewing in the schools and had been for some time. In 1988 the then Education Secretary, Kenneth Baker, had introduced a national curriculum to control and make uniform what was taught. It was the most sweeping reform of British education since the war, and it was to provoke five years of hostilities between the government and the teachers. The main problem with the Baker reforms was the detail which came to overwhelm them, showering teachers with page after page of instructions about the content of each syllabus, covering them with orders on the tests they had to carry out, and burying them in official reports on the knowledge, skills and understanding that were required.

212

It had all begun simply. Before 1988 maintained schools in England and Wales were free to choose what subjects they taught. But under the Baker reforms schoolchildren had to study nine subjects in primary school and ten in secondary school. Maths, science and English were known as core subjects, the rest as foundation subjects. The trouble was that, while this broad structure was laid down by the Education Reform Act, the actual implementation of the reforms in each subject was to be phased in gradually, the preserve of special working groups which decided the exact content of the subjects children of different ages should be compelled to learn. On top of this, special devised standard assessment tasks (or SATs) were introduced to check on children's progress at the ages of seven, eleven, fourteen and sixteen. To administer it all, there was not one but two quangos: one to deal with the coursework, the National Curriculum Council, and the other to handle the testing, the Schools Examination and Assessment Council. It all became too complex.

Mrs Thatcher had warned against the over-elaboration of the national curriculum and the accompanying tests. The original working groups packed as much as they could into each subject's curriculum. There wasn't time in the school year to do everything; school inspectors suggested that the teaching of the three Rs was being squeezed by the demands of other subjects.

Following on from Baker as Education Secretary, John MacGregor had been appointed in 1989 to ensure that the reforms would work effectively on a practical level. To Mrs Thatcher's intense annoyance, he showed every sign of listening too much to the teachers. He was even praised by the chairman of the Headmasters' Conference as the 'best Secretary of State for Education we have ever had'. The hapless MacGregor faced a whispering campaign against him from right-wing MPs, which reached the ears of the Prime Minister. The former education minister Tim Eggar, who preceded Clarke at the department by five months, found himself being told forcibly by No. 10 that the Education Act was fine structurally, but that the practical implementation of it was going wrong, and that MacGregor was not robust enough to ring the changes.

It was time to send for Clarke. Mrs Thatcher appointed him in 1990 to bring some common sense to the overall system, and also because he was 'an energetic and persuasive bruiser, very useful in a brawl or an election'.[11] He had forged his reputation for kicking the professions into shape, and she wanted some backbone to be put into a department which she always loathed. Once again, he had to take on vested interests, this time the educational establishment.

It suited Clarke to do so. Not being a theorist, he naturally had little time for educationalists. For the reforms ahead, he cited his own experience, insisting that if he just been born and still lived in Aldercar, then he would have had no more prospect of being called to the Bar than shot to the moon. The system in his days at Nottingham High School, he reflected, gave equality of opportunity to the most academically gifted but neglected the rest. So Clarke's first move was to allow his junior minister Tim Eggar to develop a vocational alternative to an essentially academic curriculum, resulting in new diplomas covering vocational qualifications and the system of national vocational qualifications for people who did not want to specialise too early on in their careers. He was still the anti-snob son of the working class, the minister who would end the distinction between polytechnics and universities and institute for them a single funding council. Against Treasury opposition and despite the recession he won the cash for the expansion of Higher Education. 'Perhaps he doesn't have a philosophy,' Eggar says, 'but he has a very deep sense of outrage at under-achievement – and I think that's something to do with the fact that he's managed to get where he has because of the educational system, and he realised that it was actually the system itself which was failing, not the kids or the parents.'

The new Education Secretary was caught up in the stronger political currents which followed Mrs Thatcher's resignation. The broad-church party which he wanted to preserve was adjusting its faith to a very different style of leadership and contemplating as it did so the general election ahead. If John Major lost, Clarke was tipped as the next leader. His stint at Education was to harm him not at all. As the right wing of the party warmed to Clarke's reforms, his enemies on the benches opposite and in the teaching unions claimed his politics were driven solely by self-interest, that he was positioning himself to take over the leadership he has always sought.

Professional politicians have to adapt to survive, but Clarke disliked his new job. He had given the subject of education little thought since his maiden speech praising Mrs Thatcher. John Clare, education editor of the *Daily Telegraph*, interviewed him a few weeks after he took office and believes that Clarke hated his new department for the first three months: 'He made no bones about it. He had no interest in education, and he was dismayed at being moved from Health, which he knew inside out. He wasn't interested, he really wasn't. To begin with, he was bored.'

Clarke had more than a little homework to do. Not long after his appointment he went to visit the British Academy, which runs, among other things, British schools overseas. On this occasion, according to one of his friends – Lord Renfrew, the Master of Jesus College, Cambridge – 'he hadn't been briefed at all. They told him there was a problem of funding – and he said in his relaxed way, can't you just charge greater fees? Of course, they don't charge fees at all. His officials look appalled.'

As Clarke gradually settled in at Education he introduced his long-held political views about the value of public services and his belief in a classless, meritocratic society. He had sent his children to state primary schools, although he had moved them to fee-paying secondary schools in Birmingham after what he calls 'classic Fabian agonies'. He belonged, he said, to the army of middle-class parents who would like to send their children to state schools but didn't because they thought they would get better education privately. The solution, he felt, was to raise the standards of the state system so that the private sector shrank.

Clarke's problem was that he might know what he wanted to do, but compared with Health, half the levers of power were missing at Education. 'I'm not a centraliser,' he claimed somewhat dis-ingenuously in the *Daily Telegraph*, 'but I'm not sure I have all the powers to control quality, raise standards and direct overall policy.' Teaching was too individual a profession to control. How could he reform the way teachers taught, when the government could not supervise the way they carried out their duties in the classroom?

His first step was to try to raise teaching standards. Within six weeks of taking up his new job, Clarke ordered the 440,000 teachers in England and Wales to submit to regular appraisal of their work for the first time. A week earlier Labour had launched its own education policy, with compulsory teacher appraisal as a central feature. The *Independent* complained: 'Mr Clarke's pitch is that of a salesman who has suddenly discovered that a rival concern has launched a competing product.' Labour's education spokesman Jack Straw had no doubts about what was going on: 'I think the policy unit in Central Office had gone berserk about the fact that I'd stolen a march on them. There was no other explanation why it was done so quickly.'

If Clarke had started with a politically astute move, he also provided a stiffer test for Straw in the House of Commons. Straw felt MacGregor had been vulnerable in debate; Clarke, however, was 'by far the best debater I've opposed on the floor of the House. He's good, no question about that – rumbustious, aggressive, but also he listens to what you have to say. He's more attentive to the argument than almost anybody on their side apart from, say, John Biffen.' Despite this, Clarke still had the same old weakness. He handed Straw a political lifeline with an impetuous intervention in the midst of what could have been an embarrassing debate for the Labour spokesman, and ended up being voted a prat by the readers of a national newspaper.

The background to this saga lies in Clarke's decision to announce that the teachers would be given a pay review body, providing they tacitly agreed not to strike for better pay and conditions in the future. This put Jack Straw in some political difficulty. The Labour Party, as a whole, was in favour of review bodies in principle and he himself had been calling for university academics to be allowed one. But there were strong differences of opinion within the Parliamentary Labour Party about whether the teachers should have one too. Although Straw himself was privately in favour, some MPs backed the stand taken by the National Union of Teachers against the idea. Straw's judgement was that he didn't have the support within the party to back the review body, but that by not supporting one he would be exposed to Tory attacks. Somehow, he had to survive a debate on the issue in the House of Commons. His solution was to prepare a speech which dealt with everything except the subject in hand.

Straw hit upon the idea of quoting an interview Clarke had given to *Woman* magazine which had been picked up by the *Daily Mirror*. Here Clarke had repeated his view that the standard of private education was higher than that of the state sector. But he did so by attacking his political opponents, who criticised Tory MPs for not following their example in sending their offspring to state schools: 'In most cases, I regard that as either hypocrisy or sacrificing their children to promote their own political careers. I have never met anybody who did not wish to send their children into independent education if they could.' It was consistent with Clarke's belief that the standards of state education needed raising, but it was also infelicitously expressed, and Straw seized upon the *Daily Mirror*'s report to dig himself out of his debating hole in the Commons.

Clarke was quick to react to Straw's intervention, too quick. 'He just popped up, intervened, as he often does, ever so quickly, and said that the *Mirror* was read by morons,' recalls Straw. He made sure one of his colleagues slipped out of the chamber to tell the newspaper what had happened.

The *Mirror* exceeded all his expectations. Striking out for the high ground of moral outrage and tabloid humour, it made sure in no uncertain terms and very large capital letters that its readers knew what Clarke called them: MORONS ('That's two fingers to 8,230,000 voters, Minister'). Clarke was pictured looking suitably unstatesman-like with his eyes shut and a large cigar in hand. Politicians should probably never smoke. They should certainly never blink.

Worse was to follow. The next day, the *Mirror* organised its own telephone poll to discover what its readers thought of Clarke. The predictable result was announced with a banner headline and a front-page spread: 'Kenneth Clarke was voted a total PRAT last night as 59,000 *Daily Mirror* readers took part in one of the most fiercely fought elections for years. The result of the phone poll came as a shock to those convinced roly-poly Education Secretary would be returned to Westminster as a MORON.' Forty-eight hours before the local elections, the *Mirror* was able to give its printers some practice at tabulating results. Thus:

> K. Clarke (Prat) 38,666
> K. Clarke (Moron) 21,855
> Prat maj 15,111

This time Clarke was pictured, as he had been at Health, with a drink as well as a cigar but he was given a dunce's hat, too. He was, the paper declared, the identikit picture of a moron himself – an overweight bully with a beer belly who smoked too much. He also appeared to have been eating solidly since he was Heath Secretary; the paper declared, with surprising precision, that he now weighed 16 st 8 lb.

Two serious points emerged from this tomfoolery. First, in his eagerness to engage the enemy, Clarke had handed a public relations victory to the Labour Party in its hour of need. As Tom King says: 'My only reservation about him is his readiness to cross the road if he sees a chance of picking a fight with somebody. It's not gratuitous violence – it's when he sees something he disagrees with strongly but other people might find it easier to pass by. Sometimes I think he's seduced by a smart line or two and he stirs offence where it isn't needed.'

Second, Clarke was not at all upset by the publicity. His friend Robert Atkins, then sports minister at the Department of Education, remembers: 'He came into work holding the front page of the *Mirror* in his hand and laughing his head off. Most ministers would go white with anger if they'd been given that sort of treatment. But he thought it was the funniest thing he'd seen.' The only time Atkins has seen Clarke angry with the media is when the *Financial Times* implied that he only pretended to be interested in cricket, though Clarke will also flare if he thinks his family is the subject of unwarranted media attention. Atkins describes him as having 'the highest boiling point of anyone in politics. The only way you ever know he's worried about something is when his eyes flick from side to side quite quickly.'

The battleground which lay ahead was enough to make any minister's eyes flick from side to side. Clarke saw clearly that the national curriculum and the tests it demanded were over-prescriptive, leaving teachers with more and more administration and less and less time to teach. Within three months of his arrival, he signalled a retreat. To try to slim down the national curriculum he decided that the full quota of ten subjects would be taught only to children aged up to fourteen, and not sixteen as originally intended. If it pleased the teachers, it was a first shot across the bows of the educational establishment; it ignored the advice of the National Curriculum Council.

The detailed syllabuses of some subjects which were to be studied under the national curriculum still had to be settled. Once more Clarke ignored the National Curriculum Council's advice when he banned quasi-political issues from geography, ruling that it must rely on facts, not opinions. He battled hard against the Schools Examination and Assessment Council too, to try to persuade it to dock GCSE marks for bad spelling. Clarke's concern was for the traditional educational basics: 'We believe that education does require children to learn facts, to learn real skills and to work hard at their lessons and homework.'[12]

In this last respect, no subject was more controversial than history. Mrs Thatcher, despite being – or perhaps because she was – a chemist by training, had held firm views on the subject, and wanted a Gradgrind approach which relied on hard facts, rather than historical skills. Clarke, who had studied medieval history at school, held equally firm views; history was something which happened in the past and came to a full stop in the 1960s. He felt there was a tendency throughout the curriculum to focus on the present day: part of a mistaken philosophy, as he saw it, that pupils had to study their immediate environment. He was also worried about the politicisation of lessons drawn from contemporary events. So in what appeared to be a surreal pastiche of *1066 and All That* he decreed that United States history ended in 1963 with the death of President Kennedy and Soviet history in 1964 with the fall of Khrushchev. Everything else Clarke deemed to be current affairs. His view was that pupils should not be legally required to study contemporary events and people, because of the difficulty of gaining a historical perspective. Eventually, he allowed the cut-off point to be a constant twenty years behind the present day, with the syllabus updating itself once every five years; in about the year 2010, therefore, British history will officially end with Mrs Thatcher's resignation.

Clarke's move to bring history to a full-stop in the 1960s was controversial, attracting opprobrium from Left and Right in equal measure. Headteachers objected; and so did the Centre for Policy Studies, arguing that he was outlawing traditional history and that his proposals were too detailed. The man who had set up the education reforms, Kenneth Baker, was not impressed either and he feels it was too rigid a demarcation to make. Overall, he considers that Clarke probably had no real feel for or deep interest in education: 'I think Ken would have turned his mind to it. But I don't think he was interested in the conceptual questions of what should be studied and how it should be studied. He's much more a nuts-and-bolts man.'

Clarke knew what he wanted, however, and if he wasn't given the answers he required then he simply ignored the findings of his advisers. He believes, John Gummer observes, 'that there's more than one way of skinning a cat, so those who tell him otherwise are probably wrong. And he's got a self-confidence which says I am not going to be led by the nose. His argument on education would be, "I'm not interested in the pupil–teacher ratio, what I want to know is do you have teachers who teach well?"'

No sooner had the government's own working group on physical education completed its report, for example, than Clarke criticised it. The group was chaired by the headmaster of Harrow, Ian Beer, and included such sporting luminaries as the athlete Steve Ovett and the footballer John Fashanu. It came out with a 76-page report, placing sporting activities in six different categories and arguing its case with exactly the kind of overblown language that Clarke detests. Expeditions were important, the report's authors considered, because they were 'a fundamental way of developing an appreciation and awareness of, and caring attitudes to, the environment'. Barely was the ink dry before Clarke declared the report to be ridden with jargon and over-prescriptive for such a practical subject.

It became clear that Clarke was heading for some sort of showdown with his advisers in the two quangos set up by Baker, the National Curriculum Council and the Schools Examination and Assessment Council. Clarke saw them as the educational establishment and part of the problem. He felt government policy was not being implemented properly and he wanted his hands on the levers of power to get people in place who would deliver what he wanted: a traditional approach, not the liberal progressive orthodoxy. 'The curriculum was too detailed,' he says, 'but it wasn't detail that ministers had guided.' The clash led to the resignation of Duncan Graham, who was chairman and chief executive of the National Curriculum Council.

Graham had been appointed by Baker in 1988. Three years on, he had offended ministers and staff. Clarke saw him as too autocratic and too complex in his instructions to schools. A minister who saw the national curriculum as overblown did not want a rival source of power. So he split Graham's job and made a senior executive with British Petroleum, David Pascall, the new chairman. Pascall had been a member of the No. 10 Policy Unit for a year and was therefore a known political quantity. Kenneth Baker says the move was unfair: 'Ken and his Ministers had become impatient with the complex detail and prescriptive nature of the curriculum. But . . . vagueness and lack of detail will allow an inadequate and lazy teacher to skip important parts.'[13] Intriguingly, it is exactly the charge that Clarke makes against Baker:

> Ken Baker's reforms were the best thing he ever did, but Ken is not a details man. I do believe despite my reputation that the devil is in the detail. He had set up all these bloody specialist committees to guide the curriculum, he'd set up quango staff who as far as I could see had come out of the Inner London Education Authority, the lot of them. There wasn't anybody there who agreed with the government's approach to education at all.

A week after Duncan Graham's departure, Clarke moved against the Schools Examination and Assessment Council. Out went the career civil servant who headed it, Philip Halsey, a man who belonged to the 1960s educational establishment which Baker had tried to appease by setting up the working groups. In came another No. 10 adviser, Lord Griffiths of Fforestfach. Clarke, the minister who had told Mrs Thatcher to her face that she must go, had now appointed the man who had advised her for five years. 'I was always struck by the irony that Griffiths had been Mrs Thatcher's creature,' remarks Jack Straw. 'They get rid of her and hey presto! Griffiths is in a more powerful position than he's ever been.' But Clarke knew that Griffiths had shared Mrs Thatcher's view that Baker's invention was too cumbersome a machine. 'A hugely bureaucratic system of assessment was being piled on top of a hugely over-prescriptive curriculum,' he says.

Besides having to tackle the two quangos, Clarke found that officials in his own department were blocking his moves. To quote one of his advisers:

> There were some very strong personalities dominating the place. It was a disaffected department, with officials who'd been there twenty years, autocrats really, absolutely determined to have their way. And you'd had a series of ministers in there who'd just

wanted a quiet life. You couldn't believe it, going into this department and seeing what was going on. It was appalling.

Clarke set out to dominate the department through the force of his personality, although he wasn't completely successful. He had to have two civil servants suspended when he discovered that they had been deliberately subverting his policies. There was much he wanted to change.

By mid-1991 Clarke had come to the conclusion that reading tests for seven-year-olds had to be drastically simplified. The tests should stay, he argued, so that parents could measure their children's progress. But he also recognised that the tests were too time-consuming for the teachers to carry out in addition to their standard classroom duties. Nowhere was Clarke's exasperation with educational experts seen more clearly than here. He rejected out of hand the intricate reading test drawn up by the Schools Examination and Assessment Council. Teachers and educationalists kept telling him, he complained, that there was more to reading than decoding the written word; they wanted a test which also took account of whether children read for enjoyment. But to Clarke the layman, the test had to be quite simple: a child should pick up a piece of writing which he or she hadn't seen before and read it.

In 1994 the chairman designate of the Schools Curriculum and Examinations Council, Sir Ron Dearing, delivered what was in effect an indictment of the national curriculum and school tests. In an 86-page report he declared that the curriculum had to be slimmed down so that it did not occupy the whole of the school timetable, and that the content of all but the three core subjects should be substantially cut. National testing was to be limited to English, maths and science and further simplified. Clarke had identified these problems but, by the time he moved on, he hadn't cured them all: 'I think we were coming along all right; I didn't make nearly as much progress as I would have liked in simplifying the form of the tests.'

Was Clarke a great escapologist, as critics maintained of Kenneth Baker, a minister who was never in one place long enough to reap the consequences of his own actions, leaving others to clear up the mess? Tim Eggar says no:

It was a question of the speed at which you could actually force a rethink. We were trying to simplify at the quickest pace we thought the teachers and the educational establishment would buy and it was always a very difficult matter of judgement how you did it. The single most important thing he did was getting the judgement right about the pace of change that would be acceptable.

But Mike Baker, education correspondent of the BBC, disagrees: 'He successfully diverted attention from the growing problems of the national curriculum and testing, but he did nothing to deal with the fundamental contradictions, particularly over testing, which were to cause problems for his successor. He had also driven teachers nearer to the point where even the more moderate of them were ready to resist.'

As well as sorting out the national curriculum, Clarke needed to make himself politically acceptable to the right wing of the party, who had made John MacGregor's life so difficult. Nowhere did this seem clearer than in his assault on the falling literacy standards in primary education. David Hart, of the headteachers' association, says:

My reading of his period as Education Secretary is that he went in with his credentials with the right wing not very well founded, and he used his time to establish those credentials. He went to Education unwillingly, and to make the best of the move he made it his prime objective to say and do things which found favour with the Right.

Later, however, Clarke assembled a powerful education manifesto group, drawn from a broad spectrum of the party.

The symbol of the apparent fall in educational standards was a modest primary school in East London. When the BBC ran a television series on a trendy primary school in Tower Hamlets it seemed that all was well in the world of progressive education. The six-part documentary, *Culloden: A Year in the Life of a City Primary School*, praised the headmaster's modern methods. Children called teachers by their first names and there were no traditional spelling tests or structured reading schemes. Children, in their mixed-ability and mixed-age classes, were merely surrounded by books in the hope that they would read them. It was about as far away from Clarke's own primary school experience in Aldercar and Bulwell as it was from Dotheboys Hall.

The *Mail on Sunday* took it upon itself to investigate this phenomenon and discovered, with a mixture of horror and delight, that half the seven-year-olds at Culloden could hardly read at all. Clarke instantly sent in school inspectors to carry out a more thorough investigation. They found that reading standards were poor in ten out of the fourteen classes, with average and less able pupils doing particularly badly. Two-thirds of the 400 pupils could not read properly. Clarke saw the wider political message at once; he needed to join battle over the whole direction of primary education and teaching methods.

The Education Secretary set his eyes on dismantling what the *Daily Mail* dubbed 'the trendy learn-as-you-play philosophy' of the 1960s. He began to earn headlines praising his back-to-basics approach two years before John Major adopted the message to try to unite a Tory Party divided over Europe. It is not that Clarke invented the slogan and gave it to the party; that honour rests with the head of the No. 10 policy unit, Sarah Hogg. But Clarke embraced the phrase at Education long before Major announced it at the 1993 party conference as his big idea. For Clarke, it means a return to practical common sense, an end to doctrinal political views. He announced an inquiry into 'progressive' teaching methods, to be headed by Professor Robin Alexander of Leeds University. It was an inquiry of sorts; Clarke already knew the answer he was going to get.

A few months earlier, in the summer of 1991, Professor Alexander had published the results of a detailed five-year study of more than 230 progressive primary schools in Leeds. He found that on average children were wasting 40 per cent of the school day: 21 per cent of the day totally distracted, 11 per cent on routine activities such as putting away books and 8 per cent waiting for the teacher's attention. He blamed group teaching for this apparent decline in purposeful activity.

Clarke gave Professor Alexander just two months to carry out his investigation but announced what he would do with the team's findings within two weeks of its starting work: 'I shall use that evidence to instigate a wide-ranging reform of teacher training colleges.'[14] The inquiry was a fig-leaf for a solution he had already decided upon.

Clarke wanted to dislodge the child-centred classroom philosophy which had dominated primary education since the Plowden Report of 1967. That report had become part of the established order of things; Lady Plowden had been a Conservative member of the Inner London Education Authority and much of her report had been implemented by the local education authorities when Mrs Thatcher was Education Secretary. Lady Plowden had suggested that children should take part in project-based learning so that they could find things out for themselves. But her critics argued that children could not be taught properly this way. Clarke said drily that he did not object in principle to pupils sticking egg boxes together, but not when they couldn't add up or read a sentence correctly. It was also a stick with which to beat what he called the 'eccentric Left' and local politicians who were 'silent allies to this subversion of standards'.[15]

Needing to tackle the way teachers taught in future, and unable to influence them in the classroom, Clarke had to tackle them at source. In October 1991 therefore he formally announced the overhaul of teacher training colleges to force students to spend more of their time in the classroom and less of it learning theory. These colleges had been the object of sustained criticism from the Conservative Right, which had long championed their reform during the Thatcher years. Clarke's dislike of union power, combined with his long-held distaste for overblown theories, merged seamlessly into a policy which made personal and political sense. It was hard to see the join between political expediency and personal conviction.

Clarke also pleased the right wing of his party with another of his long-held views – that most local authorities were barely competent. Education was seen as a crisis area for the Tories, he declared, because central government did not have adequate control over a localised school system. Education, like health, could be improved by better use of resources, not greater spending. Accordingly, a welter of Clarke-influenced schemes reduced the power of local education authorities to interfere in the running of their schools. It was entirely in character. Like Mrs Thatcher, he was prepared to grant local autonomy only so long as he could retain (and centralise) power in his own hands. It was also the way he ran the Education Department, as Robert Atkins observes: 'He has a remarkable talent to delegate to his junior ministers, and he'll back you all the way. But he's also a centralist, which is surprising in a delegator.'

'Monolithic uniformity', Clarke pronounced, 'is the curse of giant public services.'[16] The end-game, as he saw it, was to allow schools to develop their own character in response to the wishes of parents and the local communities they served, subject to his own central guidelines. By his definition, therefore, local authorities were not sufficiently responsive to local needs; they were too concerned with their own bureaucracy: 'Until we started on the reforms . . . if you wanted a window repaired, you had to ring up County Hall to get them to do it. Some councils employed more people in the head office than they employed in all their classrooms put together . . . I keep saying to people from local government, "stop defending your bureaucractic empires".'[17] Clarke also removed all further education colleges and sixth-form colleges from local government control, a move affecting some two million students. It was an important move which, as the years go by, will increasingly blur the distinction between further and higher education. Partly this was to try to liberalise and equalise educational opportunity; but partly it was the result of political prejudice against local authorities. The man who had been so shocked by local politics on coming down from Cambridge remained true to his beliefs.

'I used to think he had been dropped on his head by a Tory councillor when he was a kid, because he hated them,' comments Jack Straw. 'I remember we were having a negotiation because they were running out of time for a bill, and he asked me what my price was. I said giving the local authorities back some power, and he said "Good God! You really do care about them don't you?" – as if no sane person of either party would be interested in them. He just loathes them.'

At Education, Clarke continued to win the cheers of the Right and he seemed to court the right-wing tabloid newspapers. In a gushing *Daily Mail* interview, where political reporting appeared to meet Mills & Boon, he hinted at the move on sixth-form colleges the day before it happened: 'The whiff of revolution was in the air last night, as Education Secretary Kenneth Clarke contemplated the impending fulfilment of a dream. Puffing contentedly on a Cuban cigar, the man at the centre of the storm exuded a calm confidence.'

New plans to change the way school inspections were run also pleased the right wing. As Clarke's contribution to the Citizen's Charter, he decided to convert Her Majesty's Inspectorate into a licensing agency, which would supervise the quality of inspectors, where before it had carried out the inspections itself. In future, instead of local authorities and HMI inspecting schools, Clarke intended that the schools should purchase regular inspections, perhaps every four years. School governors would be able to buy these inspections from any agency approved by HMI.

The Education (Schools) Bill which proposed the changes to HMI was the produce of an internal review set up by Clarke in the summer of 1991, which led to criticism that the review was once again a vehicle for confirming a decision Clarke had already taken. His aim, he said, was to enhance the independence of the inspectorate, while making it more flexible to deal with grant-maintained schools and the newly independent further education colleges. It was, he maintained, part and parcel of delegating management responsibility to schools. In effect, it was a market-led solution to reforming an inspectorate which was held to be too small for its task, while circumventing the local authorities, which were held to be too incompetent. In this brave new world of the privatised market, governing bodies would be the purchasers, the free-standing inspectorate the providers. As in health, so in education.

Part of the problem, as Clarke saw it, was that parents were being deprived of vital information about schools, inhibiting their ability to make judgements about their children's education. His Parents' Charter sought not only to reform HMI but to establish an annual written report on pupil performance, as well as league tables of schools based on examination results, national curriculum tests and truancy rates. A new system of national records of achievement was to be instituted, providing a summary of every school-leaver's education, training and work experience. All this was, once again, the sound and fury of a minister tackling vested interests. 'For too long', Clarke asserted, 'education has not been open enough to the ordinary person. The operation of schools has been a closed shop that can only be entered by those already inside.'[18]

But was it fair and reasonable to try to inject the market into what was a public-sector responsibility, making schools act like private companies in hiring their own auditors when they were in fact public institutions? Clarke's imperative was clear: efficiency, again, but also dismantling the educational establishment and demystifying the profession. He wanted parents to be given a 'short, easily intelligible, jargon-free summary', followed by a statement of how the governors intended to act upon the advice of the inspectors.

Against that, however, Clarke's own review had praised the work of HMI, putting forward the option of expanding it to cope with the new demand. But its size would have to quadruple, and an enlarged version of the organisation was not to be contemplated by a man who detests bureaucracy. Local authority advisers and inspectors, opined Clarke in a television interview, were, in the view of teachers, people who could not teach 'and therefore become inspectors, or are out-of-date, or do not know enough about actual classroom experience'. Instead, the system had to be localised. Unfortunately, it was not at all clear that private inspectors would be dispassionate, objective and independent of the institutions being inspected, as the review had demanded. Schools were, in effect, being asked to be both poachers and gamekeepers.

In the end, the House of Lords defeated Clarke's plan to allow school governing bodies the right to choose and pay their own inspectors. Clarke blamed this on heavy lobbying by the unions, but there was a rare united front in the Lords against him.

Why had Clarke lumbered himself with this scheme? The idea for private competing inspectorates had originated with the Centre for Policy Studies, and one paper, published by the chief schools inspector for Mrs Thatcher's favourite council, Wandsworth, actually called for HMI to be broken up just as Clarke proposed. Was Clarke playing to the Right, therefore, in case Major lost the general election, a left-winger courting right-wing support? His opponents had no doubt; one Labour front-bencher says:

I think it was partly his gut instinct that something had gone wrong with the education system and partly cynicism, but he certainly listened very carefully to what the Tory Right was saying. People like Bob Dunn and Jim Pawsey were like pigs in shit.[19] They were over the moon that they'd got rid of MacGregor, so Ken set about trying to put into practice the right-wing agenda.

In fact, Clarke distanced himself from the hard-Right 'No Turning Back' group of Tory MPs by stating clearly that privatisation was a 'half-baked' solution for state-provided public services; but he was so trenchant in his political presentation, so pugnacious in the reforms he instituted, that the Right was convinced by what it saw and heard. He did not cynically back measures with which he disagreed purely to attract right-wing backing, yet he could read the political wind better than most and promoted those measures with which he knew the Right would agree. His favourite themes of efficiency, good management and less bureaucracy would naturally appeal to the party as a whole – nothing to do with the right wing, his adviser Tessa Keswick insists: 'He just believed that children were being short-changed on education. He went to Japan and saw enormous classes being taught in run-down shacks. But they could all read, write and add up. He's a man with common sense. He believes in really good education for the public, and that it can be delivered in a very straightforward way.' Equally, Clarke was not a consolidator, and that appealed to the Right; he still saw himself as a latter-day Iain Macleod, active, aggressive and partisan, a man who never said steady as she goes. But then Macleod's political thinking was sometimes the product of the day's debate.[20]

A curious little awards ceremony in London highlighted how far Clarke had squared the political circle. Near the end of his stay at Education, he was fêted by the Radical Society, of which Norman Tebbit was a founder member, as its Radical of the Year. Specifically, he was praised for ending the distinction between polytechnics and universities, perhaps his most forward-looking move as Education Secretary, in the encouragement it offered to students. Clarke accepted the award with some surprise and humour:

Why is a wet receiving [this award]? . . . I am one of the few survivors of the 'Long March' of the Thatcher years . . . but I always read that I was never 'one of us'. My relations with Margaret Thatcher were always, and remain, friendly and combative . . . but I was never a soulmate in the Norman Tebbit mould. Why am I being honoured in this temple of the intellectual New Right?

The answer, continued Clarke, was that the Tories had been brought closer together by the banal left-wing ideologies of the educational establishment. They were radicals all, he insisted, as politicians who wanted drastic change to restore common sense to the classrooms. Yet there was a deeper truth, which Clarke failed to mention: simply, that he was a skilful politician who played his hand on the issues which the party might support. If a measure in which he believed was politically feasible (and thus to his advantage), then the message was trumpeted loud and long.

This strategy seemed to work to Clarke's advantage. Norman Tebbit now backed him as the champion of the Thatcherites for his ability to appeal to the electorally vital 'C2' socio-economic class which had supported Mrs Thatcher but was threatening to desert John Major. It made Clarke a key contender for the leadership if Major fell at the next election.

Much, it seemed, could be achieved both personally and politically in the name of efficiency and common sense.

CHAPTER 13

Into the Jungle

*There are three classes which need sanctuary more than others – birds, wild
flowers, and Prime Ministers.*

Stanley Baldwin

On the corner of Queen Anne's Gate and Petty France, near St James's
Park in central London, there lies a charnel house. It is not designed as
one – indeed, the grey uniformity of this vast concrete structure
appears to owe more to the school of Russian hotel architecture. But a
charnel house it is, for this is the Home Office and in it lie the bones of
Home Secretaries brought down by events which fell within their
empires but beyond their control.

The Home Office is a curiosity. To be Home Secretary is to hold one
of the three great offices of state, but it is also the dustbin of politics
where the rubbish from everyday life may suddenly be tipped. Both
Kenneth Baker, with the Brixton Prison break-out, and before him
David Waddington, with the Strangeways riot, found to their cost the
difficulty of dealing with the political litter of the unexpected. In fact,
since the Second World War, only Jim Callaghan has managed to
survive the Home Office and reach the top.

So when Kenneth Clarke was sent to the Home Office after John
Major's surprise general election victory in 1992, it was a mixed
blessing. At last, after two decades on the Tory front benches, his
ambition had been rewarded with a leading Cabinet post, but at the
same time he needed to avoid having his bones interred at Queen
Anne's Gate. The former defence minister Alan Clark thought that
was precisely what John Major was aiming for: 'I may credit him with
being too Machiavellian, but it looked obvious to me. It was a clever
trick which had the fingerprints of the Chief Whip, Richard Ryder, all

over it. No one has ever emerged from the Home Office to lead the Tory Party, because it doesn't like Home Secretaries.'[1] Major understandably, denies that was his intent: 'I was in no doubt that the sleeping giant of issues out there, despite the recession, was people's understandable concern about crime. I share that concern. So I wanted a tough politician at the Home Office who would look at that issue and draft us some long-term policies.'

That Clarke survived the Home Office is a tribute to his political skill but also to the government's manifest weakness and his consequent luck in being moved on. In this period, he became less like a Home Secretary in charge of humdrum policy and more the chief defence counsel for John Major. As the ERM crisis crippled the credibility of the government, Clarke was increasingly seen as its strong man, prepared to defend it in any fight, no matter how tough the odds against him. His barristerial skills were brought firmly into play in support of his beleaguered Prime Minister. It suited his character. According to Jim Lester: 'He's a guy who you'd go into the jungle with, as we say in the Commons. He can bully or be rough, but with a smile on his face.'

Under his new leader, there was plenty of jungle for Clarke to explore, far beyond the range of his brief, and with Mrs Thatcher gone there was no one to match his hyperbolic skills. He seemed to have an uncanny knack of defusing issues through acute phraseology alone. The one-liners which had caused so much trouble when Clarke was on the attack in the health disputes now, defensively deployed, found their range. When the security services were accused of bugging the Prince and Princess of Wales to eavesdrop on their marital break-down, causing a political stir, Clarke retorted that it was more likely that the Archbishop of Canterbury was a mugger, which was the cause of mutual hilarity when the two met a few days later at the FA Cup Final. Clarke's critics failed to laugh. The question they would later pose was how far he had deliberately exploited the government's signal weakness to demonstrate his own strength.

Almost at once, there was a minor trial of strength with Norman Lamont. Lamont wanted to live in the Home Office flat while No. 11 underwent repairs, but the flat traditionally went with the job of Home Secretary. While the Clarkes and the Lamonts awaited a ruling, a woman in the Home Office told Clarke to move in, saying: 'I'm damned if Norman Lamont's going to move in, so you'd better. Possession is nine-tenths of the law.' He took the advice.

Clarke says that he expected to stay as Home Secretary for a long time and that he was appointed by Major with the 'clear purpose' of restoring public confidence in the effectiveness of the criminal justice system and to develop a new relationship of trust between the public and the police. The Conservatives had poured money into the open hands of the police for fourteen years but had little to show for it. Their 1992 manifesto claimed they now spent 74 per cent more in real terms on the police than they had in 1979. Yet recorded crime had risen to an all-time high. Crucially, a series of miscarriages of justice, especially in terrorist cases, had undermined public confidence in the police. Clarke also needed to get better value for money. There were new pressures on public spending, and the Treasury was warning that it would no longer pay billions of pounds for the criminal justice system without testing whether the cash was well spent.

The battles that followed had a familiar echo. Such was Clarke's reputation that even before he uttered a word the Police Federation sounded the alarm, fearing that he was preparing tough reforms to get better value from the £5 billion police budget. Clarke wasn't worried: 'I don't mind being seen as someone who takes on established interests. But I don't see myself as a robust bully, which my opponents call me. I think I am very laid back, but politics is a controversial business – and the one thing I have always had are very clear views of what I wanted to do.' He called on the police to show greater professionalism and integrity, to restore public confidence in the force. It was his 'gut instinct', he said, that 'middle England' wanted to see such a change.

There could be no doubt that something had gone wrong with the way the police were run. Pay had risen sharply since 1979 because of the Tories' implementation of the Edmund-Davies proposals, which gave the police an annual index-linked award. But despite the high levels of remuneration, successive reports had found that the quality of police recruits was poor, with brighter candidates put off by the need to rise through the ranks before gaining the top jobs.

As in the health service, labour costs made up most of the budget. Clarke saw the police service as a professional closed shop. However, because of the specialised nature of its work, he could not separate purchasers from providers as he had at Health. Instead, the stage was set for him, once more, to outline his favourite theme: that there was no automatic link between the level of spending and efficiency – even if for fourteen years that spending had been by his own government. It meant tackling the police head on. 'I'll say one thing for him,' declares one Labour front-bencher, 'he'll identify what's wrong and go for it. I can't imagine a Labour Home Secretary taking on the police like he did.'

Clarke moved stealthily at first. After little more than a month in office, on 20 May 1992, he travelled to Scarborough to make his first major speech, at the Police Federation's annual conference. What he would say was a closely guarded secret, and when he stood up to address the conference the 2,000 officers in the audience had no idea what was coming. They feared the worst, presenting Clarke with a fluffy toy dog, more in hope than expectation that he would belie what they termed his 'Rottweiler' reputation. Clarke rose to deliver his speech amid total silence. 'The first thing I had to decide as Home Secretary', he recalls, 'was what to do about police pay. I either got out of it now or I never got out of it. So I went to the conference and said I'm setting up this inquiry.' He left to thunderous applause.

Clarke had launched a charm offensive. In a skilfully worded speech he paid frequent tribute to police diligence and commitment. Interwoven with his fulsome praise and camouflaged by his affable manner, he slipped in a fundamental review of police pay, rank, structure and responsibilities. He had proposed one of the biggest shake-ups in the history of the police. As with the Budget speech he would deliver eighteen months later, his audience realised what had been said only too late.

Calling in Sir Patrick Sheehy to investigate the police was, on the face of it, like asking the Pope to investigate the Anglican Church; it required a leap of faith and imagination. Sir Patrick, a friend of Clarke's, was chairman of the tobacco giant BAT Industries. He knew as much about the way the police operated as any businessman, which was next to nothing. But that was the whole point of the exercise for Clarke. Like the health service and the education system, the police were just another business, which could be run on business lines. Although the police service was a national one which could not and should not be privatised, it could nevertheless be opened up to the forces of private-sector efficiency. Who better to investigate the service than a rank outsider, especially one Clarke already knew and whose managerial skills he respected? Anything less, and the vested interest – for such it was to Clarke – would strangle reform at birth. The Home Office minister Peter Lloyd backed the move: 'If you want to investigate an organisation you don't use people who've grown up in it. He wanted a clear, logical, well-thought-out view from business-men with proven management expertise, unadulterated by remarks like, "Well, I've been in the force for fifty years and I can tell you it's not going to work." '

Clarke wanted the Sheehy inquiry to devise a replacement for the 'rigid and inflexible' system of determining annual awards for the service. He did not see why weak or lazy officers should hide behind the talented ones, or why they should be protected by a national agreement. Pay had to match individual achievement. 'We must aim to make the police more effective and more efficient,' he said.

There would, of course, be a political price to pay. The police, like the teachers and the doctors before them, would resent a businessman coming in and telling them what to do. They would argue, maybe even hold rallies against reform, but at the end of the battle Clarke aimed to take more ground in one lightning attack than he could ever gain from years of patient negotiation. If he was beaten back, forced to give ground here and there, he would still hold more of the enemy's territory than when he had started. It was a well-known Clarke tactic. As he had remarked at the end of the ambulance strike: 'I'm a classic politician. Two steps forward, one step back.'[2]

Clarke was fighting simultaneously on another front. He decided to tackle the police service not just over pay and conditions but over its operational and administrative structure, too. Unsurprisingly, that meant finding some way to reduce the powers of local councillors, who had firm control over the budget of every police force in the country, except for the Metropolitan force.

Clarke wanted to end the tripartite agreement under which forces were jointly controlled by the Home Secretary, chief constables and the county police committees, replacing the system instead with centralised management from Whitehall. To do this, he suggested that elected councillors should be replaced by businessmen. He believed that police authorities, which by law were made up mainly by elected councillors and magistrates, lacked political and managerial skills. Their remit, he argued, was vague, and they needed strengthening to become truly accountable. He wanted stronger, depoliticised authorities, with fewer police forces to run, achieved through the merger of the smaller ones. In time, under a new Home Secretary, Michael Howard, the House of Lords would force the government to climb down on some of the proposed changes to the police authorities.

This was not out-and-out centralisation, nor out-and-out empowerment of the local great and good. True, Clarke was prepared to delegate to local people, but they would be subject to his strengthened control, through direct funding from the Home Office; once again he was tackling what he saw as the inadequacies of local government, and investing his hopes in the efficiency of the business community. The language of business was important to him. He told the Association of Chief Police Officers that ' "getting it right first and every time" is one of the stock phrases of quality management'.[3]

Businessmen have been held in high esteem by Clarke throughout his ministerial career. When he was Health Secretary he appointed three leading industrialists to the NHS board: Sir Graham Day, chairman of the Rover Group (known to Clarke from his time at the DTI); Sir Kenneth Durham, chairman of Kingfisher Holdings and deputy chairman of British Aerospace; and Sir Robert Scholey, chairman of British Steel. Clarke saw them as formidable figures who had shown their ability to run giant organisations. He also replaced twenty-eight health authority chairmen with Tory appointees, who were mainly councillors or businessmen, so that by March 1990 there were only four Labour chairmen left in 190 posts. According to one Health Department insider: 'He is a leading exponent of the Stalinist side of the Tory Party. He castrated the Regional Health Authority chairmen.' This showed, Clarke's critics argued, that he only appointed people who might give him the answer he wanted in the first place. 'It's all down to his time at Trade and Industry,' explains one former minister. 'He met a load of rabid business people. They wined and dined him, and he fell for it.'

If so, Clarke was also following the instinctive approach he had adopted at Education, of demystifying a profession and providing the general public with information on which it could judge performance.

At an Audit Commission conference in March 1993 he announced that league tables would be drawn up to show which police forces were performing the best in areas such as crime detection, response to 999 calls and the reduction of complaints. He called his policies today's new radicalism: 'The new accountability that we seek from our public services will not be achieved simply because men of good will and reasonableness wish it to be so. The new accountability is the new radicalism. And vested interests will always oppose radicalism.'[4]

By now the police were in full protest about the Sheehy inquiry. One senior member of the service, the President of the Association of Chief Police Officers, John Burrow, denounced plans to merge police forces as madness. It was possibly the most critical statement ever made by an ACPO chief about a Tory Home Secretary. Given Clarke's natural propensities, conflict seemed inevitable.

With war about to break out on two fronts, however, Clarke made a pragmatic retreat. He backed away from the idea of merging smaller forces in favour of legislative changes 'when the time is right'. This was a political U-turn born of experience:

> It was a question of how much you could get through at a time. I actually do think quite strongly that you should amalgamate the police forces but it's a question of how much you can carry through at once with a small majority in government and an uncertain political climate. You can sell most things to the general public but if you start to challenge local loyalties you can get yourself into really dangerous, populist politics.

Clarke's tactics were seen at Westminster as a balancing act, influenced by his desire to replace Norman Lamont as Chancellor. If the plans had been too radical, the battle could have defeated his hopes of preferment. His colleagues, such as adviser Tessa Keswick, deny this: 'Some politicians might think like that, but this man doesn't think in those terms. Do politicians really think about policy and say to themselves, "I'm going to do this and then someone's going to make me Chancellor of the Exchequer"? It just doesn't work like that. You can ruin yourself so quickly by taking that position. He backed off merging police forces because clearly it was a political nightmare – territorial disputes always are.'

By now the findings of the Sheehy inquiry were beginning to leak out. The *Daily Telegraph* disclosed that Sheehy would propose performance-related pay for the police and scrap their index-linked pay formula. There would be no 'jobs for life' but fixed-term contracts instead. This was no surprise; it had been Clarke's clear intent from the start, but it pitched his relations with the police to a new low. This time, when he went to address the annual Police Federation conference, in Blackpool on 19 May 1993, he did not escape lightly. He tried to reassure the delegates that he wanted to reform the structure of the police service, not its members, but he was jeered and heckled during his speech. Sergeant Michael Bennett of the Metropolitan Police told the conference that putting Clarke in charge of the police 'is like putting King Herod in charge of Mothercare . . . Kenneth Clarke is an arrogant, rude, social snob, an autocrat who would struggle in the modern business world.'

Clarke has been accused of many things in his political career, but he is not a snob, and it was a sign of how bad relations were with the police that they should think him one. He had been anticipating a row, specifically over his plans to make it easier to sack incompetent officers, which was his sticking point; but he didn't go out of his way to keep relations sweet. Bennett recalls how Clarke once ignored the police representatives who came to see him in his office, turning his back on them and reading the *Daily Telegraph* instead. Tom King recognises this trait in Clarke: 'The truth is that you've got weaknesses among chief constables, you've got time-servers, you've got them in all ranks, but at the same time you've got a hell of a lot of very good people and if you offend them all then everything becomes more difficult.'

Generally, however, this was how Clarke had treated the doctors, the ambulance crews and the teachers. Reform, he considered, had to be driven through. There was no point in pussy-footing around. 'I hold the establishment in the post-war British public services in a very low regard,' he says.[5] Nor was he a man for a conciliatory gesture which might have eased relations; for example, he ruled out trials of an American side-handled baton, which the police wanted, because of its 'extremely aggressive appearance'. When Michael Howard took over the Home Office, one of his first acts was to allow the trials to go ahead.

Howard had replaced Clarke as Home Secretary by the time the Sheehy team finally made public its 272 conclusions. Appropriately, Sir Patrick arrived at a London press conference to the strains of 'A Policeman's Lot Is Not a Happy One'. Nor, it might be said, was a politician's. For Michael Howard had inherited much bitterness over the Sheehy inquiry, and over the way his predecessor had handled the police. From top to bottom of the service, the police were angry at the way they had been treated. Chief constables, including Sir Hugh Annesley of the Royal Ulster Constabulary and Paul Condon, the Metropolitan Police Commissioner, warned that the Sheehy proposals could damage the morale of the service; backbench Tory MPs expressed their serious concern; and 23,000 off-duty police officers staged a rally in Wembley Stadium to demonstrate their anger and hear Clarke described by the chairman of the Police Federation, Alan Eastwood, as 'a vainglorious politician who decided that the police were fair game for a shake-up'.

Howard quickly decreed that the Sheehy recommendations were 'not cast in stone' and in October 1993 jettisoned the idea of fixed-term contracts for all ranks, lower starting salaries for new recruits and a retirement age of sixty. He kept only the less contentious proposal to abolish three management ranks, and fixed-term contracts for chief officers. The police claimed victory, although those who scrutinised the fine detail noticed that performance-related pay was to be introduced. It showed, said Michael Shersby, the MP who acts as parliamentary adviser to the Police Federation, that there was now a listening Home Secretary.

Could the same have been said of Clarke? Would he have dealt with the police as diplomatically as Howard, or would he have engaged them in a duel to the death by insisting on all of Sheehy's proposals? Peter Lloyd thought Clarke knew what he was getting into and was prepared for the fight: 'He wasn't going to shrink from a contest. He anticipated there'd be explosions of protest. He didn't expect the police to say, "Thank God! We're glad you're being so radical." ' Clarke might have played it differently from Howard, with more explosive results, but he would probably also have achieved more far-reaching reforms.

As soon as he had become Home Secretary, Clarke had perceived that reform of the police alone was not going to alter the public perception that something was rotten with the whole British system of justice. He thought there was one specific problem which no official or minister had brought to his attention: that persistent young offenders were inadequately punished, because the new Criminal Justice Act concentrated on alternatives to custody. Within months a series of widely reported youth crimes, including car hijacking, seemed to prove him right. Peter Lloyd considered that Clarke's ability to spot the problem was a tribute to his working methods:

> He reads much more than journalists allow but he won't read everything. He'll look at the front and the back, but maybe not the middle if he thinks there will be nothing interesting there. He gets the gist rapidly, but he is broad brush, and that gives him time for thinking. He quickly realised there was a gap in existing policy because he keeps his eyes and ears open and doesn't just bury himself in official papers.

In October 1992 Clarke announced that he was going to bring in new measures to lock up teenage tearaways who stole cars or burgled houses. He felt that a small number of offenders were responsible for a disproportionate amount of crime. But, as he made clear to the Tory Party conference, his action was influenced by his dislike of the stand taken by the experts he so detested: 'Some educationalists and social workers talk to me of the entitlement of young people to be able to assert their rights and express themselves as they choose. I believe young people are entitled to expect society to treat them with common sense.'[6]   Clarke made no secret of his dislike for much of the Criminal Justice Act which he inherited, questioning it in a way that more right-wing Home Secretaries, such as David Waddington, did not. Not only did he halt the Act's attempt to find alternatives to custody for juveniles; he also questioned the greater use of bail for the unconvicted, and later threw out the unit fine system – whereby offenders paid penalties in accordance with their disposable income – as well as the limitations the Act imposed on the discretion of judges over sentencing by allowing them to take only one previous conviction into account. When his officials briefed him on the Act, Clarke immediately told them that it was 'completely ridiculous' to limit a judge's sentencing power. 'I couldn't believe that when my officials first described it to me,' he says. 'Like most people who voted for that Act I had not kept in adequate touch with the detail when it went through the House of Commons.' Clarke decided with disdain that the Criminal Justice Act had been put together by wishy-washy liberal officials. A new target had replaced the educationalists in his sights: 'Have you heard the story of the sociologist who finds a member of the public who has been assaulted lying in the road in a pool of blood? He goes over, looks at the victim and says, "I must find the person who did this – he must need my help." '[7]

The Criminal Justice Act had been passed after the Conservative Party's 1987 general election victory, when Douglas Hurd was Home Secretary. Its aim was not just to reduce crime but to keep minor offenders out of prison and stabilise the number of prisoners, to keep the Treasury happy. Prison was seen as an expensive way of making bad people worse, with John Patten, then a junior Home Office minister, helping to persuade the Tory Right that punishment in the community was not a soft option. Clarke, by contrast, saw prison as a vital part of his aim to restore confidence in the government's ability to tackle crime. Prisons could be privately run – Clarke had no ideological prejudice about that – but, crucially, they should aim to reform and not just punish their inmates: 'The service I require is effective custody, enlightened regimes and genuine reformative content delivered efficiently at a reasonable cost.'[8]

So if Clarke's actions appealed to the Right, his rhetoric appealed to the Left. And just as he believed that prisons should have reformative aims, so he also held relatively liberal views on the causes of crime, a perspective he expressed as he did battle with the politician he rated as the most dangerous figure on the opposition front benches: Tony Blair.

Blair, who has a high regard for Clarke, was also new to home affairs in 1992, taking on the portfolio after the general election. But he had long recognised the potency of law and order as a political issue, and the effect crime had on making people feel insecure. For several years he had been convinced of a weakness in Labour's message. He thought the argument that poor social conditions caused crime was seen by voters as an excuse for it, denying an offender's personal responsibility. The new thinking, Blair decided, should reflect the need for social action, but only to help people accept responsibility, not as a substitute for it. It was clear that the public's first concern was that it wanted to be protected; Labour had to become tough on crime as well as on the causes of crime.

This presented Clarke with some difficulty. At a stroke, Blair had deprived him of the stick with which Labour had been ritually beaten for the past decade and more. The government could no longer condemn Labour for being soft on crime. The effect was to concentrate the political argument on why the crime rate was rising despite higher spending on the police, specifically on whether economic deprivation was a factor. John Major claimed in a speech at the start of February 1993 that inner-city crime was rooted in socialism. But in a live television debate with Tony Blair the day after Major's comment, Clarke went some way towards agreeing with Blair's position. Blair argued that it was obvious that bad housing, poor education and unemployment meant that 'crime is more likely to flourish', although it didn't excuse it.

Clarke replied: 'We're in danger of agreeing on the analysis. The difference is that we do things about it. In the inner cities, we have City Challenge, we have all the inner-city task forces, the inner-city programmes that I'm very keen on, remain keen on, for the young people who might otherwise become unemployed.'[9]

Blair seized on this statement as an admission that Clarke had, for the first time, accepted a link between crime and social conditions. In fact, it was little more than he had expressed at the Department of Employment, under Lord Young, when he said that 'enforced idleness of many of our young contributes to the complex social problems of our cities'.[10] It had also explained his interest in regenerating the inner cities, both at Employment and at the DTI. Equally, it was not quite the full acceptance of a causal link between crime and social conditions which Blair claimed. It none the less seemed very different from the Prime Minister's stand. In the same month as this television debate, John Major told his *Mail on Sunday* interviewer: 'I feel strongly . . . that society needs to condemn a little more and understand a little less.'

Common sense was still Clarke's creed, as he made clear in a speech to the Conservative Political Centre in Edinburgh. He recounted the wartime story of a twelve-year-old boy in the North of England who was caught smoking by a local policeman and given a clip round the ear by his father. Clarke evidently approved of such summary justice:

> In the unlikely event that those events were repeated in 1993 what might people say? I give you some suggestions. Inappropriate use of force on a child. Smoking by a twelve-year-old was a victimless crime. Police time and resources were being wasted. Why bother to stop a boy doing something that his parents do and which he will grow up to do anyway?
>
> Order in society is built on common sense. That is a key Conservative value – common sense that our citizens can depend upon and believe in . . . Common sense, self-discipline and order are what the United Kingdom wants and that is precisely what the Conservative Party is going to give it.[11]

They were also the values on which Kenneth Clarke had built his political career.

Government departments are cautious animals, inhabited by civil servants who are resistant to change until change has been forced through, after which they resist any change to the change. The denizens of Whitehall are diffident creatures, unwilling to challenge ministers directly. According to one of his former advisers, Clarke was once driving his red Ford XR3 in the overtaking lane of a motorway when the two civil servants accompanying him noticed that he looked as if he was about to fall asleep. They didn't tell him; while they feared for their lives, they feared a Cabinet minister's wrath even more.

Clarke, had he been more awake, would not have stood for this diffidence. He is a minister who likes to challenge civil servants directly, to put them on their mettle; he is not hidebound by departmental timidity. Yet, at the same time, he has grown up in government, having known little but politics and the law since his Cambridge days. He is the quintessential insider, even if he doesn't dress the part. 'He has always been consistently robust, but has he been robustly consistent, too?' asks Tony Blair. Certain events that took place within the Home Office itself are used by critics of Clarke's stint as Home Secretary to question the degree to which he challenges vested interests.

The first was the Matrix Churchill affair. When in October 1992 three Midlands businessmen were tried at the Old Bailey for illegally exporting £19 million worth of machine tools to Iraq between 1988 and 1990, the workings of government also came under legal scrutiny. The prosecution alleged that the trio knew that the hi-tech lathes they were exporting would be used to make weapons. But the three senior employees of the Coventry-based machine-tool manufacturers Matrix Churchill argued that the government had known exactly what was going on, and that ministers themselves had advised them on how to circumvent the export guidelines. They could prove their case, they said, if the government released secret documents which it had refused to hand over, claiming public interest immunity – in other words, that it would damage national security for the contents to become known.

The judge nevertheless ordered the disclosure of many of the government documents. Their impact – together with the notorious evidence of the former defence minister Alan Clark that government advice to the Matrix directors had been 'economical with the *actualité*' – caused the case to collapse.

The government's actions, not the three men in the dock, now stood condemned. Ministers looked as if they had been prepared to let three innocent men go to gaol to cover their own tracks. The ministers who had signed the public interest immunity certificates were Michael Heseltine, Malcolm Rifkind, Tristan Garel-Jones and Kenneth Clarke, who as Home Secretary was responsible for the security service MI5. In March 1994 Heseltine told the Scott inquiry into the affair that he had signed his certificate only after a row with the Attorney-General, Sir Nicholas Lyell, who told him it was his duty to do so. Clarke, unlike Heseltine, expressed no doubts about withholding documents, but he defends his actions firmly: 'I have personally had nothing ever to do with sales of weapons to the Iraqis and I haven't sought immunity for any documents simply on the basis that they might prejudice a prosecution or be helpful to the defence. I wouldn't dream of signing any such certificate.'[12]

So why had Clarke claimed public interest immunity? He denies that he suppressed Whitehall documents to try to cover up a secret ministerial plot to bypass the official embargo on arms sales to Iraq. He told the Scott inquiry that he was only doing his duty in accepting the advice of the Attorney-General. There is fierce legal debate about whether ministers are obliged to sign such documents, but in signing a limited certificate covering intelligence information, Clarke acted as he saw legally fit, believing that it was not for him to challenge a government law officer. So convinced is he that the case against him is flimsy that in January 1994 he declared on BBC Television's *Question Time* that he would resign if the Scott inquiry found him at fault. But Michael Heseltine emerged from the affair with great credit: his appearance before the Scott inquiry marked the start of his political renaissance and his comeback as a serious leadership contender to rival Kenneth Clarke.

There is, however, a second charge brought against Clarke by his opponents which, they argue, does show his unwillingness at times to challenge the established orthodoxy. The case they cite centres on a judicial tragedy from the past.

More than forty years ago, on the roof-top of a Croydon sweet factory, a London policeman was shot dead. The man who fired the shot received ten years in gaol; he was too young to be sentenced to death. His friend Derek Bentley, a simpleton who watched the killing, was sentenced to hang in Wandsworth Prison. Petitions were sent to the Queen and the Prime Minister pleading for a reprieve. People took to the streets; some jurors pleaded for mercy. But the Home Secretary of the day, Sir David Maxwell Fyfe, declared that the law must take its course. At nine o'clock on a cold January morning in 1953 Derek Bentley was duly hanged. It was one of the most deplorable judicial killings of the post-war period.

For four decades the dead man's sister, Iris Bentley, had campaigned for a pardon. Clarke, the man who had won selection in Rushcliffe despite his then unfashionable abhorrence of the death penalty, agreed to look at the papers. He remembered how he had followed the case 'as a reasonably political schoolboy of twelve'. As Home Secretary he came to the conclusion that Bentley should have been reprieved but that he could not simply substitute his judgement for that of the day.

Civil liberties campaigners called the decision 'extraordinary', but the explanation for it lay in Clarke's view of the law. The law said that both men were guilty of murder if they were engaged in a joint criminal enterprise in which force was used to resist arrest. There was no evidence, said Clarke, that Bentley took any action to bring the enterprise to an end.

Iris Bentley wouldn't give up. She took her case to the High Court, to challenge Clarke's view that a pardon could be given only if Bentley was morally and technically innocent of the crime for which he was convicted. She won. The three High Court judges seemed almost to bend the law to accommodate her. They had no powers themselves, they said, to direct the Home Secretary on how the royal prerogative of mercy should be exercised, but he should look at it again 'so as to give full recognition to the now generally accepted view that this young man should have been reprived'.

It was an exceptional ruling for an exceptional case. Never before had it been considered that some aspects of the royal prerogative were reviewable, and the judges stressed that this was no general ruling, but could only be decided on a case-by-case basis. Clarke firmly defends the position he took: 'I followed the precedent that a royal pardon was only given where innocence was established. The court decided that a pardon should be given where the penalty should be lifted, even if guilt is established.'

Clarke won support for his actions from Judge Stephen Tumim, the Chief Inspector of Prisons: 'There would have been no political price for a pardon; he just wanted to do the right thing legally.' Even so, as a QC and a Cabinet politician, Clarke did not speak out against the prevailing legal orthodoxy, which held him impotent to grant a pardon, even though he felt the initial verdict to be wrong. His sense of history, and also perhaps the legal force of following precedent, made it intellectually difficult for him, as a barrister, to be a reformer of the law.

The judges nevertheless had their way. In July 1993, forty years, six months and three days after he was sent to the gallows, Derek Bentley was finally granted a limited pardon.

As Home Secretary, Clarke seemed to grow in strength as the government became noticeably weaker. The central event which emasculated the government, the collapse of sterling below its fixed band in the Exchange Rate Mechanism, sent the value of Clarke soaring way above the upper limit allowed to a Home Secretary by any

Prime Minister heretofore. He reached the political equivalent of the Deutschmark level, the point at which a Cabinet minister becomes so powerful that the only sensible course for a Prime Minister to follow is to yoke their fortunes together to maintain parity. Clarke took full advantage of his licence to roam. For just over a year, until he became Chancellor of the Exchequer in May 1993, he was less and less the Home Secretary and increasingly the government's main pillar of strength.

By ranging freely over government economic policy, while a reticent Norman Lamont stayed in his Treasury bunker, Clarke became the likely beneficiary of any reshuffle, while not formally running for office. Making himself available was nothing more or less than an ambitious and astute politician might do. In the view of one minister: 'He was too smart to be bidding for the job in the conventional sense of the word, but by going out and scoring centuries he made it impossible for the selectors to ignore him.' Clarke may be a calculating politician, but his friends say he is not a devious man or a plotter. Rather, he is too self-contained to show his hand, too discreet to gossip about the way ahead. Which is fine, unless you are Norman Lamont. How does he feel about Clarke's role in his dismissal? 'I think he feels he was fucked,' declares one of his political advisers.

The single event which made Lamont's position untenable occurred on Wednesday 16 September 1992, Black Wednesday, when the government's economic policy was scuttled. Swept out to sea by a German interest rate cut of a quarter of one per cent, which was too small to hold back the Deutschmark, HM Treasury failed to make the dry land of the following weekend's French referendum on the Maastricht Treaty.

As the markets formally opened on 16 September, John Major was holding a meeting of ministers to discuss the French referendum. They met not in No. 10, where building work was in progress to install bomb-proof windows, but in the more luxurious surroundings of Admiralty House. The small gathering consisted of Clarke, the President of the Board of Trade, Michael Heseltine, the Foreign Secretary, Douglas Hurd and the Chief Whip, Richard Ryder. Norman Lamont should have been there but was delayed by the Governor of the Bank of England.

Three times the ministers met that day to fight the battle for sterling. The odds were always stacked against them. Not only did it prove impossible to shore up the pound against the tidal wave of speculators, but the ministers had no market printers or Reuters screen to guide them. They even had to send out for a transistor radio to listen to the news. When they had one, they learned that sterling was being overwhelmed by an avalanche of selling.

On the stroke of 11 a.m. Lamont put up interest rates by 2 per cent. But the pound refused to shift off its floor against the Deutschmark. At 12.45 the ministers met again over sandwiches to plot the next move. This meeting was also attended by the Chancellor, the Treasury's Permanent Secretary, Sir Terence Burns, the Governor and Deputy Governor of the Bank of England, Sarah Hogg from the No. 10 Policy Unit and Sir Robin Butler, the Cabinet Secretary. By 2.17 p.m. they had given the go-ahead for interest rates to be raised again, this time to 15 per cent, the first time the Bank of England had raised the interest rates twice in one day.

Clarke watched, appalled, as the Treasury mandarins took charge, with the politicians impotent to exert their will. At first he was shocked; later as the benefits which accrued from sterling's exit became clear, he was reconciled to the event, if not the shaming way it had happened. 'It was like being locked outside your house naked,' he told a small private dinner at the party conference later that year. 'Then you realise you always wanted to be naked but you're rather embarrassed about it.'

The speculators saw the government had no economic clothes – and so did the Home Office police officer assigned to Clarke. Clarke stepped out of Admiralty House to be greeted with the words: 'It doesn't seem to be working, does it?'

The policeman was right. By nightfall Norman Lamont had been forced to stand in King Charles Street and announce that Britain had suspended its membership of the ERM, effectively devaluing the pound by 10 per cent. With considerable understatement, he announced that it had been 'an extremely difficult and turbulent day'. He then turned on his heel and disappeared back into the Treasury, refusing all bids for television or newspaper interviews. The party chairman, Sir Norman Fowler, who is not a member of the Cabinet, was wheeled in to sell the government's line. Fowler relates how

When I turned up at Admiralty House, Norman had left. He'd sold this extraordinary idea that getting out of the ERM wasn't official until the European monetary committee had met, so neither he nor any government minister could explain our policy to the nation. So then they thought who the hell could they send? And it became me.

Lamont's retreat into a hermit-like existence was nothing new. His time as Chancellor had been marked by a reluctance to be interviewed by the media, exceeded only by his party's desire to keep him off the television screens during the 1992 general election campaign. He had a credibility problem. His critics on the back benches and in the City had suggested before 16 September that he was lucky to be Chancellor, that he had been elevated not because of political talent but because of his support for Major's leadership campaign.

After the humiliation of Black Wednesday, the government had credibility problems of its own, and that compounded Lamont's weak position. If Major had made him swap jobs with Clarke, as Jim Callaghan exchanged places with Roy Jenkins after Labour's devaluation, Lamont's Cabinet career would have been prolonged and some of the government's agony spared. But Lamont's policy was Major's; 'fool's gold', the Prime Minister had called devaluation five days before the crash, 'a betrayal of the country's future'. Lamont himself was far less enthusiastic about the ERM, and sang in his bath after Britain had been ejected. But scrubbed and cleaned and in fine voice though he was, by being allowed to stay in his job he was left hanging out to dry for half a year, growing progressively weaker while Clarke grew stronger.

It was not Lamont's fault that the government's economic policy had come crashing down around its ears. The blame lay in the attempt to make European currencies converge when the economies they represented were at widely different stages of their cycles, and also in the way the Bundesbank was forced to act as a kind of European central bank, even though its only concern was the German economy and the cost of reunification. Whatever the causes of the political débâcle, to some Black Wednesday was an economic miracle, affording a chance to slash interest rates and let sterling float. Lamont thought so too, which was why he sang in his bath. He shouldn't have

done. The media had Clarke as the front-runner to become
Chancellor, with his Cambridge rival Michael Howard second
favourite. Their apparent battle for No. 11 would dominate the
months ahead.

Within a day of sterling's ignominious exit from the ERM, interest
rates were back to where they had been before the financial whirlwind.
The government's standing could not return so easily. John Major
claimed there were 'fault lines' within the ERM which would have to
be cured before sterling returned to the fixed-rate system. But fault
lines seemed to develop at alarming speed within the Tory Party itself.
A European financial disaster rapidly became translated into a Tory
battle over the political value of European unity. The Euro-dissidents,
led by Lady Thatcher, were quick to line up to undermine Major's
promise to ratify the Maastricht Treaty, which enshrined the very
notion, now seemingly so discredited, of a single currency.

Clarke still swam with the European tide. Nothing less was
expected of a man who had been inspired by the vision of Europe he
saw as a student, and who had helped his mentor Geoffrey Howe steer
the European Act through Parliament in Ted Heath's government.
Not all his colleagues shared his enthusiasm. Immediately after
Britain's departure from the ERM, it became obvious that there were
sharp Cabinet divisions over re-entry. Both Clarke and Heseltine
made it clear that there should be no back-tracking on the government's pro-European stance, emphasising that it was unrealistic to
expect Britain to survive for long outside the ERM. The Euro-sceptic
band of Michael Howard, Peter Lilley and Michael Portillo expressed
the opposite view.

Clarke led the counter-attack on the Euro-sceptics, telling them
they must recognise that 'We are all Europeans.' In October he told a
fringe meeting of the Tory Party conference organised by the
Thatcherite 'Conservative Way Forward' group that the Maastricht
Treaty was not an exercise in damage limitation but an improvement
on the way the Community worked. Political co-operation paved the
way for greater economic liberalism, he said: 'It is not possible to have
a genuine free trade area without any political strings.'[13] Clarke's
fierce opposition to trade barriers, his free-market liberalism, lies
behind much of his pro-European thought; ownership of British
companies is unimportant to him. In November 1978 he had opposed

import controls on Japanese cars; as Minister for Trade and Industry he could see no reason why the Swiss chocolate firm Nestlé should not take over Rowntree in April 1988, nor why foreign banks could not bid for Girobank. Nor indeed, in 1994, did he worry that BMW bought Rover Cars. Even as he had swatted away opposition attacks in July 1988, when the British Aerospace take-over of Rover was held up by a last-minute snag, he had been careful not to rule out future foreign ownership.

Clarke is, therefore, an ardent European, which separates him from many on the Right of the party, despite their mutual populist tone; he once rowed fiercely with Norman Tebbit over the merits of Europe at a Jeffrey Archer party. Like most of his politics, however, Clarke's passion can be tempered with pragmatism when times demand. He has fought Britain's corner hard within Europe. In 1986, as Paymaster-General, he was praised by *The Times* for being 'one of the most adept players of the European game', after designing a rolling programme to tackle long-term unemployment (he also attacked as 'piffle' the original social proposals presented to the British presi-dency). Later, as industry minister, he saved British Steel plants from closure when the rest of Europe cut 100,000 jobs to reduce overproduction.

So while Clarke cannot be moved from his belief in Britain's membership of the European club, he is politically realistic about the rules. It enables him to change his ground when he finds the ground itself shifting under his feet, as it did on Black Wednesday. As the months went on, he exhibited an increasing acceptance that Britain could not re-enter the ERM, which made it look as if he was pitching for the Euro-sceptics' vote or, more realistically, neutralising their opposition to him. 'Yes, I think he's moved his ground,' says John Biffen:

I think he'll always remain emotionally *communautaire*, because of the loyalties he formed in the 1960s, but I think that he's got a reasonably hard-headed political judgement to know that the extent to which you can move the Conservative Party is limited. I think as his career had developed the pragmatism has burgeoned.

251

The charge against Clarke from the Lamont camp is that he shifted his ground for one reason only: to win the Treasury.

In the wake of the ERM débâcle Clarke became the biggest beast in the Tory jungle. The crisis into which the Conservatives had been pitched suited his temperament. He was the one minister who could be relied upon to put his head above the parapet as problem after problem beset the Major government, the one minister who would accept an awkward interview. 'I do not think he did too much, no,' John Major insists:

> The Chancellor was pretty engaged and so was I in the day-to-day management of what subsequently followed. Ken was a senior figure; he was available; often he was on the media. These days you can go on the media to talk about one subject and find yourself asked about quite another. And I think a bit of that gave the impression that Ken was doing a great deal, but other people did as well.

In the first week after Black Wednesday no radio or television programme seemed to be complete without Clarke's presence. It was a role he relished: 'I do it because I enjoy it. It goes back to why I'm a politician. If you're in a hell of a mess, the only way to win is to go out and try to win the argument.'

Clarke also put his foot in it. On *Target*, a Sky Television programme hosted by Lord Tebbit and the Labour MP Austin Mitchell, Tebbit thrust the blue-bound copy of the Maastricht Treaty at him. Clarke cheerfully admitted that he had never read it. He deemed it unnecessary to do so, because no one had to plough through the verbiage to understand its basic thrust, especially when he was aware of Major's negotiating position: 'Nobody out there has read it – I've never read it – you shouldn't waste your time unless you are particularly interested in the minutiae.'[14] So much for his lauded working methods. In front of two convinced Euro-sceptics, for whom the detail added up to a loss of British sovereignty, it was not the wisest of admissions, especially by a Cabinet minister with a reputation for a broad-brush approach to his job. Norman Tebbit made full use of Clarke's remark, which seemed to suggest to him that the government was staffed by ministers who were not just loyal to the European dream but, worse still, *blindly* loyal. Later Clarke ruefully admitted he had been outflanked: 'Of course I said I hadn't read it. Does anyone read their mortgage documents? Next thing I knew he had issued this statement, and my name was on the billboards. I put it down to life's rich tapestry; Norman is a very professional operator and he scored one against me.'[15]

The government's woes at this time went beyond the ERM and Maastricht. There was also unrest over John Patten's school tests, the fiasco of Michael Heseltine's pit closures, an outcry from magistrates about the new Criminal Justice Act, public resentment over rail privatisation and, to cap it all, a drubbing in the polls. In May 1993 the government was roundly defeated by the Liberal Democrats in the Newbury by-election, with a swing of more than 28 per cent. In the local elections on the same day the Tories lost control of fifteen councils and more than 470 seats.

Unlike Norman Lamont, who declared at Newbury, 'je ne regrette rien', Clarke was adroit at defending the government – though his method of defence appeared more like attack, if not on John Major's leadership, then on the Chancellor:

> We have lost the support of some of our bed-rock supporters, let alone the middle-of-the-road people whose floating votes we need. We must decide how we are going to get across our view of this country in Europe, get across our economic policy, and how we intend to sustain the recovery if we can. We have to approach the thing with common sense and decide how we are going to get out of this dreadful hole.[16]

Dreadful hole? Get across our economic policy? Sustain the recovery if we can? This was no typical speech from a Home Secretary, and no typical Home Secretary either. It reflected his general approach to politics, one which John Major professes to admire: 'He sometimes has little sense of danger. He is refreshingly frank. It is part of his persona – I would not wish to change that.'

It became clear that Clarke was the government's biggest asset even as he faced adversity in his own department. For months, magistrates had been complaining that the new Criminal Justice Act was unworkable in practice, and some had even resigned from the Bench.

The Act's sentencing policy was based upon the idea that offenders should pay 'unit fines' related to their means. But after successful pilot studies, the Treasury altered the mathematical formula used to calculate the fines – with farcical results. A motorist whose car had broken down on a double yellow line was fined £500; an unemployed man who dropped a crisp packet was fined £1,200. The loudest complaints came from people on middle incomes.

Clarke's reaction to this showed both his political pragmatism and his presentational ability to snatch victory from defeat. At the start of May he told a delegation from the Magistrates' Association that the system would be modified, but he emphasised that the principle would stay. He had always wanted it to work and was prepared to give it time to do so.

A week later, just seven months after the Act had come into force, Clarke changed his mind, scrapping unit fines to allow courts 'to exercise judgement and common sense'. The Magistrates' Association and the Association of Chief Police Officers welcomed the move, but civil libertarians argued Clarke had thrown out the baby with the bath-water. Clarke might have agreed with them; the principle accorded with his social instincts. So why did he act as he did? He did so because the middle classes were creating a furore, the government was in trouble, and his political instincts told him that when that was the case he should find a quick solution. When there was a sudden opportunity in the Commons to change the system without delay, he seized it with both hands. As in his decision to back down on merging police forces, a higher political imperative beckoned which was stronger than a principle of which he approved: 'What decided me to think "blow this for a game of soldiers, we've got to drop it" was when the Magistrates' Association and the Justices' Clerks' Society publicly fell out about what to put in place of unit fines. I took Denis Healey's view – when in a hole, stop digging.'

Clarke's climb-down showed his presentational abilities to the full. Faced with a Commons statement which could have been ridiculed by the opposition, he went on the counter-attack. First he took on Tony Blair, who made the mistake of beginning with a comment on the latest royal bugging scandal. This gave Clarke the opportunity to display a tone of moral outrage; here we all are, he suggested, discussing the great issues of the day, and all the Right Honourable gentleman can talk about is an improbable security story. Next came Robert Maclennan, for the Liberal Democrats, who was subjected to such a display of wit and savagery from Clarke that even the Tory backbenchers winced. It was pure political theatre, at which Clarke excels:

Maclennan (anxiously): *'Is it not monstrous that he should bring forward a total reversal of policy commended to this House only two years ago by another instant-governing Home Secretary as the answer to the problems of inconsistency of sentencing in order to further his own petty, personal policies at this time?'*
Clarke (cheerfully): *'Can I in response to the Honourable gentleman, firstly, when he's composed himself, ask him to go away, lie down in a darkened room, keep taking the tablets and think very carefully whether the Liberal Democrats have a single opinion one way or another on the merits of the proposals I've just made.'*

In the space of one debate, Clarke had turned disaster into triumph, cheering the backbenchers with his pugnacity and removing one of the government's political problems. The contrast with the enfeebled figure of John Patten, who earlier that week had announced the scaling down of schools tests, could not have been more marked. If you have to change course, Clarke seemed to be saying, this is the way to do it. He had somehow contrived to draw strength from a blatant policy U-turn. Of all the television news bulletins that night, only *Channel 4 News* had the space to run his exchange with Maclennan. Over the coming weeks it would be used by the other news bulletins, too, to illustrate his strength as his star waxed and John Major's waned. Clarke's view was that 'You cannot sit inside the walls of Downing Street or Admiralty House, hoping things will go away. Politics is like falling off a bicycle. If you fall off . . . it's doubly important you get back on the bloody bicycle and pedal again. It doesn't matter if you fall over again. Otherwise you lose the self-confidence to go out and face the enemy.'[17]

In March 1993 the rivalry between Clarke and Howard for Norman Lamont's job seemed to grow more heated. A stream of unattributable briefings appeared in the press, emanating, it seemed, from both camps. Howard returned from talks in Washington, fired with enthusiasm for the environmental advantages of energy taxes. Clarke was against the idea. *The Times* reported an anonymous minister as saying that Howard had 'gone native' at the Environment Department. Howard was furious at what he saw as an attempt to damage his right-wing credentials. A series of reports then appeared in newspapers suggesting that Clarke had told Major he had no interest in Norman Lamont's job.

Clarke had said no such thing. To put the record straight, he had lunch with two journalists. *The Times* duly reported Clarke's view: 'Friends of Kenneth Clarke, the Home Secretary, have taken the unusual step of denying what they say are completely erroneous reports that he has told Mr Major he has no interest in becoming Chancellor of the Exchequer.'[18]

Clarke may have been forced to take this action by what *The Times* suggested might be a dirty tricks campaign against him. But the story looked like a well-timed leak to undermine Lamont and Howard. Clarke's friends deny that was his intent. One minister insisted:

I imagine Ken would have instinctively judged that to campaign against Howard would have been the wrong tactic. Actually, in those months there was some pretty clumsy bidding going on from the Department of the Environment – I always assumed it was from John Redwood. The press was getting a lot of briefings, and one or two newspapers, like the *Mail on Sunday*, were pretty overtly in the Howard corner. But I'm sure Ken just got on with his job. If he wasn't going to become Chancellor, that was the best way to protect his back. If he was going to be in with a shout, that was the best way to make his point.

Two months later Clarke made what looked like an even more overt move. Interviewed on the BBC Television *Breakfast with Frost* programme, he underlined his commitment to the ERM but ruled out a return to it before the end of the present Parliament. If his remark showed his political acuity – the realisation that the Tory Party would be broken by any return to the ERM – it also looked like an attempt to secure support across the whole of the Conservative Party, to disarm the right wing, who saw him as too much of an ERM man to be Chancellor. 'Norman shares the widespread view that Kenneth

Clarke was campaigning to be Chancellor,' declares one of the former Chancellor's advisers:

> The reshuffle was more about satisfying Clarke's ambition than it was about replacing Norman Lamont. Clarke gave the impression of being a highly active politician who wasn't being Home Secretary most of the time he opened his mouth. What he did very well was to persuade the right wing that he was right-wing friendly. He impresses them because they're prissy, fastidious people and he's a brute and a bully. They think that because someone is crude he's got to be right-wing. It says more about them than it does about Clarke, but their reaction helped him.

Not true, according to Clarke's friends, one of whom remarks: 'Ken is ambitious and sophisticated and would never lose sight of opportunities that might be coming along, and if there was a forceful speech to be made he would make it. That is a world apart from conniving and pulling strings.' Jim Lester concurs: 'He talked to me about all the interviews he was doing and said, "I'm worried – I seem to be doing Home Office, Chancellor and everything else. But I keep clearing it with Downing Street and they keep saying go and do it." He didn't campaign; that's just not his style.' Nor did the Prime Minister feel that Clarke was running for No. 11: 'Ken Clarke is straight – he was Home Secretary; it was a good job, and he was not campaigning against Norman Lamont. I am quite sure he was not.'

It seems, then, that Clarke did not run a covert campaign against Norman Lamont; but being an astute politician he calculated his chances: 'I genuinely didn't want Norman Lamont to go, but towards the end it was obvious he wasn't going to survive. He wasn't going to be allowed to. He just didn't defend himself. He retreated from the world while the press hammered on about all sorts of silly things, like his credit cards.' Clarke discussed the possibilities with his adviser Tessa Keswick, although he told her he thought John MacGregor would get the job if Lamont went:

> I knew I was being canvassed by some people who wanted Norman to go but I had done nothing to encourage that. I'd supported Norman publicly and privately although I didn't

think his survival chances were great. I thought John would keep me as Home Secretary for the entire Parliament. John now tells me that was not his intention – that he was going to reshuffle halfway through the Parliament, in the summer of 1994, and that he was going to make me Chancellor then. The problems with Norman accelerated that.

Clarke none the less made himself available for selection by doing what he does best – fighting his, or the government's, corner. The contrast between his political style and Norman Lamont's appeared all the sharper. According to a No. 10 political adviser:

The problem was that not only did Norman Lamont not do interviews – he stopped other Treasury ministers doing them too. It was one of our biggest sources of complaint. There was a period when everyone except the Chancellor was talking about economic policy. Even when he did, he wasn't very good at it. It was cumulative. He was discredited in the City, and the whips were reporting that the party thought the same way. Keeping him there was holding back the recovery, because it needed confidence and he wasn't providing it. Lamont was prickly to work with, and lugubrious with it. He didn't make people feel chirpy. Then there's Clarke – a man who's bouncy, strong, a fluent personality. Who would you rather have?

On 27 May 1993 John Major decided he knew the answer: Kenneth Clarke. In Major's words: the economy was turning, getting more up-beat.

Apart from the fact that I considered technically he would be a very good Chancellor, I think he will present the changing circumstances very well. He is a very bullish, up-beat presenter. Presentation is an important part of politics but it is not the most important part. He is interested in policy for its own sake, and that is very important in a Chancellor.

An unsuspecting Norman Lamont was called into No. 10 and offered the job of Environment Secretary. He declined, bitterly, and left the government. Kenneth Clarke became Chancellor, and Michael Howard had to make do with the Home Office: revenge, indeed, for the Cambridge Union defeat Clarke had suffered more than three decades earlier.

CHAPTER 14

Long-Distance Runner

You can always overtake on long-distance running without letting the others smell the hurry in you; and when you've used your craft like this to reach the two or three up front then you can do a big dash later that puts everybody else's hurry in the shade.

Alan Sillitoe, *The Loneliness of the Long-Distance Runner*

When a government sacks a Chancellor there seems little merit in discussing the quality of the new incumbent's tie: his economic beliefs (or lack of them) in monetary aggregates, public spending and inflation, yes, but not his sartorial elegance. That the salmon-pink and lime-green striped tie which Kenneth Clarke sported as he posed for his first press call on the Treasury steps should be the cause of controversy within the Tory Party was in its own curious way a sign of the political divide the new Chancellor had to bridge.

The tie in question was perhaps not the most appropriate choice for a sober-suited and suede-shoed Chancellor, but Clarke deemed it 'a glorious tie to go with the mood of optimism' in the City. It is, in fact, the tie of the Garrick Club, to which he had just been elected. The club regards itself as a haven for actors and men, though not women, of education and refinement. Clarke's enemies on the right wing were quick to sneer. 'He thinks if you're wearing a Garrick tie it's a splendid club so it must be right,' says a former Cabinet minister. 'He thought, "Christ! you can't be smarter than be a member of the Garrick and I'm proving I am one." But what an awful tie and what an awful combination!'

The Right had no reason to love Kenneth Clarke and every reason to fear him. Although latterly he had made rightward sorts of noises on the ERM, he was of its wing only in the trenchant way in which he could sell or defend policies. Lord Parkinson accords him 'that combination of toughness and unreasonableness which actually at the moment is absolutely vital'. That made him a harder politician for the Right to define. The party had grown used to right-wing populists, but not to politicians like Clarke who could speak the language of a Tebbit. In the febrile Westminster atmosphere caused by the collapse of sterling and Lamont's departure, Clarke was aware of the political balancing act he had to perform. Not only did the Right need placating; but, more by Lamont's accident than Major's design, Clarke had to work hand in glove with their champion, the Chief Secretary to the Treasury, Michael Portillo: 'I think John Major stumbled on to a pretty good combination in Michael Portillo and myself, just like David Young and myself years before.' Clarke presented himself as being in the middle of the party: 'The politics I bring to the Treasury are not those of the soft centre, the dead centre, the left of centre or the right of centre. They are the politics of the hard centre.'[1]

Clarke brought with him to the Treasury his special adviser Tessa Keswick, which also attracted the Right's scorn. Mrs Keswick is nothing if not well connected. She is the daughter of the seventeenth Lord Lovat, who distinguished himself on the Dieppe raid and in the Normandy landings. She was a founder shareholder in Cluff Oil, was once married to the fourteenth Lord Reay and is now married to one of the richest men in Britain, Henry Keswick. It is not a background naturally associated with Clarke; when his previous adviser, Jonathan Hill, phoned Mrs Keswick to let her know Clarke was appointing her, he was answered by the butler. Some right-wing Tories cannot reconcile Keswick with Clarke's beer-and-skittles approach to life. 'What the hell's she doing advising someone like him?' asks one. 'She's a grandee married to a grandee who spends the whole of her time rubbing shoulders with minor royals, and she's meant to be advising this man-of-the-people.'

The attacks on Clarke were sharp because the Right could see that the pragmatism which made him a hard politician to pigeon-hole would be brought to bear at the Treasury. The battle to reduce the huge £50 billion public spending deficit was not going to be fought by a man wedded to the simple Thatcherite nostrum 'cutting spending – good; raising taxes – bad'. Lurking below the surface of this political debate, and sometimes above it, was the threat Clarke posed to

Major's enfeebled leadership. Major had promoted his closest rival. David Mellor, a friend of both men, had long urged the Prime Minister to trust Clarke: 'I personally always said to John that Kenneth Clarke is a man who would not do anything underhand and is a strong man, with whom the closest relationship is entirely desirable.'

Clarke's friend John Barnes considers that 'He expects Major to stand down before the next election. But he's shrewd enough to know that he can't be seen as the assassin. I don't think he expects Major to last the pace – too thin-skinned – but the liking is very genuine.'

It was clear at once that Clarke would bring a very different style to the Treasury. He abolished 'purdah', the sacred period of retreat before a Budget in which Chancellors have traditionally deemed themselves to be too involved in the intricacies of economic problem-solving to talk to the real world. It was an obvious target for Clarke's scorn: 'I never thought for a moment that Ken would want "purdah" to interfere with a pint of beer and a cigar at the end of a hard day,' says Mellor.

Then there was the question of the Chancellor's grace-and-favour retreat: Dorneywood, the seventeenth-century Buckinghamshire mansion which boasts 45 rooms and 214 acres of garden. Kenneth Baker, as Home Secretary, was granted the use of Dorneywood by John Major, but it was given to Lamont, not Clarke, after the 1992 election. Clarke (who called No. 11 the 'best tied cottage in London') was unbothered. When he finally inherited the house as Chancellor, he didn't even know where it was. As Jim Lester recalls: 'I was with Ken at Trent Bridge after he became Chancellor, and I asked him about his weekend. Gillian is a big tennis fan and they said they were going down to Wimbledon for the finals. I asked if they were staying in London and Ken said, "No, we thought we might try Dorneywood – if we can find it. Gillian's got the map."'

Clarke's opponents on the Right of the party also alleged that he needed an economic guidebook to steer him around the Treasury. In fact, he brought with him to the Treasury less economic baggage than almost any Chancellor since Jim Callaghan. According to his friends, he isn't much good at his own finances either. His Birmingham barrister friend David Jones remembers him as 'always pretty hopeless with money':

He'd always been a spender, a very generous chap. Like me, money burns a hole in his pocket. So when he was appointed Chancellor I sent him a short note saying, 'As the only other person I know whose personal finances are as chaotic as mine, I can't help but derive enormous satisfaction from the realisation that this is no bar to obtaining the highest fiscal office in the land.' He wrote straight back to me saying, 'I strongly resent your criticism of my ability in my present post. You and I know more about borrowing money than anyone else I know!'

There was, therefore, something symbolic about the way the Permanent Secretary to the Treasury, Sir Terence Burns, greeted Clarke on the building's steps for the benefit of the cameras, and then steered him indoors. It mattered little; Clarke was not a man to be bound by economic theory, even if he understood it, which his more unkind critics suggested he did not. 'Norman Lamont spent half his career at the Treasury,' says one of the former Chancellor's advisers. 'Lawson's whole career was spent preparing for it. Howe had five years in opposition. Clarke feels very uncomfortable with finance and economics. It's a way of thinking – you either have it or you don't. What gives it away is when he talks about the real economy. It tells me he's suspicious of economic concepts.'

That analysis is true as far as it goes. At no stage of his career has Clarke been a slavish adherent to concepts. Once at the Treasury, he positively *revelled* in his role as the outsider, railing gently against the system, as once he had at school. He did make an attempt to establish his economic credentials in his first speech as Chancellor, when he spoke of his past membership of the Star Chamber and his present membership of the 'EDX' committee of Cabinet ministers which had replaced it. But he also stressed his *anti*-Treasury credentials: 'I am not a City man, although I can just about find my way around it. My interests are in the real economy of business and commerce.'[2]

Instead, Clarke looked set to be the most political Chancellor of recent times – a Treasury outsider, but a government insider, trying to straddle the political divide within his party. Political prudence, not economic theory, dictated his moves. The great debunker had arrived at the Exchequer. He complained that he was being bombarded with economic advice, and that his job as 'an intelligent political layman' was to compare it with the messages he received from his contacts in industry – 'the people out there actually trying to earn a living'. Although he had enormous respect for Nigel Lawson's Chancellorship, he would offer pragmatic solutions to specific problems, not an economic philosophy. Indeed, to his friends he likened being Chancellor to driving in a thunderstorm without windscreen wipers, saying that he had to move forward by feel. The remit was clear: to deal with the public-sector borrowing requirements or PSBR, to restrict public-sector pay and to keep inflation down.

It was obvious, however, that Clarke stood by the welfare state in a way in which the Right did not. He might be prepared to crack down on scroungers, as he had first suggested before Mrs Thatcher became leader, and he might be prepared to restrict some of the welfare state's provisions, but it still remained for him a cornerstone of society. 'Anyone who thought I came into politics to be party to the dismantling of the welfare state has not the slightest idea where I came from,' he declared. 'The fact is that I am not remotely interested in dismantling it. I have spent my entire life seeking to modernise it, improve it, and give it a chance of survival.'[3]

Clarke none the less could provide the strong leadership the Right wanted, so lacking under the disaster-prone Lamont. Lamont, Clarke considered, had got himself into a 'dreadful situation where nobody took the slightest notice of anything he said on economic policy'.[4] Though not Treasury-schooled like Lamont, he would never lack political credibility, because of his ability to perform on camera and at the despatch box.

On 9 June 1993 John Major was subjected to a withering resignation speech from his sacked Chancellor, who accused the government of being in office but not in power. In the economic debate which followed, where Major was lacklustre, Clarke was coruscating. The shadow Chancellor, Gordon Brown, in a powerful speech, had accused the Tories of breaking election promises by imposing value added tax on fuel, but Clarke was his match. Brown's speech 'had about as much policy content as the average telephone directory,' he quipped. 'The best parts of it were when you were quoting me.'[5] Who needed a Lawson-esque knowledge of the velocity of circulation of M4 on the logarithmic scale, when speed of insult would suffice? For Clarke: 'Politics is a kind of spectator sport. If you get the adrenalin going and you feel suitably relaxed, and you've prepared properly for it, I find usually you can survive.' So completely did the new Chancellor outshine his leader in this debate that a feeling grew among some right-wingers that they could accept him as Prime Minister. Later they became more cautious about Clarke's abilities. 'He doesn't have either the dour industry of a Geoffrey Howe or the very high-grade intelligence of Nigel Lawson,' as Nicholas Budgen puts it. 'He's got a good but not great mind and he's very quick at picking up the central point. When you get to the stage he's at, you are tested to destruction. So far his row-in-the-pub style has done very well, but whether it will see him through every situation is yet to be tested.'

Within a month of becoming Chancellor, Clarke had to deliver the annual Mansion House speech to a City audience at Guildhall. It is traditionally a speech where the Chancellor sets out his view of the economic road ahead. Clarke, new to the job, could hardly be expected to do that. Instead, he drew upon the experiences which had formed his political career. The speech reflected the three ages of Ken. First, there was the shopkeeper's son: 'I stand before you not as a Londoner; my whole life has been spent in the industrial Midlands where I have acquired a deep and abiding respect for all those engaged in the difficult business of commerce.' Then, there was public-sector man, the One Nation Tory: 'I know how socially destructive inflation can be . . . it destroys the budgets of the National Health Service and other great public services.' Finally, from his time under Lord Young, there emerged enterprise man, whose social concerns and belief in private-sector efficiency merged into one seamless policy: 'We sold our ideas hard. We restored respect for entrepreneurship, the profession of management and the skills of wealth creation in this country. We created the enterprise economy.'

Why did Clarke feel the need to don the Midlands mantle? He has never forgotten his roots (indeed, he still takes his watch, which was a 21st-birthday present from his parents, to be serviced in his father's old shop), but he had never stressed them before in his speeches. It was partly because, dressed in white tie and tails and without his regulation Hush Puppies, he looked indistinguishable from his privileged City audience, and he likes to be different. But it was partly because the policies he was espousing were essentially the same as his predecessor's. The inflation target remained in place, and the public finances were to be balanced over the medium term – the policy mix which Major and Lamont lit upon after the ERM disaster. So Clarke tried to demonstrate the qualities which set him apart from the merchant banker and Surrey MP who until a month before had been due to make the speech. He said he wanted to be judged on how he could help industry and commerce, and much of both was to be found in the Midlands. The Lamont team were scornful: 'He wants the Treasury to be a sort of super-DTI. He goes on about encouraging industry. But that's not what the Treasury is about. It's about money, and controlling inflation.'

Clarke's Guildhall début was also the speech of a pragmatic Chancellor, a politician who wanted to debunk the very institution in which he worked. 'The conduct of monetary policy outside a fixed exchange rate is very much an art, not a science,' he declared, summing up his approach to the Treasury; and he insisted: 'The Chancellor of the Exchequer is essentially a political post.'[6] He was determined to force the Treasury, blinking, into the full glare of the world outside, to make it less academic and more practical; and so the Treasury staff had to get used to a different routine. Clarke held fewer set-piece meetings than Lamont to discuss the more arcane aspects of monetary policy. Whereas Lamont might hold two such meetings a day, involving up to ten officials, Clarke made do with a couple a week. One Treasury official observes: 'He doesn't get bogged down in the jargon. And he doesn't seem to care very much about the Treasury as an institution. He'll go out and talk to the outside world, rather than look inwards. So he brought a breath of fresh air to the place.'

The new Chancellor also brought a new spirit of confidence to a Treasury battered by the storms of the ERM, because he was so obviously the strongest minister in the Cabinet. His style nevertheless came as something of a shock to officials used to the tight-lipped rule of Howe, Lawson, Major and Lamont. In 1994 Clarke authorised the publication of the minutes of meetings held with the Governor of the Bank of England Eddie George, and from the beginning of his period as Chancellor when travelling abroad for finance meetings defied convention by briefing reporters personally rather than hiding behind an unattributable quote. The *Guardian*'s finance editor reported from Washington that Clarke had introduced the global monetary community to the phenomenon of high finance as a platform for banter, politics and blunt speaking: 'He has become something of a hero. Normally uninterested commentators from the European and American press, fed on a diet of inanities, have only one question on their minds – "Where's Clarke?"'[7]

Impressing the foreign financial community was one thing, however; the main battle lay ahead as Clarke prepared for the first unified Budget, to be delivered in November 1993. To put the Budget together successfully, he had to perform political gymnastics. He was like a circus rider whose act is to bestride two horses as they travel around the ring, while restraining the animals from veering off in different directions. Either he cut public spending or he raised taxes. Each policy had its backers from the different wings of the party. Clarke initially decided he was not going to cut public spending, and wanted to prepare the public for the worst:

> I'd decided that the Budget I had to introduce could only be sold if you got people's expectations right. So I began to talk about the £50 billion spending deficit, myself, right away. Madness, you might have thought – why's the *Chancellor* going round telling everybody how much we're borrowing? Well, it was to prepare people for tough decisions because I was convinced in my first Budget that I couldn't do anything as Chancellor unless I began to get the public finances sorted out.

But Clarke was also concerned that he might be blamed for the tax hike announced by Lamont earlier in the year. So he made sure that, whenever possible, he explained the details of Lamont's changes.

Accordingly he gave an interview to the *Daily Telegraph* in which he extolled the virtues of the 1981 Budget, which put up taxes at the height of the recession (and which he initially opposed), praising it as 'the finest Budget of the 1980s'. He also declared that he would not back down on Lamont's controversial Budget decision to put VAT on heating fuel. 'An extremely tough spending remit had to be balanced by some tax increases,' Clarke insists. 'I always thought that. But I underestimated what the climate would do to my colleagues.'

The reaction from the Right was immediate. The vice-chairman of the Tory finance committee, David Shaw, warned that he could not support any increase on the standard rate of tax. Indirect taxes, such a VAT, had been 'pushed to the limit'. Instead, there should be a re-examination of public expenditure. Sir George Gardiner, then a member of the executive of the 1922 Committee, also joined the call against tax increases. The threat from the Right was real. With Major's Commons majority down to seventeen, the warnings could not be ignored. The party chairman, Sir Norman Fowler, ordered Clarke to do the rounds of television interviews to keep the lid on the controversy he had stirred. It had concentrated minds wonderfully but it had done nothing for party popularity.

By the middle of September the polls showed the Tories barely ahead of the Liberal Democrats, some eighteen percentage points behind Labour. For a government only halfway through its second year in office, it was scarcely fatal. But the perceived weakness of Major's leadership, the renewed sniping by Norman Lamont in newspaper articles and Kenneth Baker's newly published memoirs reopened old wounds. Ahead lay the party conference and Lady Thatcher's own memoirs, which hung Damocles-like over the Prime Minister as he prepared for a six-day tour of Japan, Malaysia and Monaco.

Major's trip was an unmitigated political disaster. It began badly and grew worse. Even as he left Britain the *Sunday Times* was comparing his excursion with Margaret Thatcher's final foray to Paris. From Tokyo, Major was compelled to make an extraordinary demand of his own MPs, telling them to stop their 'stupid internecine squabbling', and describing the trouble-makers privately as 'devils on the fringe, living out past glories'.

Clarke was left to play the part of the loyal Chancellor, talking of the government's 'overwhelming desire' to get behind the Prime Minister. He also described reports of a leadership challenge as 'unreal and not real news . . . it appears in the newspapers, but there is nobody out there actually canvassing it'. The *Daily Mail*, more than a touch ingeniously, interpreted this as implying that he was being pressed to stand for the leadership. Clarke said and meant no such thing; his view is that the Tory Party is a broad church which has to act as a unified body. Sir Norman Fowler rejects the idea that Clarke would act deviously: 'He wouldn't dream of leading a coup. It's not in his nature.' But these events brought into sharper focus his relationship, as the strongest man in the government, with John Major, his enfeebled leader. 'John was aware of Ken breathing down his neck throughout this period,' according to one former Cabinet minister. But Major denies it: 'Ken is beside me, not behind me; the former minister should realise that.'

Clarke insists that he and Major are politically close:

> Our political instincts are exactly the same. There are very few issues where he and I differ. We often do things by just exchanging our first broad-brush instinct, and the number of times we start from a different point of view is quite small. The very nature of the current crisis makes me closer to him. Just in terms of the politics of it, the destruction of another leader inside four years could be the destruction of the Conservative Party. I think the idea that John is thrown out and someone takes over in a calm and settled succession is nonsense. It would be a dreadful crisis if we had a change of leadership, and I always tell him that I'd like to be Prime Minister – but in his time not mine. One of the best things going for John Major is that every now and again his critics suddenly realise that they are in serious danger, if they were to succeed in their desire of getting him out, of putting me in his place, and I think that's quite a useful protection for him.

For his part, John Major agrees that they are politically close and insists that he trusts Clarke 'completely': 'I see him as Chancellor of the Exchequer, a good friend with whom I work closely and for whom I have great respect.' While relations between the two work on a professional level, they do not appear instinctively close personally. Sir Norman Fowler describes them as 'temperamentally different', while denying that they are opponents. The two men share a similar background, but Clarke gained from his upbringing an intellectual self-confidence which Major lacks. Major, says one former minister, is

> an administrator. He doesn't have the same intellectual power or education as Kenneth Clarke. John sees politics purely in terms of keeping the party together, without realising that if he had a vision the party would follow. He's too busy calculating the fourth move ahead. Clarke's not like that; he's a trained fighter, and hits out at what's in front of him.

Clarke's robustness, and Major's apparent lack of it, seemed to compound the latter's difficulties. 'Clarke has zipp, pizzazz. He needs a dresser but that's part of his charm,' says Sir Bernard Ingham. 'John Major is a very grey politician, too nice for it by half. Nobody would accuse Kenneth Clarke of being too nice for it.' Kenneth Baker agrees that Major's apparent lack of leadership caused problems: 'Ken said to me after our first Cabinet meeting under John Major, "How refreshing to have a discussion, if we'd only had it eighteen months ago, we wouldn't have had so much trouble." Well, we've got into deeper trouble than Margaret got into with this great consensual approach.'

By the time of the October 1993 party conference in Blackpool no one was more aware than Clarke himself how his perceived strength was in almost inverse proportion to the perceived weakness of Major. The *Daily Mail* had already shown how a protestation of loyalty to John Major could be turned into a stick with which to beat the Prime Minister. Clarke could not even afford to make himself available for selection, as he had done for the Chancellorship.

In the circumstances it was perhaps unfortunate that Blackpool's Imperial Hotel, aided by a local jeweller, should give Cabinet ministers and selected delegates commemorative knives to mark the party conference. But Clarke refused to play Brutus with his silver-plated gift and delivered what was by any standards a low-key conference address. Part of the reason for the dullness of his delivery that day is explained by his dislike of set-piece speeches, and the proximity of the Budget: 'What I had in mind was a speech on the economy, saying life is hard, life is earnest, we have a hell of a mess here.' He also needed to deflect some of the media attention which was centred on him. This was not the time for the ringing Clarke phrase – except for one. 'Any enemy of John Major is an enemy of mine,' he declared roundly.

This message of support for the Prime Minister was written by Clarke himself and designed to neutralise the press campaign which had built up against Major and for himself. Yet it also seemed to be a measure of the Prime Minister's weakness, and Clarke's strength, that the latter should have to issue such a statement of loyalty. For John Major this is not the case: 'He had told me that that was how he felt and that was what he was going to say. I do not think it is remotely surprising. Around the Cabinet table we have collective responsibility, we work together. It is only surprising for people who do not understand politics, I think.' Clarke himself is convinced that

> It's the kiss of death when you're said to be the most likely candidate for the leadership. To be third or fourth favourite, that's safe. I find myself written up day by day as the dauphin. Once you emerge as the man who's going to be the next Prime Minister your enemies have no one to go at but you, and that position has been a dangerous one in politics for as long as I can remember. My approach to it is good luck to the Prime Minister in that his dauphin is someone he can trust – and we have to trust each other, and we do trust each other. The other thing is that if I'm to keep the dauphin position I have to make a success of my job, and that means economic recovery.

But Clarke is also interested, he says, in becoming Foreign Secretary – the only great office of state he has not occupied: 'If I have a long stint as Chancellor, and somebody wants to move me, I certainly wouldn't say no to being Foreign Secretary.'

In Blackpool, if Clarke's reputation had been built up any further, there was a danger that the party might see him as a divisive figure – and perceive his strength as adding to its fractures, rather than just being the result of them. The other danger, Clarke recognised, was that the same reporters who had praised him for six months would turn against him. 'Politics is a very roller-coaster game. It is the inevitable habit of journalists to build up reputations . . . to reduce them again, so I expect to be extremely unpopular with the press in a few months' time,' he told *Crossbow* magazine.[8] He also maintained in Blackpool that he did not seek to become Prime Minister in these circumstances. 'Who wants a pot of cold tea?' he asked at a private dinner the night before his conference speech. He expressed the view that John Major would not leave office when he was down, but that he would go as soon as he was up, when he could get out with dignity. 'Whoever becomes leader of the party, in my experience, depends entirely on the events of the previous fortnight,' Clarke insists. 'It just depends why the party suddenly needs a new leader and what the particular candidates have been doing in the last six months – whether they're up or down.'

The ritual gathering of the party faithful by the seaside could not disguise John Major's troubles. The leaking of Lady Thatcher's memoirs to the *Daily Mirror* when the conference was under way only emphasised how Major could not shake off her shadow, attenuated though it was. ('Someone's got to kick that woman's head in,' said one minister privately.) Senior ministers openly expressed their disen-chantment to journalists; Michael Heseltine, recovered from his heart attack, even spoke of retiring to his splendid arboretum although its fascination for him seemed to have withered by the spring of 1994 when his political renaissance was in full flower and he was again viewed as a possible party leader. The Foreign Secretary, Douglas Hurd, too, railed privately against the poor intake of new MPs, the inadequacy of new ministers and the lack of leadership from Major. Major was, he opined, obsessed with what people thought about him, and spent all his time reading what the papers said about his performance.

At the conference the party's divide was plain to see. Peter Lilley and Michael Portillo spoke out for Thatcherite values, while Hurd (who considered that Lilley had been behaving abominably) elegantly repudiated their stand, stating that the party should not indulge in a perpetual 'cultural revoluton' in the public services. Indeed, Major's own clarion call for unity – that the party must get 'back to basics' – was soon subverted by right-wing ministers who made single mothers the target for their attacks. That was partly the fault of the idea's original vagueness; but it also reflected the Right's agenda within the party. Clarke was unmoved, observing: 'If there *are* people who become pregnant after consulting their welfare rights officer, then there are very few of them.'[9]

The party's splits and its small majority made the Budget calculations even more of a balancing act. As Michael Portillo's negotiations as Chief Secretary to the Treasury went on, it became clear that the departmental settlements were coming in under the goverment's public spending target of £253.6 billion, and that the contingency reserve would not be needed. The right wing's standard bearer had delivered. 'When we started, Portillo was much more confident that we could undershoot than I was. I'd underestimated both the climate and the new EDX spending system,' says Clarke. 'The figures kept on unfolding in our favour. It was a lucky bonus.'

The undershoot was kept secret from Cabinet colleagues who were not on the EDX spending committee – they were told only at the end of the round. In Tessa Keswick's view:

> Kenneth genuinely thought there was going to be a much bigger tax hike than there was. He didn't bring about the eventual undershoot in public spending because of the Right. He did it because it was possible to have an undershoot much more easily than he expected. He doesn't like cutting public expenditure – he believes in public services – but then it also became clear that the recovery was pretty patchy.

It was only ten days before the Budget that the size of the undershoot became clear. It happened very late on, according to Mrs Keswick: 'I remember Michael Portillo coming in and saying I think we're going to get an undershoot – we all nearly fell off our chairs with excitement!' The negotiations were complete; the stage was set for Clarke's first Budget.

At the start of his Commons speech Clarke likened a politician presenting his first Budget to a 'lion tamer trying out his act for the first time'. Swaying on his feet in his usual rotary manner, sipping whisky and water and occasionally punching the air with his right hand to emphasise points, he tamed his own backbenchers with the sheer gusto of his performance, his evident enjoyment of being centre-stage. Simon Heffer wrote in the *Spectator*: 'The most important considerations for Mr Clarke were (in ascending order of gravity) that he do nothing to impair the recovery, nothing to inflame Tory supporters further, and nothing to damage his standing as heir apparent to Mr Major.' He appeared to succeed in all three.

Clarke's Budget was an undoubted political success, pleasing the two wings of his party and neutralising the VAT issue. He had little leeway, with rebels waiting in the wings to overturn Lamont's two-stage tax. He had to find a way to eat into the PSBR deficit without slavish adherence to one solution, for fear of alienating either wing of the party. And he had to deliver a Budget which would enhance his reputation.

So Clarke tightened up the rules on unemployment benefit, which pleased the Right, but there was a new child-care allowance, which satisfied the Left. Michael Portillo, the Right's champion, was praised, but so too was the European Union. Clarke spoke with the voice of the caring Left, while cutting £2.5 billion from the social security budget, which pleased the Right. It was a Budget both paternalistic and tough, a balancing act which also reflected Clarke's character as an individualistic politician, hard to define.

In effect, the whole Budget was a summation of Clarke's career to date. He showed himself to be politically astute, fiscally tough, the supporter of small business and the welfare state – providing it was tightly run. The abolition of unemployment benefit in favour of a job-seekers' allowance would, he said, make for a much closer link between the benefit and the claimant's professed willingness to work. The restrictions on invalidity benefit would stop it being claimed by 'people who are not genuine invalids'. While his immediate political priority was to restrict the burgeoning social security budget, he could always justify it by recourse to the war on scroungers he had first launched two decades earlier, and also to his wish, first expressed at the Llandudno party conference of 1962 and repeated in his first term in Parliament, to see 'an increasingly selective approach in social welfare'.[10]

All politicians like to claim they are defenders of the welfare state, and Labour saw Clarke's moves as a sharp attack on its provisions, but he genuinely does not believe in a minimalist welfare state, unlike his Chief Secretary. So there was another £1.5 billion for the health service, a rise of 1.5 per cent in real terms; pensions, his early interest as a Mansfield candidate and as a One Nation Tory, were to rise above inflation for the first time since the late 1970s and would, he said, remain the cornerstone of the welfare state. He declared: 'This Government will never take part in any attempt to dismantle the welfare state', even if there had to be means-testing of some benefits. Some sort of battle-line had been drawn up against those who argued for its continued reduction – Portillo, Lilley and Redwood.

The most political, and vital, decision of the Budget was Clarke's move to buy the government out of its great VAT imbroglio with a £1 billion compensation package. As Clarke reported back to the Prime Minister every fortnight on the progress of his deliberations in the run-up to the Budget, he was left in no doubt that this was what his leader wanted: 'As Harold Wilson said, it's the Prime Minister's duty to warn and advise. As John had changed his Chancellor, it was important to him and important to me that I did what I wanted, so he did not crawl over every bit of the Budget. But his advice included strong encouragement to put together a big compensation package.'

For the rest, the tax pain was shared out widely. There was no underlying taxation philosophy but, as in much of Clarke's career, a response to a specific problem, this time to the goverment's fiscal difficulties. Equally, there was no single tax measure which attracted the opprobrium earned by Lamont's imposition of VAT on heating fuel. Instead, two new indirect taxes were introduced, on insurance premiums and air travel. Excise duties raised another £1 billion, and income tax allowances were frozen for the second year running. Mortgage tax relief was further eroded to 15 per cent from 1995. Each taxation measure, in isolation, looked modest. Together they added up to a swingeing £6 billion in extra taxation by 1997.

This was the biggest tax increase and the biggest cut in public spending since the war, and yet the Chancellor was hailed – at the time – by his party as a hero. It had happened partly because of his tactic of preparing people for the worst and then delivering something short of it. It was also an adroit budget; the £3.6 billion underspend and the VAT package bought off both wings of the party, even if the former relied on an unprecedented raid on the contingency reserve. But at its heart it was a performer's Budget, the Budget of a Chancellor who looked and sounded confident. In delivery, he hurried through the awkward passages on tax increases, while savouring the jokes.

Clarke compares his Budget speech with the speech he made to the Police Federation the year before, when he sold the idea of the Sheehy inquiry, without his audience quite realising what had happened:

In both cases, I was down the road before the penny dropped. I put a lot of effort into distilling the Budget speech down to make it *my* speech, a political speech, because I thought I had a real selling job on my hands. The key thing was saving the spending cuts until the end. But I still thought the time had come to put my tin hat on. I was astonished it got the euphoric reception it did. The debate we had later about the tax rises was the debate I thought I'd be seriously stuck into between November and Christmas.

Initially, at least, the lions had been tamed.

The day after the Budget, the *Daily Telegraph* printed a letter from a Hampshire vicar which seemed to sum up the national mood: 'Sir – The popularity of the Chancellor of the Exchequer and his uncanny ability "to get away with it" is, indeed, hard to pin down. He does for me have an uncanny likeness to the late singer Matt Monroe; no great shakes as an image but, to quote Frank Sinatra, "the only limey who could sing".'

Clarke's critics acknowledge his presentational skills, which delayed the opposition to the tax increases until a few months later, opposition that was stoked by his relaxed suggestion that the tax rises were the equivalent of three pints of beer each week. But they argue that they don't know what he stands for, except perhaps for himself. 'Motherhood, apple pie, everything will be all right if we stick together, that sort of thing,' says the former Transport Secretary, David Howell. Clarke is irritated by such remarks:

> I am an old Bow Grouper. I believe in a free-market economy and enlightened social reform. I think it is extremely unwise to sail under false colours. If you're going to become an MP, you do have to tell your constituents you are against hanging. If you are going to take on one day the leadership of the party, you do need to tell people you are in favour of our continuing membership of the European Union. It doesn't work to dissemble.

Clarke's beliefs are, effectively, the fusion of North American free enterprise and a European approach to welfare. Each side of his protean political personality has come to his aid in his long career, allowing him to claim consistency of purpose: 'It constantly gets asked – it's *bound* to be asked of somebody who's been a minister under Heath, Thatcher and Major – how far have I changed. I think I've been as constant as the northern star.' But he is, at the same time, ecumenical with the truth. His political parameters, of caring and market discipline, are sufficiently wide to allow generous room for manoeuvre. He has stood firm throughout his career for a national health service, the welfare state and Europe. But change can always be justified, in new political circumstances, by recourse to efficiency and common sense.

Common sense is an undefined base for a political career, and all politicians, of whatever persuasion, feel they have it. Yet in many ways it is apt for Clarke, indicating a common touch, a sensible approach to life, the ultimate hallmark of a pragmatic politician – although he dislikes this description, believing that pragmatism implies opportunism and a lack of a sense of overall direction. Above all else, politics for Clarke is the art of the possible.

The consequence is that in his much reshuffled career Clarke has devoted himself to problem-solving, the approach of his Birmingham Bow Group days. In Cabinet he has a view on everything but not necessarily a vision which might unite his troops. David Mellor suggests this in comparing the attributes of Major and Clarke:

> I think they are very similar in many ways. They're both self-made men who remain in touch with the warp and woof of British society in the sense that they have interests, lifestyles, that mirror where they come from rather than the ruling class. Ken perhaps rides more easily with the punches and is more robust, but essentially there isn't much between them in terms of their outlook and what they represent. In Cabinet, however, I always thought John was better than Ken at privately determining where he wanted to go and going for it with an ostensibly open mind.

Major, blessed initially with Mrs Thatcher's imprimatur, was inscrutable enough for the Thatcherites to read into him what they wanted to see, even if the effect wore off. Clarke never sought, nor was granted, such a blessing; by that token he is less of a unifying figure. Like Major, he is not a conviction politician; but unlike Major, he appears to have the courage of his pragmatism. He *sounds* like a conviction politician in that he convinces by force of argument – he appears to be a strong leader. It is still not enough for the true Thatcherite believers, who seek a return to conviction politics. 'He wouldn't horse around like Michael Heseltine, leading a dotty crusade in the inner cities,' Alan Clark remarks. 'But I wouldn't ride in his cavalry, because I don't know what he'd do. If the gunfire got too heavy he might turn round. Mrs Thatcher never would. I think he makes it up as he goes along.'

For Kenneth Clarke, politics is a hugely enjoyable activity. It has always been so – from his early campaigning days in Mansfield to his present high office. Like any barrister, he enjoys the performance as much as the content of his brief. This does not mean that he makes it up as he goes along, as Alan Clark suggests; he has fixed points on his compass. But it is the political process itself, rather than its content, which fascinates Clarke above all. To his fingertips he is a House of Commons man. When ministerial life is over, it is hard to imagine him ending his political days as Lord Clarke of Rushcliffe.

For such an ambitious politician, Clarke bears an uncanny resemblance to a human being, by virtue of his cheerful aspect and his hinterland of interests. There is no side to him; he is as hard as they come, but as affable as he seems. Unlike most politicians, however, Clarke is prepared to declare his ambition, which appears to make him a more straightforward character than his rivals. It is not so. Clarke's rounded good humour may make him stand out as a rare species in the Westminster jungle, but it also does much to provide the inner man with a natural camouflage. Ultimately, Clarke approaches politics as he approaches life – on his own terms.

It is a long journey from Aldercar to Downing Street, longer by far than the journey from Brixton to No. 10. If Clarke's route has been smoother than John Major's, there have none the less been unven times along the way. This is partly because Mrs Thatcher changed the direction of the Conservative Party's signposts for a decade or more; but Clarke's own character – in which the caution of high ambition is married to a stronger impulse, an incautious love of debate – has also been a factor. His talent for disputation has been the very foundation stone of his success, yet it has pitched him into trouble in the past, and will do so again in the futre. Politics will never be dull with Clarke at the helm.

In his dreams, Clarke plays the tenor saxophone as fluently as one of his heroes, Sonny Rollins: 'He is, I think, the best improviser in jazz. He's a perfect, technically relaxed musician. He is always slightly a loner, on his own.' Clarke plays politics with the same mixture of improvisation, relaxation and solitude. He also admires the bass player Charlie Mingus – a wilder, more gregarious musician, who caused the occasional riot – because he 'puts a bit of fire back in your belly'.[11] There is some of that in Clarke, too: 'The places I most enjoy in politics are inside the chamber of the House of Commons and inside a television studio, and they're both very dangerous places.'

The two sides of Clarke's personality – the loner and the gregarious combatant – are wrapped into a self-contained man, at one with himself. In this way he has survived the vicissitudes of front-bench politics for more than two decades: the Tories' long-distance runner. 'With Clarke as Prime Minister I think you'll get a Just William form of government,' Bernard Ingham concludes. 'It will be pretty untidy. It will very informal and quite relaxed. And it will be very voluble.'

Notes and References

1 The Journey
1 *Eastwood & Kimberley Advertiser*, 11.11.38.
2 *Daily Telegraph*, 29.1.90.
3 *Mail on Sunday*, 26.11.93.
4 Quoted Peter Riddell, *Honest Opportunism: The Rise of the Career Politician*, London, Hamish Hamilton, 1993, p. 47.
5 *Nottingham Evening Post*, 5.10.93.
6 David Peters, who kindly provided some of the factual information in this chapter, died in February 1994.
7 Jazz FM, 19.2.93.

2 The Right People
1 *Varsity*, 6.3.92.
2 Ibid.
3 *Independent*, 26.9.92.
4 *Sunday Telegraph* debate, Blackpool, 7.10.93.
5 John Barnes, writing in the *Cambridge Review*, 2.2.63.
6 *Varsity*, 9.2.63.
7 Ibid., 16.6.62.
8 Ibid., 6.3.92.
9 Ibid., 19.1.63.
10 *Sunday Times* advertisement, 14.10.61.
11 Cambridge Union Society, Record of Debates, 22.11.61.
12 Cambridge Union Society, Record of Debates, 17.3.63.

3 This Little Socialist Outpost
1 *Mansfield Chronicle Advertiser*, 21.5.64.
2 Ibid., 16.4.64.
3 Letter, ibid., 30.4.64.
4 Ibid., 11.6.64
5 Ibid., 17.9.64.
6 Ibid., 8.10.64.
7 *Nottingham Guardian Journal*, 15.3.66.

4 Graduates on the Make
1 *Nottingham Evening Post*, 19.9.88.
2 *Impact*, Young Conservatives' news magazine, February 1965.

3 Quoted in Judy Hillman and Peter Clarke, *Geoffrey Howe: A Quiet Revolutionary*, London, Weidenfeld, 1988, pp. 46–7.
4 Brian Lapping, *The Labour Government, 1964–70*, London, Penguin, 1970, p. 111.
5 Bow Group, *Immigration, Race and Politics*, London, 1966.
6 Bow Group, *Regional Government*, London, 1968.
7 *Crossbow*, January–March 1969, pp. 13–15.
8 *Beeston Gazette & Echo*, 12.6.70.

5 Glittering Prizes
1 Hansard, 8.7.70, col. 694.
2 *Nottingham Evening Post*, 9.7.70.
3 Hansard, 14.1.71, cols 365–82.
4 John Campbell, *Edward Heath*, London, Cape, 1993, p. 364.
5 *Nottingham Evening Post*, 7.12.70.
6 Hansard, May 1971, col. 610.
7 M. Tomison, 'Thatcherism – a fundamental departure?', unpublished MA thesis, City of London Polytechnic, 1983.
8 *Nottingham Evening Post*, 14.4.72.
9 Barbara Castle, *The Castle Diaries 1974–6*, London, Weidenfeld & Nicolson, 1980, p. 53.
10 Ibid.
11 *Nottingham Evening Post*, 8.11.74.
12 Castle, op. cit.

6 The Counter-Revolution
1 Hugo Young, *One of Us*, London, Macmillan, 1989, p. 98.
2 *Nottingham Evening Post*, 11.3.75.
3 Young, *One of Us*, p. 103.
4 Preston, 24.9.75.
5 *Nottingham Evening Post*, 22.3.76.
6 *British Leyland: The Next Decade*.
7 Beeston Conservative Club, 24.9.77.
8 Hartlepool Civic Centre, 10.2.78.
9 Bow Group talk, House of Commons, 5.2.79.
10 Edwalton Young Conservatives, 19.1.79.
11 Cotgrave Conservative Association, 2.2.79.
12 *Nottingham Evening Post*, 27.1.79.
13 *Financial Times*, 25.4.79.

7 At the Sultan's Court
1 Harrogate, 30.10.79.
2 DoT press release, 17.3.80.

3 Norman Fowler, *Ministers Decide: A Personal Memoir of the Thatcher Years*, London, Chapmans, 1991, p. 202.
4 Westminster Lecture, Tory Reform Group, London, 24.11.92.
5 *Nottingham Evening Post*, 19.7.82.
6 *Jimmy Young Programme*, BBC Radio 2, 9.9.83.
7 Alan Clark, *Diaries*, London, Weidenfeld, 1993. p. 71.
8 *The Times*, 7.5.84.
9 *Sun*, 21.5.84.

8 The Odd Couple
1 Margaret Thatcher, *The Downing Street Years*, London, Harper Collins, 1993, p. 418.
2 Lord Young, *The Enterprise Years: A Businessman in the Cabinet*, London, Headline, 1990, pp. 41, 155. Unless noted, Young's comments are from my own interview.
3 Oxford, 11.4.86.
4 Institute of Personnel Management, London, 25.9.85.
5 Ibid.
6 Thatcher, *The Downing Street Years*, p. 567.
7 Ian Gilmour, *Dancing with Dogma: Britain under Thatcherism*, London, Simon & Schuster, 1992, p. 46.
8 Blackpool, 11.10.85.
9 Ibid.
10 *Sun*, 31.8.86.
11 *The Times*, 22.5.86.
12 *Test Match Special*, BBC Radio 5, 3.7.93.

9 Dressing the Part
1 Tory Reform Group, London, 24.11.92.
2 *The Times*, 7.1.88.
3 Eastbourne, 13.2.88.
4 *Breakfast with Frost*, BBC Television, 31.10.93.
5 Centre for Policy Studies, *The Free Market and the Inner Cities*, London, October 1987.
6 Nigel Lawson, *The View from No. 11*, London, Bantam Press, 1992, p. 291.
7 Penny Junor, *The Major Enigma*, London, Michael Joseph, 1993, p. 145.
8 Hansard, 13.7.88, cols 361, 365, 368.

10 A Monumental Row
1 Robert Carr, Home Secretary 1973–4, was renowned for his verbosity.

2 *Daily Express*, 19.5.89.
3 *Sunday Times*, 20.11.88.
4 Lawson, *The View from No. 11*, p. 615.
5 Bournemouth, 9.10.90.
6 Nicholas Ridley, *My Style of Government*, London, Hutchinson, 1991, p. 97.
7 *Test Match Special*, BBC Radio 5, 3.7.93.
8 St Stephen's Club, London, 6.6.89.
9 Blackpool, 10.10.89.
10 *Independent*, 20.7.89.
11 Thatcher, *The Downing Street Years*, pp. 616–17.
12 *Guardian*, 8.3.89.

11 A Postcard and a Letter
1 Hansard, 7.3.89.
2 Edwina Currie, *Life Lines*, London, Sidgwick & Jackson, 1989, p. 265.
3 Kenneth Baker, *The Turbulent Years*, London, Faber, 1993, p. 276.
4 Hansard, 5.12.88.
5 *Financial Times*, 14.12.89.
6 *Sunday Express*, 12.11.89.
7 Ibid.
8 Ibid.
9 *Daily Express*, 3.1.90.
10 *Guardian*, 3.1.90.
11 Clark, *Diaries*, p. 273.
12 Junor, *The Major Enigma*, p. 187.
13 *Guardian*, 4.1.90.
14 Channel 4 News, 26.1.90.
15 *Breakfast with Frost*, BBC Television, 31.10.93.
16 Thatcher, *The Downing Street Years*, p. 624.

12 The End of History
1 Alan Watkins, *A Conservative Coup*, London, Duckworth, 1991, p. 213.
2 Ibid., p. 4.
3 Thatcher, *The Downing Street Years*, p. 852.
4 *The Downing Street Years*, BBC Television, October 1993.
5 BBC Radio 1, 1.2.94.
6 *Pursuit of Power*, Channel 4, 21.7.91.
7 Baker, *The Turbulent Years*, p. 406.
8 *The Downing Street Years*, BBC Television, October 1993.
9 Clark, *Diaries*, pp. 365, 384.

10 Second Westminster Lecture, Tory Reform Group, London, 12.6.91.
11 Thatcher, *The Downing Street Years*, p. 835.
12 Sixty-First Conservative Women's Conference, London, 28.6.91.
13 Baker, *The Turbulent Years*, p. 198.
14 *Daily Mail*, 16.12.91.
15 Ibid.
16 Leeds, 4.1.91.
17 *On the Record*, BBC Television, 21.4.91.
18 *The Times*, 28.9.91.
19 Bob Dunn: former under-secretary at Education; James Pawsey: chairman of Tory backbench education committee.
20 See Bruce Anderson, *John Major: The Making of the Prime Minister*, London, Fourth Estate, 1991, p. 222.

13 Into the Jungle
1 Clark was slightly adrift on this point. Churchill led the Tories after being a Liberal Home Secretary.
2 *Financial Times*, 14.12.89.
3 Association of Chief Police Officers, Bramshill, 8.12.92.
4 Audit Commission conference, London, 5.3.93.
5 *Spectator*, April 1993
6 Brighton, 7.10.92.
7 Harrogate, 6.3.93.
8 *Independent*, 22.12.92.
9 Channel 4 News, 4.2.93.
10 Institute of Personnel Management, London, 25.9.85.
11 Conservative Political Centre, Edinburgh, 12.5.93.
12 BBC Radio 4, 11.11.92.
13 Blackpool, 6.10.92.
14 Sky Television, 6.10.92.
15 *Observer* magazine, 28.11.93.
16 BBC Radio 4, 8.5.93.
17 Junor, *The Major Enigma*, p. 279.
18 *The Times*, 6.3.93.

14 Long-Distance Runner
1 Parliamentary press gallery lunch, London, 9.6.93.
2 Ibid.
3 *Crossbow*, October 1993.
4 Ibid.
5 Hansard, 9.6.93, col. 360.
6 *Financial Times*, 25.6.93.

7 *Guardian*, 29.9.93.
8 *Crossbow*, October 1993.
9 Channel 4 News, 15.11.93.
10 Hansard, 26.4.71, col. 95.
11 Jazz FM, 19.2.93.

Index